UNIVERSITY CASEBOOK SERIES®

2021 SUPPLEMENT TO

FEDERAL COURTS AND THE LAW OF FEDERAL-STATE RELATIONS

NINTH EDITION

PETER W. LOW
Hardy Cross Dillard Professor of Law Emeritus
University of Virginia

JOHN C. JEFFRIES, JR.
David and Mary Harrison Distinguished Professor of Law
University of Virginia

CURTIS A. BRADLEY
Professor of Law
University of Chicago

TARA LEIGH GROVE
Charles E. Tweedy, Jr., Endowed Chairholder of Law
University of Alabama

FOUNDATION
PRESS

University Casebook Series is a trademark registered in the U.S. Patent and Trademark Office.

© 2019, 2020 LEG, Inc. d/b/a West Academic
© 2021 LEG, Inc. d/b/a West Academic
  444 Cedar Street, Suite 700
  St. Paul, MN 55101
  1-877-888-1330

Printed in the United States of America

ISBN: 978-1-64708-847-7

PREFACE

This Supplement brings the 9th edition up to date through the end of the Supreme Court's Term in the summer of 2021. It carries forward three new main cases that were added in prior supplements, and it adds another main case decided in 2021.

Jesner v. Arab Bank (2018) replaces *Kiobel v. Royal Dutch Petroleum* (2013), which was a main case in the 9th edition. In *Kiobel*, the Supreme Court construed the Alien Tort Statute in light of the presumption against extraterritoriality and found that it did not reach certain actions in Nigeria having no direct connection with the United States. The Second Circuit had reached the same conclusion but on different grounds. That court had ruled that the Alien Tort Statute did not provide for suits against corporations, 621 F.3d 111 (2d Cir. 2010), a conclusion that was obviated but not overruled by the Supreme Court's reliance on extraterritoriality. In *Jesner*, the Supreme Court accepted the Second Circuit's reasoning in *Kiobel* in part and held that the Alien Tort Statute has no application to foreign corporations.

Rucho v. Common Cause (2019) is a new main case on the political question doctrine. After backing and filling for years on whether political gerrymandering could be attacked in federal court, the Supreme Court ruled that such claims are non-justiciable, primarily for the lack of "judicially manageable standards" for determining how much political influence on redistricting is too much. Justice Kagan authored a passionate dissent. The 9th edition already has two main cases on the political question doctrine, *Nixon v. United States* (1993) and *Zivotofsky v. Clinton* (2012). Both deal with important contexts, impeachment in *Nixon* and foreign affairs in *Zivotofsky*. It may be that having three main cases on this doctrine will prove unsustainable in the long run, but for now we thought it best to provide an opportunity to study the most recent case, especially given its impact on upcoming elections. Each case is interesting, and there is very little overlap.

Franchise Tax Bd v. Hyatt (2019) overruled Nevada v. Hall, 440 U.S. 410 (1979). The Court held that state immunity against private suits in the courts of other states was "preserved in the constitutional design." The decision in *Franchise Tax Bd* was the third time the litigation of this issue reached the Supreme Court. In 2003, the Court upheld a civil suit against California in a Nevada state court on the authority of *Nevada v. Hall*. In 2016, after the death of Justice Scalia, the case returned to the Supreme Court, which split four-four on whether *Hall* should be overruled. The question was reargued and resolved in *Franchise Tax Board*, with the liberal-conservative alignment that has long dominated state sovereign immunity cases.

Edwards v. Vannoy (2021) concerned the retroactive application of new rules in habeas corpus proceedings. Such retroactive application is generally disallowed under Teague v. Lane, 489 U.S. 288 (1989), but the

Court had indicated before *Edwards* that there were two exceptions: for new "substantive" rules, and for new "watershed" rules of criminal procedure. The Court had never upheld a claim of retroactivity under the watershed exception, and the Court in *Edwards* eliminated this exception altogether. This change to the doctrine is sufficiently significant that we have rewritten the section of the casebook on the retroactive application of rights in habeas and organized it around *Edwards* as a main case. We have included additional notes on the remaining substantive exception to *Teague*.

* * * * *

In addition to the new main cases, the Supplement has notes on a number of other recent cases, including cases involving third-party standing by abortion providers, the availability of *Bivens* actions, suits against domestic corporations under the Alien Tort Statute, and nationwide injunctions. It also has notes discussing recent debates about Supreme Court reform, the standing issues that arose in litigation over the 2020 presidential election, and proposals to restrict qualified immunity. Finally, it has citations to recently published literature.

PERMISSION TO DUPLICATE

There are many intersections between **Federal Courts and the Law of Federal-State Relations** (9th ed. 2018) and Jeffries, Karlan, Low & Rutherglen, **Civil Rights Actions: Enforcing the Constitution** (4th ed. 2018). A teacher using one book may wish to use material from the other book or its supplement. To facilitate such borrowings, we authorize teachers who have adopted either book to duplicate limited portions of the other or its annual supplement for distribution to their students. We are grateful to Foundation Press for agreeing to make this option available.

PWL
JCJ, JR.
CAB
TLG

Charlottesville, Virginia
Chicago, Illinois
Tuscaloosa, Alabama
July 2021

TABLE OF CONTENTS

TABLE OF CASES

The principal cases are in bold type.

TABLE OF AUTHORITIES

UNIVERSITY CASEBOOK SERIES®

2021 SUPPLEMENT TO

FEDERAL COURTS AND THE LAW OF FEDERAL-STATE RELATIONS

NINTH EDITION

CHAPTER I

CHOICE OF LAW IN THE FEDERAL SYSTEM

SECTION 1. STATE LAW IN FEDERAL COURT

Page 15, add at the end of footnote d:

In 2018, the Akron Law Review published a wide-ranging symposium entitled *Erie* at Eighty: Choice of Law Across the Disciplines. Of particular interest to Federal Courts students are Ernest A. Young, *Erie* as a Way of Life, 52 Akron L. Rev. 193 (2018); Craig Green, *Erie* and Constitutional Structure: An Intellectual History, 52 Akron L. Rev. 259 (2018); and Laura Little, *Erie's* Unintended Consequence: Federal Courts Creating State Law, 52 Akron L. Rev. 275 (2018).

Page 19, add at the end of footnote k:

Compare the analysis of the source of law that should govern the tolling of statutes of limitations in federal class action litigation in Stephen B. Burbank and Tobias Barrington Wolfe, Class Actions, Statutes of Limitation and Repose, and Federal Common Law, 167 U. Pa. L. Rev. 1 (2018). The authors conclude that:

> Careful attention to the source of the tolling rule applied in [prior cases], to sources of authority for federal law, and to the distinction between sources of authority and sources of rules, leads us to reaffirm that the tolling rule announced [by the Supreme Court] is a rule of federal common law. . . . Rule 23 [of the Federal Rules of Civil Procedure] is not the source [of the] tolling [principle], but it is the source of the procedural policies that the federal courts are carrying into effect through their authority to promulgate federal common law.

Page 25, add at the end of footnote b:

See also Jeffrey L. Rensberger, The Metasplit: The Law Applied After Transfer in Federal Question Cases, 2018 Wis. L. Rev. 847.

Page 33, add at the end of footnote e:

For a study of the use of certification procedures over the past twenty-five years that finds that courts have increasingly found certification to be a useful tool, see Hon. Kenneth F. Ripple & Kari Anne Gallagher, Certification Comes of Age: Reflections on the Past, Present, and Future of Cooperative Judicial Federalism, 95 Notre Dame L. Rev. 1927 (2020).

Page 33, add after the carryover paragraph:

In Mckesson v. Doe, 592 U.S. ___, 141 S.Ct. 48 (2020), the Supreme Court, in a per curiam opinion, directed the U.S. Court of Appeals for the Fifth Circuit to certify a question of state law. The issue before the Court was whether the Fifth Circuit's application of Louisiana tort law created a conflict with the First Amendment, but the Court concluded that "the Fifth Circuit's interpretation of state law is too uncertain a premise on which to address the question presented." While noting that the federal courts generally have discretion about whether to certify issues of state law, and that "[o]ur system of 'cooperative judicial federalism' presumes federal and state courts alike are competent to apply federal and state law," the Court observed that "[i]n exceptional instances . . . certification is advisable before addressing a constitutional issue." The Court emphasized that in this case "the dispute presents novel issues of state law peculiarly calling for the exercise of judgment by the state courts," and that "certification would ensure that any conflict in this case between state law and the First Amendment is not purely hypothetical." Justice Thomas dissented without opinion.

SECTION 2. FEDERAL LAW IN STATE COURT

Page 48, insert before "—[Footnote by eds.]" at the end of footnote b:

In Ann Woolhandler & Michael G. Collins, State Jurisdictional Independence and Federal Supremacy, 72 Fla. L. Rev. 73 (2020), the authors "take[ ] issue with suggestions that the state courts have broad duties to entertain federal causes of action, whether statutory or constitutional. There is little early support for requiring state courts to entertain such claims and considerable evidence against it. . . . Neither the Supremacy Clause nor related arguments justify such compulsion."

Page 69, add to the second sentence of footnote e:

; Ann Woolhandler & Michael G. Collins, State Jurisdictional Independence and Federal Supremacy, 72 Fla. L. Rev. 73 (2020) (elaborating on the weakness of arguments and historical evidence for the *Testa* result).

SECTION 3. SUPREME COURT REVIEW OF STATE COURT DECISIONS

Page 88, add at the end of footnote a:

For a unique and interesting suggested application of *Brand*, see Michael L. Wells, Wrongful Convictions, Constitutional Remedies, and *Nelson v. Colorado*, 86 Fordham L. Rev. 2199, 2210–15 (2018).

CHAPTER II

THE POWER OF FEDERAL COURTS TO CREATE FEDERAL LAW

SECTION 1. FEDERAL COMMON LAW

Page 155, add at the end of Note 6:

For a critique of the idea of a more wide-ranging federal common law of foreign relations, see Paul B. Stephan, One Voice in Foreign Relations and Federal Common Law, 60 Va. J. Int'l L. 1 (2019).

SECTION 3. RIGHTS OF ACTION TO ENFORCE CONSTITUTIONAL RIGHTS

Page 211, omit Note 3.

Page 212, add at the end of Note 4:

For an empirical analysis of who bears the financial burden of successful *Bivens* claims, finding that individual officials rarely have to use their own resources to pay the damage awards, see James E. Pfander, Alexander A. Reinert & Joanna C. Schwartz, The Myth of Personal Liability: Who Pays When *Bivens* Claims Succeed, 72 Stan. L. Rev. 561 (2020).

Page 212, add a new Note:

4A. NATIONWIDE INJUNCTIONS

The *Bivens* line of cases concerns only the ability to sue for damages. It is well accepted that private parties may seek prospective relief to stop federal government action violative of federal law, assuming they meet standing and other justiciability requirements. In recent years, however, there has been much discussion of the propriety of nationwide federal-court injunctions that have the effect of halting executive branch programs or activities throughout the country. When issued in cases that have not been certified as class actions, these injunctions affect government interactions with many individuals who are not before the court.

For example, in 2015, a federal district court judge in Texas issued a nationwide injunction against President Obama's Deferred Action for Parents of Americans and Lawful Permanent Residents (DAPA) program that would have given many aliens who were illegally present in the United States an exemption from deportation and access to a renewable work permit. In 2017 several federal district courts issued nationwide injunctions against President Trump's "travel ban" orders that were designed to restrict the ability of individuals from certain countries to enter the United States.

Also in 2017, courts issued nationwide injunctions against the Trump administration's allowance of religious exemptions to statutory health insurance requirements, pursuant to which employers would have been able to opt out of paying for contraceptives.

Critics contend that such injunctions give individual district court judges too much authority to affect national policy, lead to forum shopping by plaintiffs, unduly politicize the judiciary, and prevent the useful percolation of issues among the circuits prior to potential Supreme Court review. They also contend that such injunctions are a modern phenomenon that is inconsistent with historical understandings of the proper scope of equitable relief. See, for example, Samuel L. Bray, Multiple Chancellors: Reforming the National Injunction, 131 Harv. L. Rev. 417 (2017).

Defenders of district court discretion to issue such injunctions contend that they are sometimes needed either to provide a plaintiff with complete relief, because the rights being asserted are not divisible, or to avoid undue confusion in the implementation of federal programs. Such injunctions are also claimed to promote rule-of-law values by ensuring that individuals who are in similar situations are treated the same by the government as those before the court. See, for example, Amanda Frost, In Defense of Nationwide Injunctions, 93 N.Y.U. L. Rev. 1065 (2018). Some commentators have also defended these injunctions from a historical perspective. See, for example, Mila Sohoni, The Lost History of the "Universal" Injunction, 133 Harv. L. Rev. 920 (2020).

In Trump v. Hawaii, 585 U.S. ___, 138 S.Ct. 2392 (2018), the Supreme Court reversed a nationwide preliminary injunction directed against one of President Trump's travel ban orders. But it did so because it found that the plaintiffs had not established a likelihood of success on the merits, and thus it did not address the general propriety of this form of relief. Justice Thomas wrote a concurrence, however, that specifically questioned nationwide injunctions, which he referred to as "universal injunctions." Relying heavily on Bray's article and other scholarship, Thomas reasoned that nothing in either existing statutes or in the inherent equitable authority of the federal courts provides support for universal injunctions, and that such injunctions are inconsistent with "traditional limits on equity and judicial power."

There have been suggestions that Congress should address the phenomenon of nationwide injunctions through legislation. Some proposals envision that Congress might use its authority to regulate federal court jurisdiction to simply disallow courts from issuing nationwide injunctions. Other proposals envision more structural reforms, such as the creation of three-judge district courts to decide on the injunctions, with direct appeals to the Supreme Court, similar to what was in place from 1910–1976 to address injunctive challenges to state laws. To date, none of the legislative proposals has been enacted.

For additional discussion of these and related issues, see Spencer E. Amdur & David Hausman, Nationwide Injunctions and Nationwide Harm, 131 Harv. L. Rev. F. 49 (2017); Zachary D. Clopton, National Injunctions and Preclusion, 118 Mich. L. Rev. 1 (2019); Bradford Mank & Michael E.

Solimine, State Standing and National Injunctions, 94 Notre Dame L. Rev. 1955 (2019); Michael T. Morley, Nationwide Injunctions, Rule 23(B)(2), and the Remedial Powers of the Lower Courts, 97 B.U. L. Rev. 615 (2017); Jonathan Remy Nash, State Standing for Nationwide Injunctions Against the Federal Government, 94 Notre Dame L. Rev. 1985 (2019); Zayn Siddique, Nationwide Injunctions, 117 Colum. L. Rev. 2095 (2017); Alan M. Trammell, Demystifying Nationwide Injunctions, 98 Tex. L. Rev. 67 (2019); Howard M. Wasserman, Precedent, Non-Universal Injunctions, and Judicial Departmentalism: A Model of Constitutional Adjudication, 23 Lewis & Clark L. Rev. 1077 (2020).

For articles in a recent symposium issue on nationwide injunctions, see Charlton C. Copeland, Seeing Beyond Courts: The Political Context of the Nationwide Injunction, 91 U. Colo. L. Rev. 789 (2020); David Hausman, When Congress Requires Nationwide Injunctions, 91 U. Colo. L. Rev. 835 (2020); Suzette Malveaux, National Injunctions: What Does the Future Hold?, 91 U. Colo. L. Rev. 779 (2020); Portia Pedro, Toward Establishing a Pre-Extinction Definition of "Nationwide Injunctions," 91 U. Colo. L. Rev. 847 (2020); David Rendleman, Preserving the Nationwide National Government Injunction to Stop Illegal Executive Branch Activity, 91 U. Colo. L. Rev. 887 (2020); Alan M. Trammell, The Constitutionality of Nationwide Injunctions, 91 U. Colo. L. Rev. 977 (2020); Howard W. Wasserman, Concepts, Not Nomenclature: Universal Injunctions, Declaratory Judgments, Opinions, and Precedent, 91 U. Colo. L. Rev. 999 (2020).

Page 213, add the following new Notes:

5A. *HERNANDEZ V. MESA*

Mesa, a U.S. border patrol agent, shot and killed Hernandez, a fifteen-year-old Mexican national, while Hernandez was in Mexico just across the border from Texas. Apparently, Hernandez and some friends had run over to the U.S. side of a culvert along the border and, after one of the friends was detained, Hernandez ran back to the Mexican side where he was shot. The Justice Department investigated the incident, concluded that Mesa had not violated official policy or training, and decided not to bring charges or otherwise take action against him. Mexico was not satisfied with this outcome and requested that Mesa be extradited to Mexico, a request that the United States denied. Hernandez's parents eventually brought suit against Mesa in a federal district court in Texas, seeking damages for violation of Hernandez's Fourth and Fifth Amendment rights.

In Hernandez v. Mesa, 589 U.S. ___, 137 S.Ct. 2003 (2020), the Supreme Court, in a five–four decision, denied a *Bivens* remedy. In an opinion by Justice Alito, the Court began by emphasizing the "tension between this practice [of allowing damage claims for constitutional violations] and the Constitution's separation of legislative and judicial power," and it observed that "for almost 40 years, we have consistently rebuffed requests to add to the claims allowed under *Bivens*." While it did not suggest overturning *Bivens*, the Court expressed disagreement with its reasoning, stating, for example, that "[w]ith the demise of federal general common law, a federal court's authority to recognize a damages remedy must rest at bottom on a statute enacted by Congress, . . . and no statute expressly creates a *Bivens* remedy."

As in *Ziglar v. Abbasi*, the Court considered whether this case involved a "new context" and concluded that it did. Although the plaintiffs' claims were similar to the constitutional claims at issue in *Bivens* and *Davis*, the Court said that it was "glaringly obvious that petitioners' claims involve a new context, i.e., one that is meaningfully different." The Court noted that "*Bivens* concerned an allegedly unconstitutional arrest and search carried out in New York City [and] *Davis* concerned alleged sex discrimination on Capitol Hill," and it said that "[t]here is a world of difference between those claims and petitioners' cross-border shooting claims, where 'the risk of disruptive intrusion by the Judiciary into the functioning of other branches' is significant."

Because it found the context to be new, the Court proceeded to consider whether there were "factors that counsel hesitation," and it concluded that there were. One factor was the foreign relations context:

> A cross-border shooting is by definition an international incident; it involves an event that occurs simultaneously in two countries and affects both countries' interests. Such an incident may lead to a disagreement between those countries, as happened in this case. . . .

> Both the United States and Mexico have legitimate and important interests that may be affected by the way in which this matter is handled. The United States has an interest in ensuring that agents assigned the difficult and important task of policing the border are held to standards and judged by procedures that satisfy United States law and do not undermine the agents' effectiveness and morale. Mexico has an interest in exercising sovereignty over its territory and in protecting and obtaining justice for its nationals. It is not our task to arbitrate between them.

Another factor counseling hesitation, said the Court, was the national security aspect of border protection:

> One of the ways in which the Executive protects this country is by attempting to control the movement of people and goods across the border, and that is a daunting task. The United States' border with Mexico extends for 1,900 miles, and every day thousands of persons and a large volume of goods enter this country at ports of entry on the southern border. The lawful passage of people and goods in both directions across the border is beneficial to both countries.

The Court also said that its reluctance to allow a *Bivens* claim was "reinforced by our survey of what Congress has done in statutes addressing related matters," noting that "Congress has repeatedly declined to authorize the award of damages for injury inflicted outside our borders." For example, 42 U.S.C. § 1983 can be invoked only by "citizen[s] of the United States or other person[s] within the jurisdiction thereof." And, because of the Westfall Act, state-law tort claims brought against federal officials generally will trigger application of the Federal Tort Claim Act (FTCA), which bars "[a]ny claim arising in a foreign country." The Court also noted that, in order to avoid causing foreign relations consequences not intended by the political branches, it generally presumes that statutes do not apply abroad. "If this danger provides a reason for caution when Congress has enacted a statute but has not provided expressly whether it applies abroad," reasoned the Court, "we have even greater reason for hesitation in deciding whether to extend a judge-made cause of action beyond our borders."

Justice Thomas, joined by Justice Gorsuch, concurred in the Court's opinion but wrote separately to suggest that "the time has come to consider discarding the *Bivens* doctrine altogether." He noted that "[t]he foundation for *Bivens*—the practice of creating implied causes of action in the statutory context—has already been abandoned" and that the Court "has consistently refused to extend the *Bivens* doctrine for nearly 40 years, even going so far as to suggest that *Bivens* and its progeny were wrongly decided." In Thomas's view, "[f]ederal courts lack the authority to engage in the distinctly legislative task of creating causes of action for damages to enforce federal positive law," and he said that he "see[s] no reason for us to take a different approach if the right asserted to recover damages derives from the Constitution, rather than from a federal statute."

Justice Ginsburg dissented and was joined by Justices Breyer, Sotomayor, and Kagan. Ginsburg rejected the proposition that this case presented a new context:

> Plaintiffs' *Bivens* action arises in a setting kin to *Bivens* itself: Mesa, plaintiffs allege, acted in disregard of instructions governing his conduct and of Hernandez's constitutional rights. . . . Using lethal force against a person who "poses no immediate threat to the officer and no threat to others" surely qualifies as an unreasonable seizure. Tennessee v. Garner, 471 U.S. 1, 11 (1985). The complaint states that Mesa engaged in that very conduct; it alleged, specifically, that Hernandez was unarmed and posed no threat to Mesa or others. For these reasons, as Mesa acknowledged at oral argument, Hernandez's parents could have maintained a *Bivens* action had the bullet hit Hernandez while he was running up or down the United States side of the embankment.

> The only salient difference here: the fortuity that the bullet happened to strike Hernandez on the Mexican side of the embankment. But Hernandez's location at the precise moment the bullet landed should not matter one whit. . . . Mesa's allegedly unwarranted deployment of deadly force occurred on United States soil. It scarcely makes sense for a remedy trained on deterring rogue officer conduct to turn upon a happenstance subsequent to the conduct—a bullet landing in one half of a culvert, not the other.

Ginsburg further argued that, even if the context were new, there was no good reason to deny a damages claim in this case. As an initial matter, she noted that, "[a]s in *Bivens*, plaintiffs [in this case] lack recourse to alternative remedies." While acknowledging that "the absence of alternative remedies, standing alone, does not warrant a *Bivens* action," Ginsburg argued that "it remains a significant consideration under *Abbasi*'s guidelines." As for the foreign relations aspects of this case, she observed that the damages action here is "no different from one a federal court would entertain had the fatal shot hit Hernandez before he reached the Mexican side of the border." She also argued that the Court was not escaping foreign relations considerations by refusing to allow a *Bivens* claim, since that refusal was likely to create additional friction with Mexico and undermine the United States' compliance with international commitments. As for national security considerations, Ginsburg complained that "the Court speaks with generality of the national-security involvement of Border Patrol officers. It does not home in on how a *Bivens* suit for an unjustified killing would in fact undermine security at the border."

As for the position of Congress on all this, Ginsburg noted that "Congress, although well aware of the Court's opinion in *Bivens*, . . . has not endeavored to dislodge the decision." The limitations in 42 U.S.C. § 1983, she pointed out, relate to "its provenance [in] Reconstruction-era policies aiming to secure to former slaves federal rights and to ward off state and local incursion on those rights." As for the FTCA, she said that its disallowance of claims arising in a foreign country stems from "Congress's 'unwilling[ness] to subject the United States to liabilities depending upon the laws of a foreign power,'" whereas here "the suit arises under U.S. law." Finally, with respect to the general presumption against applying U.S. laws extraterritorially, she noted that the "plaintiffs in this case allege a tort stemming from stateside conduct" and thus "seek the application of U.S. law to conduct occurring inside our borders."

5B. JUDGMENT BAR OF THE FEDERAL TORTS CLAIMS ACT

The Federal Torts Claims Act (FTCA) authorizes damages claims against the United States for negligent actions by government employees acting within the scope of their employment under circumstances where the United States, if a private person, would be liable under the law of the place where the act or omission occurred. It contains a judgment bar provision that reads:

> "The judgment in an action under section 1346(b) of this title shall constitute a complete bar to any action by the claimant, by reason of the same subject matter, against the employee of the government whose act or omission gave rise to the claim."

28 U.S.C. § 2676. The Court noted in Simmons v. Himmelreich, 578 U.S. 621, 630 n.5 (2016), that:

> The judgment bar provision supplements common-law claim preclusion by closing a narrow gap: At the time that the FTCA was passed, common-law claim preclusion would have barred a plaintiff from suing the United States after having sued an employee but not vice versa. The judgment bar provision applies where a plaintiff first sues the United States and then sues an employee.

The judgment bar has arisen in situations where a plaintiff brings an FTCA claim against the government and a *Bivens* action against the federal employee involved in the FTCA suit. The Court addressed the circumstances under which the judgment bar is triggered in *Simmons* as well as in Brownback v. King, 592 U.S. ___, 141 S.Ct. 740 (2021). See also James E. Pfander & Neil Aggarwal, *Bivens*, the Judgment Bar, and the Perils of Dynamic Textualism, 8 U. St. Thomas L.J. 417 (2011) ("In the hands of textualist judges acting with a measure of skepticism towards *Bivens* litigation, the judgment bar has . . . become an important burden on the right of individuals to pursue constitutional tort claims against the federal government.").

Page 213, add at the end of Note 6:

For a rich set of symposium essays commemorating the fiftieth anniversary of *Bivens*, see Katherine Mims Crocker, A Scapegoat Theory of *Bivens*, 96 Notre Dame L. Rev. 1943, 1946 (2021) ("explor[ing] the possibility that the *Bivens* regime's beginnings countered various exercises in scapegoating and that the *Bivens* regime's abatement constitutes an exercise in scapegoating"); Andrew Kent, Lessons for *Bivens* and Qualified Immunity Debates from Nineteenth-Century Damages Litigation Against Federal Officers, 96 Notre Dame L. Rev. 1755, 1787 (2021) (explaining that "[w]hen bureaucratic sophistication, speedier communications and modes of travel, professionalization of the civil service, and salarization came to characterize U.S. government over the course of the nineteenth century and early twentieth century, the United States began turning away from personal officer liability for damages"); Randy J. Kozel, Stare Decisis as Authority and Aspiration, 96 Notre Dame L. Rev. 1971, 1975 (2021) (arguing that *Bivens* "is a powerful candidate for reaffirmance under the doctrine of stare decisis"); Joanna C. Schwartz, Alexander Reinert, and James E. Pfander, Going Rogue: The Supreme Court's Newfound Hostility to Policy-Based *Bivens* Claims, 96 Notre Dame L. Rev. 1835, 1838 (2021) (critiquing "the *Ziglar* Court's suggestion that plaintiffs may not seek damages for injuries caused by an unconstitutional federal government policy"); Gregory Sisk, Recovering the Tort Remedy for Federal Official Wrongdoing, 96 Notre Dame L. Rev. 1789, 1791 (2021) (contending that "[t]he modern Federal Tort Claims Act (FTCA) roughly replicates the original regime for official wrongdoing by imposing liability directly on the government through the traditional medium of tort" and that "[t]hrough modest revisions to the FTCA, most claims for abuse of federal government power can be adequately addressed through a common-law tort cause of action"); Carlos M. Vazquez, *Bivens* and the *Ancien Regime*, 96 Notre Dame L. Rev. 1923, 1924 (2021) (arguing that "the federal damage remedy recognized in *Bivens* could have been framed—and should now be understood—as the post-*Erie* manifestation of the general common-law remedial regime that prevailed since the Founding"); Stephen I. Vladeck, The Inconsistent Originalism of Judge-Made Remedies Against Federal Officers, 96 Notre Dame L. Rev. 1869, 1872 (2021) (contending that "the Supreme Court's modern hostility to judge-made damages remedies against federal officers, in contrast to its solicitude toward judge-made injunctive relief," is "affirmatively antithetical to originalism as a modality of constitutional interpretation"); Ann Woolhandler and Michael G. Collins, Was *Bivens*

Necessary?, 96 Notre Dame L. Rev. 1893, 1920 (2021) (arguing that "*Bivens* was supported by the Framers' expectations that trespass actions against officials would be a means of implementing the Constitution").

SECTION 4. CUSTOMARY INTERNATIONAL LAW AND THE ALIEN TORT STATUTE

Page 224, add a footnote at the end of the second full paragraph:

ᵉ Anthony J. Bellia, Jr. and Bradford R. Clark, The Law of Nations and the United States Constitution (2017), reflects the authors' views on these issues relating to the domestic status of the law of nations. This book was the subject of a 2018 symposium in the Georgetown Law Journal. See William S. Dodge, Customary International Law, Change, and the Constitution, 106 Georgetown L.J.1559 (2018); David M. Golove and Daniel J. Hulsebosch, The Law of Nations and the Constitution: An Early Modern Perspective, 106 Georgetown L.J.1593 (2018); John Harrison, The Constitution and the Law of Nations, 106 Georgetown L.J.1659 (2018); Thomas H. Lee, The Law of Nations and the Judicial Branch, 106 Georgetown L.J. 1707 (2018); Michael D. Ramsey, The Constitution's Text and Customary International Law, 106 Georgetown L.J. 1747 (2018); Paul B. Stephan, Inferences of Judicial Lawmaking Power and the Law of Nations, 106 Georgetown L.J. 1793 (2018); Ingrid Wuerth, The Future of the Federal Common Law of Foreign Relations, 106 Georgetown L.J. 1825 (2018). A response to these articles can be found in Anthony J. Bellia, Jr. and Bradford R. Clark, Why Federal Courts Apply the Law of Nations Even Though It Is Not the Supreme Law of the Land, 106 Georgetown L.J. 1915 (2018).

Page 242, omit Note 3 and renumber the remaining Notes.

Page 248, replace *Kiobel* and its Notes, pages 248–61, with the following:

Jesner v. Arab Bank, PLC

Supreme Court of the United States, 2018.
584 U.S. ___, 138 S.Ct. 1386.

■ JUSTICE KENNEDY announced the judgment of the Court and delivered the opinion of the Court with respect to Parts I, II-B-1, and II-C, and an opinion with respect to Parts II-A, II-B-2, II-B-3, and III, in which THE CHIEF JUSTICE and JUSTICE THOMAS join.

Petitioners in this case, or the persons on whose behalf petitioners now assert claims, allegedly were injured or killed by terrorist acts committed abroad. Those terrorist acts, it is contended, were in part caused or facilitated by a foreign corporation. Petitioners now seek to impose liability on the foreign corporation for the conduct of its human agents, including its then-chairman and other high-ranking management officials. The suits were filed in a United States District Court under the Alien Tort Statute, commonly referred to as the ATS. See 28 U.S.C. § 1350.

The foreign corporation charged with liability in these ATS suits is Arab Bank, PLC; and it is respondent here. Some of Arab Bank's officials, it is alleged, allowed the Bank to be used to transfer funds to terrorist groups in the Middle East, which in turn enabled or facilitated criminal acts of terrorism, causing the deaths or injuries for which petitioners now seek compensation. Petitioners seek to prove Arab Bank helped the terrorists receive the moneys in part by means of currency clearances and bank transactions passing through its New York City offices, all by means of electronic transfers.

It is assumed here that those individuals who inflicted death or injury by terrorism committed crimes in violation of well-settled, fundamental precepts of international law, precepts essential for basic human-rights protections. It is assumed as well that individuals who knowingly and purposefully facilitated banking transactions to aid, enable, or facilitate the terrorist acts would themselves be committing crimes under the same international-law prohibitions.

Petitioners contend that international and domestic laws impose responsibility and liability on a corporation if its human agents use the corporation to commit crimes in violation of international laws that protect human rights. The question here is whether the Judiciary has the authority, in an ATS action, to make that determination and then to enforce that liability in ATS suits, all without any explicit authorization from Congress to do so.

The answer turns upon the proper interpretation and implementation of the ATS. The statute provides: "The district courts shall have original jurisdiction of any civil action by an alien for a tort only, committed in violation of the law of nations or a treaty of the United States." § 1350. The Court must first ask whether the law of nations imposes liability on corporations for human-rights violations committed by its employees. The Court must also ask whether it has authority and discretion in an ATS suit to impose liability on a corporation without a specific direction from Congress to do so.

I

A

. . . During the pendency of this litigation, there was an unrelated case that also implicated the issue whether the ATS is applicable to suits in this country against foreign corporations. See Kiobel v. Royal Dutch Petroleum Co., 621 F.3d 111 (2d Cir. 2010). That suit worked its way through the trial court and the Court of Appeals for the Second Circuit. The Kiobel litigation did not involve banking transactions. Its allegations were that holding companies incorporated in the Netherlands and the United Kingdom had, through a Nigerian subsidiary, aided and abetted the Nigerian Government in human-rights abuses. In Kiobel, the Court of Appeals held that the ATS does not extend to suits against corporations. This Court granted certiorari in Kiobel.

After additional briefing and reargument in Kiobel, this Court held that, given all the circumstances, the suit could not be maintained under the ATS. Kiobel v. Royal Dutch Petroleum Co., 569 U.S. 108, 114, 124–25 (2013). The rationale of the holding, however, was not that the ATS does not extend to suits against foreign corporations. That question was left unresolved. The Court ruled, instead, that "all the relevant conduct took place outside the United States." Dismissal of the action was required based on the presumption against extraterritorial application of statutes.

So while this Court in *Kiobel* affirmed the ruling that the action there could not be maintained, it did not address the broader holding of the Court of Appeals that dismissal was required because corporations may not be sued under the ATS. Still, the courts of the Second Circuit deemed that broader holding to be binding precedent. As a consequence, in the instant case the District Court dismissed petitioners' ATS claims based on the earlier *Kiobel* holding in the Court of Appeals; and on review of the dismissal order the Court of Appeals, also adhering to its earlier holding, affirmed. This Court granted certiorari in the instant case.

Since the Court of Appeals relied on its *Kiobel* holding in the instant case, it is instructive to begin with an analysis of that decision. The majority opinion in *Kiobel*, written by Judge Cabranes, held that the ATS does not apply to alleged international-law violations by a corporation. Judge Cabranes relied in large part on the fact that international criminal tribunals have consistently limited their jurisdiction to natural persons.

Judge Leval filed a separate opinion. He concurred in the judgment on other grounds but disagreed with the proposition that the foreign corporation was not subject to suit under the ATS. Judge Leval conceded that "international law, of its own force, imposes no liabilities on corporations or other private juridical entities." But he reasoned that corporate liability for violations of international law is an issue of "civil compensatory liability" that international law leaves to individual nations. Later decisions in the Courts of Appeals for the Seventh, Ninth, and District of Columbia Circuits agreed with Judge Leval and held that corporations can be subject to suit under the ATS. The respective opinions by Judges Cabranes and Leval are scholarly and extensive, providing significant guidance for this Court in the case now before it.

With this background, it is now proper to turn to the history of the ATS and the decisions interpreting it.

B

[In this section of its opinion, the Court reviewed the history of the ATS as recounted in Sosa v. Alvarez-Machain, 542 U.S. 692 (2004). It also described the evolution of ATS litigation from *Filartiga* to *Kiobel*.]

II

With these principles in mind, this Court now must decide whether common-law liability under the ATS extends to a foreign corporate defendant. It could be argued, under the Court's holding in *Kiobel*, that even if, under accepted principles of international law and federal common law, corporations are subject to ATS liability for human-rights crimes committed by their human agents, in this case the activities of the defendant corporation and the alleged actions of its employees have insufficient connections to the United States to subject it to jurisdiction under the ATS. Various amici urge this as a rationale to affirm here, while the Government argues that the Court should remand this case so the Court of Appeals can address the issue in the first instance. There are substantial arguments on both sides of that question; but it is not the question on which this Court granted certiorari, nor is it the question that has divided the Courts of Appeals.

The question whether foreign corporations are subject to liability under the ATS should be addressed; for, if there is no liability for Arab Bank, the lengthy and costly litigation concerning whether corporate contacts like those alleged here suffice to impose liability would be pointless. In addition, a remand to the Court of Appeals would require prolonging litigation that already has caused significant diplomatic tensions with Jordan for more than a decade. So it is proper for this Court to decide whether corporations, or at least foreign corporations, are subject to liability in an ATS suit filed in a United States district court.

Before recognizing a common-law action under the ATS, federal courts must apply the test announced in *Sosa*. An initial, threshold question is whether a plaintiff can demonstrate that the alleged violation is "of a norm that is specific, universal, and obligatory." 542 U.S. at 732. And even assuming that, under international law, there is a specific norm that can be controlling, it must be determined further whether allowing this case to proceed under the ATS is a proper exercise of judicial discretion, or instead whether caution requires the political branches to grant specific authority before corporate liability can be imposed. See id. at 732–33 and nn. 20–21. "[T]he potential implications for the foreign relations of the United States of recognizing such causes should make courts particularly wary of impinging on the discretion of the Legislative and Executive Branches in managing foreign affairs." Id. at 727.

It must be said that some of the considerations that pertain to determining whether there is a specific, universal, and obligatory norm that is established under international law are applicable as well in determining whether deference must be given to the political branches. For instance, the fact that the charters of some international tribunals and the provisions of some congressional statutes addressing international human-rights violations are specifically limited to individual wrongdoers, and thus foreclose corporate liability, has significant bearing both on the content of the norm being asserted and the question whether courts should defer to Congress. The two inquiries inform each other and are, to that extent, not altogether discrete.

With that introduction, it is proper now to turn first to the question whether there is an international-law norm imposing liability on corporations for acts of their employees that contravene fundamental human rights.

A

Petitioners and Arab Bank disagree as to whether corporate liability is a question of international law or only a question of judicial authority and discretion under domestic law. [At this point the Court considered various materials relating to corporate liability under international law.]

[T]he Court need not resolve the questions whether corporate liability is a question that is governed by international law, or, if so, whether international law imposes liability on corporations. There is at least sufficient doubt on the point to turn to *Sosa*'s second question—whether the Judiciary must defer to Congress, allowing it to determine in the first instance whether that universal norm has been recognized and, if so, whether it is prudent and necessary to direct its enforcement in suits under the ATS.

B

1

Sosa is consistent with this Court's general reluctance to extend judicially created private rights of action. The Court's recent precedents cast doubt on the authority of courts to extend or create private causes of action even in the realm of domestic law, where this Court has "recently and repeatedly said that a decision to create a private right of action is one better left to legislative judgment in the great majority of cases." 542 U.S. at 727 (citing Correctional Services Corp. v. Malesko, 534 U.S. 61, 68 (2001); Alexander v. Sandoval, 532 U.S. 275, 286–87 (2001)). That is because "the Legislature is in the better position to consider if the public interest would be served by imposing a new substantive legal liability." Ziglar v. Abbasi, 582 U.S. ___, ___, 137 S.Ct. 1843, 1857 (2017). Thus, "if there are sound reasons to think Congress might doubt the efficacy or necessity of a damages remedy, . . . courts must refrain from creating the remedy in order to respect the role of Congress." Id. at ___, 137 S.Ct. at 1858.

This caution extends to the question whether the courts should exercise the judicial authority to mandate a rule that imposes liability upon artificial entities like corporations. Thus, in *Malesko* the Court held that corporate defendants may not be held liable in *Bivens* actions. See Bivens v. Six Unknown Fed. Narcotics Agents, 403 U.S. 388 (1971). Allowing corporate liability would have been a "marked extension" of *Bivens* that was unnecessary to advance its purpose of holding individual officers responsible for "engaging in unconstitutional wrongdoing." *Malesko*, 534 U.S. at 74. Whether corporate defendants should be subject to suit was "a question for Congress, not us, to decide." Id. at 72.

Neither the language of the ATS nor the precedents interpreting it support an exception to these general principles in this context. In fact, the separation-of-powers concerns that counsel against courts creating private rights of action apply with particular force in the context of the ATS. The political branches, not the Judiciary, have the responsibility and institutional capacity to weigh foreign-policy concerns. That the ATS implicates foreign relations "is itself a reason for a high bar to new private causes of action for violating international law." *Sosa*, 542 U.S. at 727.

In *Sosa*, the Court emphasized that federal courts must exercise "great caution" before recognizing new forms of liability under the ATS. In light of the foreign-policy and separation-of-powers concerns inherent in ATS litigation, there is an argument that a proper application of *Sosa* would preclude courts from ever recognizing any new causes of action under the ATS. But the Court need not resolve that question in this case. Either way, absent further action from Congress it would be inappropriate for courts to extend ATS liability to foreign corporations.

2

Even in areas less fraught with foreign-policy consequences, the Court looks to analogous statutes for guidance on the appropriate boundaries of judge-made causes of action. Doing so is even more important in the realm of international law, where "the general practice has been to look for legislative guidance before exercising innovative authority over substantive law." *Sosa*, 542 U.S. at 726.

Here, the logical place to look for a statutory analogy to an ATS common-law action is the [Torture Victim Protection Act (TVPA)]—the only cause of action under the ATS created by Congress rather than the courts. . . .

The key feature of the TVPA for this case is that it limits liability to "individuals," which, the Court has held, unambiguously limits liability to natural persons. Mohamad v. Palestinian Authority, 566 U.S. 449, 453–56 (2012). Congress's decision to exclude liability for corporations in actions brought under the TVPA is all but dispositive of the present case. That decision illustrates that significant foreign-policy implications require the courts to draw a careful balance in defining the scope of actions under the ATS. It would be inconsistent with that balance to create a remedy broader than the one created by Congress. Indeed, it "would be remarkable to take a more aggressive role in exercising a jurisdiction that remained largely in shadow for much of the prior two centuries." *Sosa*, 542 U.S. at 726. . . .

Petitioners contend that, instead of the TVPA, the most analogous statute here is the Anti-Terrorism Act. That Act does permit suits against corporate entities. See 18 U.S.C. §§ 2331(3), 2333(d)(2). In fact, in these suits some of the foreign plaintiffs joined their claims to those of United States nationals suing Arab Bank under the Anti-Terrorism Act. But the Anti-Terrorism Act provides a cause of action only to "national[s] of the United States," and their "estate, survivors, or heirs." § 2333(a). In contrast, the ATS is available only for claims brought by "an alien." 28 U.S.C. § 1350. A statute that excludes foreign nationals (with the possible exception of foreign survivors or heirs) is an inapt analogy for a common-law cause of action that provides a remedy for foreign nationals only.

To the extent, furthermore, that the Anti-Terrorism Act is relevant it suggests that there should be no common-law action under the ATS for allegations like petitioners'. Otherwise, foreign plaintiffs could bypass Congress's express limitations on liability under the Anti-Terrorism Act simply by bringing an ATS lawsuit. The Anti-Terrorism Act . . . is part of a comprehensive statutory and regulatory regime that prohibits terrorism and terrorism financing. The detailed regulatory structures prescribed by Congress and the federal agencies charged with oversight of financial institutions reflect the careful deliberation of the political branches on when, and how, banks should be held liable for the financing of terrorism. It would be inappropriate for courts to displace this considered statutory and regulatory structure by holding banks subject to common-law liability in actions filed under the ATS.

In any event, even if the Anti-Terrorism Act were a suitable model for an ATS suit, Congress's decision in the TVPA to limit liability to individuals still demonstrates that there are two reasonable choices. In this area, that is dispositive—Congress, not the Judiciary, must decide whether to expand the scope of liability under the ATS to include foreign corporations.

3

Other considerations relevant to the exercise of judicial discretion also counsel against allowing liability under the ATS for foreign corporations, absent instructions from Congress to do so. It has not been shown that corporate liability under the ATS is essential to serve the goals of the statute. As to the question of adequate remedies, the ATS will seldom be the only way for plaintiffs to hold the perpetrators liable. See, e.g., 18 U.S.C. § 1091 (criminal prohibition on genocide); § 1595 (civil remedy for victims of slavery). And plaintiffs still can sue the individual corporate employees responsible for a violation of international law under the ATS. If the Court were to hold that foreign corporations have liability for international-law violations, then plaintiffs may well ignore the human perpetrators and concentrate instead on multinational corporate entities.

. . . [I]n the context of criminal tribunals international law itself generally limits liability to natural persons. Although the Court need not decide whether the seeming absence of a specific, universal, and obligatory norm of corporate liability under international law by itself forecloses petitioners' claims against Arab Bank, or whether this is an issue governed by international law, the lack of a clear and well-established international-law rule is of critical relevance in determining whether courts should extend ATS liability to foreign corporations without specific congressional authorization to do so. That is especially so in light of the TVPA's limitation of liability to natural persons, which parallels the distinction between corporations and individuals in international law.

If, moreover, the Court were to hold that foreign corporations may be held liable under the ATS, that precedent-setting principle "would imply that other nations, also applying the law of nations, could hale our [corporations] into their courts for alleged violations of the law of nations." *Kiobel*, 569 U.S. at 124. This judicially mandated doctrine, in turn, could subject American corporations to an immediate, constant risk of claims seeking to impose massive liability for the alleged conduct of their employees and subsidiaries around the world, all as determined in foreign courts, thereby "hinder[ing] global investment in developing economies, where it is most needed." Brief for United States as Amicus Curiae in *American Isuzu Motors, Inc.* v. *Ntsebeza*, O.T. 2007, No. 07–919, p. 20.

In other words, allowing plaintiffs to sue foreign corporations under the ATS could establish a precedent that discourages American corporations from investing abroad, including in developing economies where the host government might have a history of alleged human-rights violations, or where judicial systems might lack the safeguards of United States courts. And, in consequence, that often might deter the active corporate investment that contributes to the economic development that so often is an essential foundation for human rights.

It is also true, of course, that natural persons can and do use corporations for sinister purposes, including conduct that violates international law. That the corporate form can be an instrument for inflicting grave harm and suffering poses serious and complex questions both for the international community and for Congress. So there are strong arguments for permitting the victims to seek relief from corporations themselves. Yet the urgency and complexity of this problem make it all the more important that Congress determine whether victims of human-rights abuses may sue foreign corporations in federal courts in the United States. Congress, not the Judiciary, is the branch with "the facilities necessary to make fairly such an important policy decision where the possibilities of international discord are so evident and retaliative action so certain." *Kiobel*, 569 U.S. at 116. As noted further below, there are many delicate and important considerations that Congress is in a better position to examine in determining whether and how best to impose corporate liability. And, as the TVPA illustrates, Congress is well aware of the necessity of clarifying the proper scope of liability under the ATS in a timely way.

C

The ATS was intended to promote harmony in international relations by ensuring foreign plaintiffs a remedy for international-law violations in circumstances where the absence of such a remedy might provoke foreign nations to hold the United States accountable. Brief for United States as Amicus Curiae 7. But here, and in similar cases, the opposite is occurring.

Petitioners are foreign nationals seeking hundreds of millions of dollars in damages from a major Jordanian financial institution for injuries suffered in attacks by foreign terrorists in the Middle East. The only alleged connections to the United States are [electronic currency clearance] transactions in Arab Bank's New York branch and a brief allegation regarding a charity in Texas. The Court of Appeals did not address, and the Court need not now decide, whether these allegations are sufficient to "touch and concern" the United States under *Kiobel*.

At a minimum, the relatively minor connection between the terrorist attacks at issue in this case and the alleged conduct in the United States well illustrates the perils of extending the scope of ATS liability to foreign multinational corporations like Arab Bank. For 13 years, this litigation has "caused significant diplomatic tensions" with Jordan, a critical ally in one of the world's most sensitive regions. Brief for United States as Amicus Curiae 30. "Jordan is a key counterterrorism partner, especially in the global campaign to defeat the Islamic State in Iraq and Syria." Id. at 31. The United States explains that Arab Bank itself is "a constructive partner with the United States in working to prevent terrorist financing." Id. at 32 (internal quotation marks omitted). Jordan considers the instant litigation to be a "grave affront" to its sovereignty. See Brief for Hashemite Kingdom of Jordan as Amicus Curiae 3.

This is not the first time, furthermore, that a foreign sovereign has appeared in this Court to note its objections to ATS litigation. . . . These are the very foreign-relations tensions the First Congress sought to avoid.

Petitioners insist that whatever the faults of this litigation—for example, its tenuous connections to the United States and the prolonged diplomatic disruptions it has caused—the fact that Arab Bank is a foreign corporate entity, as distinct from a natural person, is not one of them. That misses the point. As demonstrated by this litigation, foreign corporate defendants create unique problems. And courts are not well suited to make the required policy judgments that are implicated by corporate liability in cases like this one.

Like the presumption against extraterritoriality, judicial caution under *Sosa* "guards against our courts triggering . . . serious foreign policy consequences, and instead defers such decisions, quite appropriately, to the political branches." *Kiobel*, 569 U.S. at 124. If, in light of all the concerns that must be weighed before imposing liability on foreign corporations via ATS suits, the Court were to hold that it has the discretion to make that determination, then the cautionary language of *Sosa* would be little more than empty rhetoric. Accordingly, the Court holds that foreign corporations may not be defendants in suits brought under the ATS.

III

With the ATS, the First Congress provided a federal remedy for a narrow category of international-law violations committed by individuals. Whether, more than two centuries on, a similar remedy should be available against foreign corporations is similarly a decision that Congress must make.

The political branches can determine, referring to international law to the extent they deem proper, whether to impose liability for human-rights violations upon foreign corporations in this Nation's courts, and, conversely, that courts in other countries should be able to hold United States corporations liable. Congress might determine that violations of international law do, or should, impose that liability to ensure that corporations make every effort to deter human-rights violations, and so that, even when those efforts cannot be faulted, compensation for injured persons will be a cost of doing business. If Congress and the Executive were to determine that corporations should be liable for violations of international law, that decision would have special power and force because it would be made by the branches most immediately responsive to, and accountable to, the electorate.

It is still another possibility that, in the careful exercise of its expertise in the field of foreign affairs, Congress might conclude that neutral judicial safeguards may not be ensured in every country; and so, as a reciprocal matter, it could determine that liability of foreign corporations under the ATS should be subject to some limitations or preconditions. Congress might deem this more careful course to be the best way to encourage American corporations to undertake the extensive investments and foreign operations that can be an important beginning point for creating the infrastructures that allow human rights, as well as judicial safeguards, to emerge. These delicate judgments, involving a balance that it is the prerogative of the political branches to make, especially in the field of foreign affairs, would, once again, also be entitled to special respect, especially because those careful distinctions might themselves advance the Rule of Law. All this underscores the important separation-of-powers concerns that require the Judiciary to refrain from making these kinds of decisions under the ATS. The political branches, moreover, surely are better positioned than the Judiciary to determine if corporate liability would, or would not, create special risks of disrupting good relations with foreign governments.

Finally, Congress might find that corporate liability should be limited to cases where a corporation's management was actively complicit in the crime. Cf. ALI, Model Penal Code § 2.07(1)(c) (1985) (a corporation may be held criminally liable where "the commission of the offense was authorized, requested, commanded, performed or recklessly tolerated by the board of directors or by a high managerial agent acting on behalf of the corporation within the scope of his office or employment"). Again, the political branches are better equipped to make the preliminary findings and consequent conclusions that should inform this determination.

These and other considerations that must shape and instruct the formulation of principles of international and domestic law are matters that the political branches are in the better position to define and articulate.

For these reasons, judicial deference requires that any imposition of corporate liability on foreign corporations for violations of international law must be determined in the first instance by the political branches of the Government.

The judgment of the Court of Appeals is affirmed.

It is so ordered.

■ JUSTICE THOMAS, concurring.

I join the Court's opinion in full because it correctly applies our precedents. I also agree with the points raised by my concurring colleagues. Courts should not be in the business of creating new causes of action under the Alien Tort Statute (Gorsuch, J., concurring in part and concurring in judgment), especially when it risks international strife (Alito, J., concurring in part and concurring in judgment). And the Alien Tort Statute likely does not apply to suits between foreign plaintiffs and foreign defendants (opinion of Gorsuch, J.).

■ JUSTICE ALITO, concurring in part and concurring in the judgment.

Creating causes of action under the Alien Tort Statute against foreign corporate defendants would precipitate exactly the sort of diplomatic strife that the law was enacted to prevent. As a result, I agree with the Court that we should not take that step, and I join Parts I, II-B-1, and II-C of the opinion of the Court. I write separately to elaborate on why that outcome is compelled not only by "judicial caution," but also by the separation of powers. . . .

For the reasons articulated by Justice Scalia in Sosa v. Alvarez-Machain, 542 U.S. 692 (2004), and by Justice Gorsuch today, I am not certain that *Sosa* was correctly decided. But even taking that decision on its own terms, this Court should not create causes of action under the ATS against foreign corporate defendants. As part of *Sosa*'s second step, a court should decline to create a cause of action as a matter of federal common law where the result would be to further, not avoid, diplomatic strife. Properly applied, that rule easily resolves the question presented by this case.*

Sosa interpreted the ATS to authorize the federal courts to create causes of action as a matter of federal common law. We have repeatedly emphasized that "in fashioning federal [common law] principles to govern areas left open by Congress, our function is to effectuate congressional policy." United States v. Kimbell Foods, Inc., 440 U.S. 715, 738 (1979). Fidelity to congressional policy is not only prudent but necessary: Going beyond the bounds of Congress's authorization would mean unconstitutionally usurping part of the "legislative Powers." U.S. Const., Art. I, § 1. Accordingly, the objective for courts in every case requiring the

---

* Because this case involves a foreign corporation, we have no need to reach the question whether an alien may sue a United States corporation under the ATS. And since such a suit may generally be brought in federal court based on diversity jurisdiction, 28 U.S.C. § 1332(a)(2), it is unclear why ATS jurisdiction would be needed in that situation.

creation of federal common law must be "to find the rule that will best effectuate the federal policy." Textile Workers v. Lincoln Mills of Ala., 353 U.S. 448, 457 (1957).

The ATS was meant to help the United States avoid diplomatic friction. The First Congress enacted the law to provide a forum for adjudicating that "narrow set of violations of the law of nations" that, if left unaddressed, "threaten[ed] serious consequences" for the United States. *Sosa*, 542 U.S. at 715. Specifically, the First Congress was concerned about offenses like piracy, violation of safe conducts, and infringement of the rights of ambassadors, each of which "if not adequately redressed could rise to an issue of war." Id. That threat was existentially terrifying for the young Nation. To minimize the danger, the First Congress enacted the ATS, "ensur[ing] that the United States could provide a forum for adjudicating such incidents" and thus helping the Nation avoid further diplomatic imbroglios. Kiobel v. Royal Dutch Petroleum Co., 569 U.S. 108, 114, 124 (2013).

Putting that objective together with the rules governing federal common law generally, the following principle emerges: Federal courts should decline to create federal common law causes of action under *Sosa*'s second step whenever doing so would not materially advance the ATS's objective of avoiding diplomatic strife. And applying that principle here, it is clear that federal courts should not create causes of action under the ATS against foreign corporate defendants. All parties agree that customary international law does not *require* corporate liability as a general matter. But if customary international law does not require corporate liability, then declining to create it under the ATS cannot give other nations just cause for complaint against the United States.

To the contrary, ATS suits against foreign corporations may provoke—and, indeed, frequently *have* provoked—exactly the sort of diplomatic strife inimical to the fundamental purpose of the ATS. Some foreign states appear to interpret international law as foreclosing civil corporate liability for violations of the law of nations. Creating ATS causes of action against foreign corporate defendants would put the United States at odds with these nations. Even when states do not object to this sort of corporate liability as a *legal* matter, they may be concerned about ATS suits against their corporations for political reasons. For example, Jordan considers this suit "a direct affront" to its sovereignty and one that "risks destabilizing Jordan's economy and undercutting one of the most stable and productive alliances the United States has in the Middle East." Brief for Hashemite Kingdom of Jordan as Amicus Curiae 4. Courting these sorts of problems—which seem endemic to ATS litigation—was the opposite of what the First Congress had in mind.

In response, the dissent argues merely that any diplomatic friction "can be addressed with a tool more tailored to the source of the problem than a blanket ban on corporate liability." Even on its own terms, that argument is problematic: Many of the "more tailored" tools offered by the dissent will still be hotly litigated by ATS plaintiffs, and it may be years before incorrect initial decisions about their applicability can be reviewed by the courts of appeals.

In any event, the dissent misunderstands the relevant standard. The question before us is whether the United States would be embroiled in fewer international controversies if we created causes of action under the ATS against foreign corporate defendants. Unless corporate liability would actively *decrease* diplomatic disputes, we have no authority to act. On that score, the dissent can only speculate that declining to create causes of action against foreign corporate defendants "might" lead to diplomatic friction. But the dissent has no real-world examples to support its hunch, and that is not surprising; the ATS already goes further than any other statute in the world in granting aliens the right to sue civilly for violations of international law, especially in light of the many other avenues for relief available. It would be rather rich for any other nation to complain that the ATS does not go far enough. Indeed, no country has. . . .

Creating causes of action under the ATS against foreign corporate defendants would be a no-win proposition. Foreign corporate liability would not only fail to meaningfully advance the objectives of the ATS, but it would also lead to precisely those "serious consequences in international affairs" that the ATS was enacted to avoid. *Sosa*, 542 U.S. at 715. Under those circumstances, federal courts have a duty to refrain from acting. Although that may make it more difficult for aliens to hold foreign corporations liable for human rights abuses, we have repeatedly rejected the view that the ATS was meant to transform the federal courts into forums for the litigation of all human rights suits. Declining to extend the ATS to foreign corporate defendants is thus not about "[i]mmunizing corporations that violate human rights," but rather about furthering the purpose that the ATS was actually meant to serve—avoiding diplomatic strife.

■ JUSTICE GORSUCH, concurring in part and concurring in the judgment.

I am pleased to join the Court's judgment and Parts I, II-B-1, and II-C of its opinion. Respectfully, though, I believe there are two more fundamental reasons why this lawsuit must be dismissed. A group of foreign plaintiffs wants a federal court to invent a new cause of action so they can sue another foreigner for allegedly breaching international norms. In any other context, a federal judge faced with a request like that would know exactly what to do with it: dismiss it out of hand. Not because the defendant happens to be a corporation instead of a human being. But because the job of creating new causes of action and navigating foreign policy disputes belongs to the political branches. For reasons passing understanding, federal courts have sometimes treated the Alien Tort Statute as a license to overlook these foundational principles. I would end ATS exceptionalism. We should refuse invitations to create new forms of legal liability. And we should not meddle in disputes between foreign citizens over international norms. I write because I am hopeful that courts in the future might pause to consider both of these reasons for restraint before taking up cases like this one. Whatever powers courts may possess in ATS suits, they are powers judges should be doubly careful not to abuse.

First adopted in 1789, the current version of the ATS provides that "[t]he district courts shall have original jurisdiction of any civil action by an alien for a tort only, committed in violation of the law of nations or a treaty of the United States." 28 U.S.C. § 1350. More than two hundred years later, the meaning of this terse provision has still "proven elusive." Sosa v. Alvarez-Machain, 542 U.S. 692, 719 (2004). At the same time, this Court has suggested that Congress enacted the statute to afford federal courts jurisdiction to hear tort claims related to three violations of international law that were already embodied in English common law: violations of safe conducts extended to aliens, interference with ambassadors, and piracy. Id. at 715; 4 W. Blackstone, Commentaries on the Laws of England 68 (1769) (Blackstone); see also Anthony J. Bellia, Jr. & Bradford R. Clark, The Alien Tort Statute and the Law of Nations, 78 U. Chi. L. Rev. 445 (2011) (arguing that the ATS meant to supply jurisdiction over a slightly larger set of claims involving intentional torts by Americans against aliens).

In this case, the plaintiffs seek much more. They want the federal courts to recognize a new cause of action, one that did not exist at the time of the statute's adoption, one that Congress has never authorized. While their request might appear inconsistent with Sosa's explanation of the ATS's modest origin, the plaintiffs say that a caveat later in the opinion saves them. They point to a passage where the Court went on to suggest that the ATS may also afford federal judges "discretion [to] conside[r] [creating] new cause[s] of action" if they "rest on a norm of international character accepted by the civilized world and defined with a specificity comparable to the features of the [three] 18th-century" torts the Court already described. Sosa, 542 U.S. at 725.

I harbor serious doubts about Sosa's suggestion. In our democracy the people's elected representatives make the laws that govern them. Judges do not. . . . Adopting new causes of action may have been a "proper function for common-law courts," but it is not appropriate "for federal tribunals" mindful of the limits of their constitutional authority. Alexander v. Sandoval, 532 U.S. 275, 287 (2001).

Nor can I see any reason to make a special exception for the ATS. As Sosa initially acknowledged, the ATS was designed as "a jurisdictional statute creating no new causes of action." 542 U.S. at 724. And I would have thought that the end of the matter. A statute that creates no new causes of action . . . creates no new causes of action. To the extent Sosa continued on to claim for federal judges the discretionary power to create new forms of liability on their own, it invaded terrain that belongs to the people's representatives and should be promptly returned to them.

But even accepting *Sosa*'s framework does not end the matter. As the Court acknowledges, there is a strong argument that "a proper application of *Sosa* would preclude courts from ever recognizing any new causes of action under the ATS." I believe that argument is correct. For the reasons just described, separation of powers considerations ordinarily require us to defer to Congress in the creation of new forms of liability. This Court hasn't yet used *Sosa*'s assertion of discretionary authority to recognize a new cause of action, and I cannot imagine a sound reason, hundreds of years after the statute's passage, to start now. For a court inclined to claim the discretion to enter this field, it is a discretion best exercised by staying out of it. . . .

Another independent problem lurks here. This is a suit by foreigners against a foreigner over the meaning of international norms. Respectfully, I do not think the original understanding of the ATS or our precedent permits federal courts to hear cases like this. At a minimum, both those considerations and simple common sense about the limits of the judicial function should lead federal courts to require a domestic defendant before agreeing to exercise any *Sosa*-generated discretion to entertain an ATS suit.

Start with the statute. What we call the Alien Tort Statute began as just one clause among many in § 9 of the Judiciary Act of 1789, which specified the jurisdiction of the federal courts. 1 Stat. 76–78. . . . Like today's recodified version, 28 U.S.C. § 1350, the original text of the ATS did not expressly call for a U.S. defendant. But I think it likely would have been understood to contain such a requirement when adopted.

That is because the First Congress passed the Judiciary Act in the shadow of the Constitution. The Act created the federal courts and vested them with statutory authority to entertain claims consistent with the newly ratified terms of Article III. Meanwhile, under Article III, Congress could not have extended to federal courts the power to hear just any suit between two aliens (unless, for example, one was a diplomat). Diversity of citizenship was required. So, because Article III's diversity-of-citizenship clause calls for a U.S. party, and because the ATS clause requires an alien plaintiff, it follows that an American defendant was needed for an ATS suit to proceed.

Precedent confirms this conclusion. In Mossman v. Higginson, 4 U.S. 12, 14 (1800), this Court addressed the meaning of a neighboring provision of the Judiciary Act. Section 11 gave the circuit courts power to hear, among other things, civil cases where "an alien is a party." 1 Stat. 78. As with § 9, you might think § 11's language could be read to permit a suit *between* aliens. Yet this Court held § 11 must instead be construed to refer only to cases "where, indeed, an alien is one party, but a citizen is the other." *Mossman*, 4 Dall. at 14 (internal quotation marks omitted). That was necessary, *Mossman* explained, to give the statute a "constructio[n] consistent" with the diversity-jurisdiction clause of Article III. And as a matter of precedent, I cannot think of a good reason why we would now read § 9 differently than *Mossman* read § 11. . . .

Nor does it appear the ATS meant to rely on any other head of Article III jurisdiction. You might wonder, for example, if the First Congress considered a "violation of the law of nations" to be a violation of, and thus "arise under," federal law. But that does not seem likely. . . . While this Court has called international law "part of our law," The Paquete Habana, 175 U.S. 677, 700 (1900), and a component of the "law of the land," The Nereide, 13 U.S. 388 (1815), that simply meant international law was no different than the law of torts or contracts—it was "part of the so-called general common law," but *not* part of federal law. *Sosa*, 542 U.S. at 739–40 (opinion of Scalia, J.). See Curtis A. Bradley & Jack L. Goldsmith, Customary International Law as Federal Common Law: A Critique of the Modern Position, 110 Harv. L. Rev. 815, 824, 849–50 (1997); see also Ernest A. Young, Sorting Out the Debate Over Customary International Law, 42 Va. J. Int'l L. 365, 374–75 (2002). . . .

Any attempt to decipher a cryptic old statute is sure to meet with challenges. For example, one could object that this reading of the Act does not assign to the ATS the work of addressing assaults by aliens against foreign ambassadors on our soil, even though *Sosa* suggested the statute was enacted partly in response to precisely such a case: the "Marbois incident of May 1784, in which a French adventurer, De Longchamps, verbally and physically assaulted the Secretary of the French Legion in Philadelphia." 542 U.S. at 716. Many thought that the States' failure to provide a forum for relief to the foreign minister was a scandal and part of what prompted the framers of the Constitution to strengthen the national government.

But worries along these lines may be misplaced. The ATS was never meant to serve as a freestanding statute, only as one clause in one section of the Judiciary Act. So even if you think *something* in the Judiciary Act must be interpreted to address the Marbois incident, that doesn't mean it must be the ATS clause. And, as it happens, a different provision of the Act *did* deal expressly with the problem of ambassadorial assaults: Section 13 conferred on this Court "original, but not exclusive jurisdiction of all suits brought by ambassadors, or other public ministers, or in which a consul, or vice consul shall be a party." 1 Stat. 80–81. That implemented Article III's provision empowering us to hear suits "affecting Ambassadors, other public ministers and Consuls." § 2. And given that § 13 deals with the problem of "ambassadors" so directly, it is unclear why we must read § 9 to address that same problem. See Thomas H. Lee, The Safe-Conduct Theory of the Alien Tort Statute, 106 Colum. L. Rev. 830, 855–58 (2006).

Along different but similar lines, some might be concerned that requiring a U.S. defendant in ATS suits would leave the problem of piracy inadequately addressed, given that *Sosa* suggested that piracy was one of the three offenses the ATS may have meant to capture, and many pirates were foreigners. But here the response is much the same. A separate clause of § 9 gave the district courts "exclusive original cognizance of all civil causes of admiralty and maritime jurisdiction." 1 Stat. 77. That statute has long been given a broad construction covering "all maritime contracts, torts and injuries," DeLovio v. Boit, 7 F. Cas. 418, 442 (No. 3,776) (CC Mass. 1815) (Story, J.), along with "prize jurisdiction, which probably included almost all 'piracy' cases after 1789," Lee, supra, at 867. So it is not clear why it's necessary to cram the problem of piracy into the ATS. If anything, it may be necessary *not* to do so. . . .

If doubt lingers on these historical questions, it is a doubt that should counsel restraint all the same. Even if the ATS might have meant to allow foreign *ambassadors* to sue foreign defendants, or foreign plaintiffs to sue foreign *pirates*, what would that prove about more mine-run cases like ours, where none of those special concerns are implicated? There are at least serious historical arguments suggesting the ATS was not meant to apply to suits like this one. And to the extent *Sosa* affords courts discretion to proceed, these arguments should inform any decision whether to exercise that discretion. . . .

Any consideration of *Sosa*'s discretion must also account for proper limits on the judicial function. As discussed above, federal courts generally lack the institutional expertise and constitutional authority to oversee foreign policy and national security, and should be wary of straying where they do not belong. Yet there are degrees of institutional incompetence and constitutional evil. It is one thing for courts to assume the task of creating new causes of action to ensure *our* citizens abide by the law of nations and *avoid* reprisals against this country. It is altogether another thing for courts to punish *foreign* parties for conduct that could not be attributed to the United States and thereby *risk* reprisals against this country. If a foreign state or citizen violates an "international norm" in a way that offends another foreign state or citizen, the Constitution arms the President and Congress with ample means to address it. Or, if they think best, the political branches may choose to look the other way. But in all events, the decision to impose sanctions in disputes between foreigners over international norms is not ours to make. It is a decision that belongs to those answerable to the people and assigned by the Constitution to defend this nation. If they wish our help, they are free to enlist it, but we should not ever be in the business of elbowing our way in.

■ JUSTICE SOTOMAYOR, with whom JUSTICE GINSBURG, JUSTICE BREYER, and JUSTICE KAGAN join, dissenting.

The Court today holds that the Alien Tort Statute (ATS), 28 U.S.C. § 1350, categorically forecloses foreign corporate liability. In so doing, it absolves corporations from responsibility under the ATS for conscience-shocking behavior. I disagree both with the Court's conclusion and its analytic approach. The text, history, and purpose of the ATS, as well as the long and consistent history of corporate liability in tort, confirm that tort claims for law-of-nations violations may be brought against corporations under the ATS. Nothing about the corporate form in itself raises foreign-policy concerns that require the Court, as a matter of common-law discretion, to immunize all foreign corporations from liability under the ATS, regardless of the specific law-of-nations violations alleged. I respectfully dissent. . . .

The plurality assumes without deciding that whether corporations can be permissible defendants under the ATS turns on the first step of the two-part inquiry set out in Sosa v. Alvarez-Machain, 542 U.S. 692 (2004). But by asking whether there is "a specific, universal, and obligatory norm of liability for corporations" in international law, the plurality fundamentally misconceives how international law works and so misapplies the first step of Sosa. . . .

Sosa's norm-specific first step is inapposite to the categorical question whether corporations may be sued under the ATS as a general matter. International law imposes certain obligations that are intended to govern the behavior of states and private actors. Among those obligations are substantive prohibitions on certain conduct thought to violate human rights, such as genocide, slavery, extrajudicial killing, and torture. Substantive prohibitions like these are the norms at which Sosa's step-one inquiry is aimed and for which Sosa requires that there be sufficient international consensus.

Sosa does not, however, demand that there be sufficient international consensus with regard to the mechanisms of enforcing these norms, for enforcement is not a question with which customary international law is concerned. Although international law determines what substantive conduct violates the law of nations, it leaves the specific rules of how to enforce international-law norms and remedy their violation to states, which may act to impose liability collectively through treaties or independently via their domestic legal systems. . . .

Instead of asking whether there exists a specific, universal, and obligatory norm of corporate liability under international law, the relevant inquiry in response to the question presented here is whether there is any reason—under either international law or our domestic law—to distinguish between a corporation and a natural person who is alleged to have violated the law of nations under the ATS. . . . The text, history, and purpose of the ATS plainly support the conclusion that corporations may be held liable.

Beginning "with the language of the statute itself," United States v. Ron Pair Enterprises, Inc., 489 U.S. 235, 241 (1989), two aspects of the text of the ATS make clear that the statute allows corporate liability. First, the text confers jurisdiction on federal district courts to hear "civil action[s]" for "tort[s]." 28 U.S.C. § 1350. Where Congress uses a term of art like tort, "it presumably knows and adopts the cluster of ideas that were attached to [the] borrowed word in the body of learning from which it was taken and the meaning its use will convey to the judicial mind unless otherwise instructed." Morissette v. United States, 342 U.S. 246, 263 (1952).

Corporations have long been held liable in tort under the federal common law. This Court "has assumed that, when Congress creates a tort action, it legislates against a legal background of ordinary tort-related . . . rules and consequently intends its legislation to incorporate those rules." Meyer v. Holley, 537 U.S. 280, 285 (2003). The presumption, then, is that, in providing for "tort" liability, the ATS provides for corporate liability.

Second, whereas the ATS expressly limits the class of permissible plaintiffs to "alien[s]," § 1350, it "does not distinguish among classes of defendants," Argentine Republic v. Amerada Hess Shipping Corp., 488 U.S. 428, 438 (1989). That silence as to defendants cannot be presumed to be inadvertent. That is because in the same section of the Judiciary Act of 1789 as what is now the ATS, Congress provided the federal district courts with jurisdiction over "all suits against consuls or vice-consuls." § 9, 1 Stat. 76–77. Where Congress wanted to limit the range of permissible defendants, then, it clearly knew how to do so.

Nothing about the historical background against which the ATS was enacted rebuts the presumption that the statute incorporated the accepted principle of corporate liability for tortious conduct. Under the Articles of Confederation, the Continental Congress was unable to provide redress to foreign citizens for violations of treaties or the law of nations, which threatened to undermine the United States' relationships with other nations. The First Congress responded with, *inter alia*, the ATS. Although the two incidents that highlighted the need to provide foreign citizens with a federal forum in which to pursue their grievances involved conflicts between natural persons, . . . there is "no reason to conclude that the First Congress was supremely concerned with the risk that natural persons would cause the United States to be drawn into foreign entanglements, but was content to allow formal legal associations of individuals, i.e., corporations, to do so," Doe v. Exxon Mobil Corp., 654 F.3d 11, 47 (D.C. Cir. 2011), vacated on other grounds, 527 Fed. Appx. 7 (D.C. Cir. 2013). Indeed, foreclosing corporations from liability under the ATS would have been at odds with the contemporaneous practice of imposing liability for piracy on ships, juridical entities. . . .

[Justice Gorsuch's] concurrence suggests that federal courts may lack jurisdiction to entertain suits between aliens based solely on a violation of the law of nations. It contends that ATS suits between aliens fall under neither the federal courts' diversity jurisdiction nor our federal question jurisdiction. The Court was not unaware of this argument when it decided *Sosa*. . . . The Court nonetheless proceeded to decide the case, which it could not have done had it been concerned about its Article III power to do so. That decision forecloses the argument the concurrence now makes, as *Sosa* authorized courts to "recognize private claims *under federal common law* for violations of" certain international law norms. 542 U.S. at 732 (emphasis added).

Sosa was correct as a legal matter. Moreover, our Nation has an interest not only in providing a remedy when our own citizens commit law of nations violations, but also in preventing our Nation from serving as a safe harbor for today's pirates. . . . To the extent suits against foreign defendants may lead to international friction, that concern is better addressed under the presumption the Court established in *Kiobel* against extraterritorial application of the ATS than it is by relitigating settled precedent.

. . . Nothing about the corporate form in itself justifies categorically foreclosing corporate liability in all ATS actions. Each source of diplomatic friction that respondent Arab Bank and the plurality identify can be addressed with a tool more tailored to the source of the problem than a blanket ban on corporate liability.

Arab Bank contends that foreign citizens should not be able "to sue a Jordanian corporation in New York for events taking place in the Middle East." Brief for Respondent 42. The heart of that qualm was already addressed in *Kiobel*, which held that the presumption against extraterritoriality applies to the ATS. . . .

Arab Bank also bemoans the unfairness of being sued when others— namely, the individuals and organizations that carried out the terrorist attacks—were "the direct cause" of the harm petitioners here suffered. Brief for Respondent 41. That complaint, though, is a critique of the imposition of liability for financing terrorism, not an argument that ATS suits against corporations generally necessarily cause diplomatic tensions.

Arab Bank further expresses concern that ATS suits are being filed against corporations in an effort to recover for the bad acts of foreign governments or officials. But the Bank's explanation of this problem reveals that the true source of its grievance is the availability of aiding and abetting liability. . . . Yet not all law-of-nations violations asserted against corporations are premised on aiding and abetting liability; it is possible for a corporation to violate international-law norms independent of a foreign state or foreign state officials. In this respect, too, the Court's rule is ill fitted to the problem identified.

Notably, even the Hashemite Kingdom of Jordan does not argue that there are foreign-policy tensions inherent in suing a corporation generally. Instead, Jordan contends that this particular suit is an affront to its sovereignty because of its extraterritorial character and because of the role that Arab Bank specifically plays in the Jordanian economy.

The majority also cites to instances in which other foreign sovereigns have "appeared in this Court to note [their] objections to ATS litigation," but none of those objections was about the availability of corporate liability as a general matter.

As the United States urged at oral argument, when international friction arises, a court should respond with the doctrine that speaks directly to the friction's source. In addition to the presumption against extraterritoriality, federal courts have at their disposal a number of tools to address any foreign-relations concerns that an ATS case may raise. This Court has held that a federal court may exercise personal jurisdiction over a foreign corporate defendant only if the corporation is incorporated in the United States, has its principal place of business or is otherwise at home here, or if the activities giving rise to the lawsuit occurred or had their impact here. See Daimler AG v. Bauman, 571 U.S. 117 (2014). Courts also can dismiss ATS suits for a plaintiff's failure to exhaust the remedies available in her domestic forum, on forum non conveniens grounds, for reasons of international comity, or when asked to do so by the State Department.

Several of these doctrines might be implicated in this case, and I would remand for the Second Circuit to address them in the first instance. The majority, however, prefers to use a sledgehammer to crack a nut. I see no need for such an ill-fitting and disproportionate response. Foreclosing foreign corporate liability in all ATS actions, irrespective of circumstance or norm, is simply too broad a response to case-specific concerns that can be addressed via other means. . . .

The plurality extrapolates from Congress's decision regarding the scope of liability under the TVPA a rule that it contends should govern all ATS suits. But there is no reason to think that because Congress saw fit to permit suits only against natural persons for two specific law-of-nations violations, Congress meant to foreclose corporate liability for all law-of-nations violations. . . .

To infer from the TVPA that no corporation may ever be held liable under the ATS for any violation of any international-law norm, moreover, ignores that Congress has elsewhere imposed liability on corporations for conduct prohibited by customary international law. For instance, the Antiterrorism Act of 1990 (ATA) created a civil cause of action for U.S. nationals injured by an act of international terrorism and expressly provides for corporate liability. 18 U.S.C. § 2333. That Congress foreclosed corporate liability for torture and extrajudicial killing claims under the TVPA but permitted corporate liability for terrorism-related claims under the ATA is strong evidence that Congress exercises its judgment as to the appropriateness of corporate liability on a norm-by-norm basis, and that courts should do the same when considering whether to permit causes of action against corporations for law-of-nations violations under the ATS. . . .

Moreover, even if there are other grounds on which a suit alleging conduct constituting a law-of-nations violation can be brought, such as a state-law tort claim, the First Congress created the ATS because it wanted foreign plaintiffs to be able to bring their claims in federal court and sue for law-of-nations violations. A suit for state-law battery, even if based on the same alleged conduct, is not the equivalent of a federal suit for torture; the latter contributes to the uptake of international human rights norms, and the former does not.

Furthermore, holding corporations accountable for violating the human rights of foreign citizens when those violations touch and concern the United States may well be necessary to avoid the international tension with which the First Congress was concerned. Consider again the assault on the Secretary of the French Legation in Philadelphia by a French adventurer. Would the diplomatic strife that followed really have been any less charged if a corporation had sent its agent to accost the Secretary? Or, consider piracy. If a corporation owned a fleet of vessels and directed them to seize other ships in U.S. waters, there no doubt would be calls to hold the corporation to account. Finally, take, for example, a corporation posing as a job-placement agency that actually traffics in persons, forcibly transporting foreign nationals to the United States for exploitation and profiting from their abuse. Not only are the individual employees of that business less likely to be able fully to compensate successful ATS plaintiffs, but holding only individual employees liable does not impose accountability for the institution-wide disregard for human rights. Absent a corporate sanction, that harm will persist unremedied. Immunizing the corporation from suit under the ATS merely because it is a corporation, even though the violations stemmed directly from corporate policy and practice, might cause serious diplomatic friction. . . .

In categorically barring all suits against foreign corporations under the ATS, the Court ensures that foreign corporations—entities capable of wrongdoing under our domestic law—remain immune from liability for human rights abuses, however egregious they may be. . . .

Immunizing corporations that violate human rights from liability under the ATS undermines the system of accountability for law-of-nations violations that the First Congress endeavored to impose. It allows these entities to take advantage of the significant benefits of the corporate form and enjoy fundamental rights, without having to shoulder attendant fundamental responsibilities.

I respectfully dissent.

NOTES ON JESNER V. ARAB BANK

1.   CORPORATE ATS LIABILITY

Since the 1990s, numerous ATS suits have been brought against private corporations on the theory that the corporations either have violated one of the few international human rights norms that apply to private actors (such as the prohibition on slavery) or that the corporations have "aided and abetted" violations of international human rights law committed by foreign governments. The allegations in these cases have varied, ranging from claims that corporations were merely doing business with oppressive regimes to claims that the corporations were knowingly participating in abuses. The lower courts generally assumed in such cases that corporations could be sued, although there was substantial debate over the proper standards for liability.

In Kiobel v. Royal Dutch Petroleum Co., 621 F.3d 111 (2d Cir. 2010), the Second Circuit held that ATS suits could not be brought against private corporations. The court reasoned that, in order for a defendant's conduct to be actionable under the ATS, the conduct must violate international law, and it concluded that international human rights law did not extend to conduct by corporations. This decision created a conflict in the circuits. The Supreme Court granted certiorari to resolve the conflict, but, as discussed in the next Note, it ultimately decided the case on other grounds. In the meantime, other circuit courts continued to disagree with the Second Circuit.

As noted earlier in this section, in 1992 Congress enacted the Torture Victim Protection Act (TVPA), which creates a cause of action for claims of torture and "extrajudicial killing" under color of foreign law. The TVPA, which is codified as a note to the ATS, refers to claims by an "individual" against another "individual." Because of this language, the Court held in Mohamad v. Palestinian Authority, 566 U.S. 449 (2012), that the TVPA authorizes suit only against natural persons. The Court observed that, because the ATS does not use the term "individual," it "offers no comparative value here regardless of whether corporate entities can be held liable in a federal common-law action brought under that statute."

2.   *KIOBEL* AND THE PRESUMPTION AGAINST EXTRATERRITORIALITY

The Supreme Court ordinarily presumes that federal statutes apply only to conduct occurring inside the United States. In EEOC v. Arabian American Oil Co., 499 U.S. 244 (1991), the Court applied this "presumption against extraterritoriality" in holding that Title VII of the Civil Rights Act did not apply to a U.S. corporation's alleged discriminatory treatment of a U.S. citizen in Saudi Arabia. In Morrison v. National Australia Bank Ltd., 561 U.S. 247 (2010), the Court applied the presumption in holding that Section 10(b) of the Securities Exchange Act did not apply to claims of alleged misconduct in connection with securities traded on foreign exchanges. The Court explained that the presumption "rests on the perception that Congress ordinarily legislates with respect to domestic, not foreign matters," *Morrison*, 561 U.S. at 255, and that it also "serves to protect against unintended clashes between our laws and those of other nations which could result in international discord," *Arabian American Oil*, 499 U.S. at 248.

Despite the presumption against extraterritoriality, most lower courts prior to 2013 assumed that claims could be brought under the ATS for foreign conduct. One reason they may have made this assumption is that the ATS is limited to torts that violate international law. Since international law applies globally, it may not seem "extraterritorial" for a U.S. court to apply it to adjudicate a dispute concerning conduct abroad.

In Kiobel v. Royal Dutch Petroleum Co., 569 U.S. 108 (2013), however, the Supreme Court "conclude[d] that the presumption against extraterritoriality applies to claims under the ATS, and that nothing in the statute rebuts that presumption." In that case, a group of Nigerian citizens residing in the United States had filed an ATS action in federal court against various non-U.S. corporations, alleging that the corporations had aided and abetted the Nigerian government in committing human rights violations in Nigeria. While the Court acknowledged that it had typically applied the presumption only to statutes that directly regulate conduct, whereas the ATS is a jurisdictional statute that "allows federal courts to recognize certain causes of action," it reasoned that "the principles underlying the canon of interpretation similarly constrain courts considering causes of action that may be brought under the ATS." If anything, said the Court, "the danger of unwarranted judicial interference in the conduct of foreign policy is magnified in the context of the ATS, because the question is not what Congress has done but instead what courts may do."

The Court then proceeded to examine the text, history, and purposes of the ATS, and it concluded that they did not suggest that Congress intended for extraterritorial application of the statute. Among other things, the Court reasoned that there was nothing in the historical context of the ATS that "suggests that Congress . . . intended federal common law under the ATS to provide a cause of action for conduct occurring in the territory of another sovereign." As a result, the Court affirmed the dismissal of this case:

> On these facts, all the relevant conduct took place outside the United States. And even where the claims touch and concern the territory of the United States, they must do so with sufficient force to displace the presumption against extraterritorial application. . . . Corporations are often present in many countries, and it would reach too far to say that mere corporate presence suffices. If Congress were to determine otherwise, a statute more specific than the ATS would be required.

Justice Kennedy observed in a short concurrence that the decision left open "significant questions regarding the reach and interpretation of the Alien Tort Statute" and that "the presumption against extraterritorial application may require some further elaboration and explanation" in cases covered "neither by the TVPA nor by the reasoning and holding of today's case." In a separate concurrence, Justice Alito, joined by Justice Thomas, expressed the view that "a putative ATS cause of action will fall within the scope of the presumption against extraterritoriality—and will therefore be barred—unless the domestic conduct is sufficient to violate an international law norm that satisfies [the] requirements [in Sosa v. Alvarez-Machain, 542 U.S. 692 (2004)] of definiteness and acceptance among civilized nations."

Justice Breyer, writing for himself and Justices Ginsburg, Sotomayor, and Kagan, concurred in the judgment upholding dismissal of the case but disagreed with the majority's reasoning. Instead of applying a presumption against extraterritoriality to the ATS, Breyer argued that ATS suits should be allowed in three situations: "where (1) the alleged tort occurs on American soil, (2) the defendant is an American national, or (3) the defendant's conduct substantially and adversely affects an important American national interest, and that includes a distinct interest in preventing the United States from becoming a safe harbor (free of civil as well as criminal liability) for a torturer or other common enemy of mankind." He agreed with the majority, however, that in this case "the parties and relevant conduct lack sufficient ties to the United States for the ATS to provide jurisdiction."

Kiobel imposed a substantial territorial limitation on ATS litigation. There was debate, however, over how broadly to construe this limitation. In particular, there has been disagreement over what must be shown in order to establish that a plaintiff's claims "touch and concern the territory of the United States." If all of the defendant's activities connected to the case occurred abroad, then presumably the "touch and concern" test is not met. Less clear, however, are situations in which it is alleged that the defendant has engaged in conduct in the United States that has helped to facilitate foreign tortious conduct. It was not clear, for example, whether the plaintiffs' claims in *Jesner v. Arab Bank* (which included allegations that electronic transactions were channeled by the defendant bank through its New York City offices) met the "touch and concern" test. The Court in *Jesner* declined to resolve that issue.

3.   QUESTIONS AND COMMENTS ON *JESNER V. ARAB BANK*

After *Kiobel* and *Jesner*, what suits can be brought under the ATS? *Kiobel* disallows at least many ATS suits involving foreign conduct, and *Jesner* disallows ATS suits against foreign corporations. Do these limitations reflect sensible interpretations of the ATS? In imposing these limitations, the Court has emphasized separation-of-powers considerations. Justice Alito gave even greater emphasis to such considerations in his concurrence in *Jesner*. To what extent are these considerations similar to the ones reflected in the Court's decisions on the other topics covered in this chapter—federal common law, implied statutory rights of action, and *Bivens* remedies? Is the decision in *Jesner* best viewed as leaving an important policy question to be decided by Congress in the first instance, as the majority maintains, or as immunizing corporations from the reach of a generally-worded statute, as the dissent maintains? Note that the Court does not resolve whether *U.S.* corporations may be sued under the ATS. Does its analysis nevertheless suggest an answer to that question?

In his concurrence, Justice Gorsuch suggests that the ATS may have been intended to be limited to cases involving U.S.-citizen defendants. Such an interpretation would provide an easy answer to the question of how ATS suits fall within the Article III jurisdiction of the federal courts: they would fall within Article III "alienage diversity" jurisdiction. Given prior precedents, is it too late for the Court to adopt such an interpretation? For academic commentary supporting this diversity interpretation of the ATS, see Curtis A. Bradley, The Alien Tort Statute and Article III, 42 Va. J. Int'l L. 587 (2002), and Anthony J. Bellia, Jr. & Bradford R. Clark, The Alien Tort Statute and the Law of Nations, 78 U. Chi. L. Rev. 445 (2011). For a critique of such an interpretation, see William S. Dodge, The Constitutionality of the Alien Tort Statute: Some Observations on Text and Context, 42 Va. J. Int'l L. 687 (2002).

4. *NESTLE USA, INC. V. DOE*

Although the Court granted certiorari to decide the issue of domestic corporate liability under the ATS in Nestle USA, Inc. v. Doe, 593 U.S. ___, 141 S.Ct. 1931 (2021), it ended up resolving the case on extraterritoriality grounds. In that case, the plaintiffs alleged that they had been enslaved as child laborers on cocoa farms in the West African country of Ivory Coast, and that the defendant U.S. corporations had aided and abetted this practice. In an opinion by Justice Thomas that was joined by seven other Justices, the Court held that the suit could not be maintained under the ATS:

> Nearly all the conduct that [the plaintiffs] say aided and abetted forced labor—providing training, fertilizer, tools, and cash to overseas farms—occurred in Ivory Coast. . . .

> As we made clear in *Kiobel*, a plaintiff does not plead facts sufficient to support domestic application of the ATS simply by alleging "mere corporate presence" [in the United States] of a defendant. Pleading general corporate activity is no better. Because making "operational decisions" is an activity common to most corporations, generic allegations of this sort do not draw a sufficient connection between the cause of action respondents seek—aiding and abetting forced labor overseas—and domestic conduct.

Thomas, now writing only for himself and Justices Gorsuch and Kavanaugh, also argued that the Court lacked the authority to recognize a cause of action to govern this case. "Our decisions since *Sosa*, as well as congressional activity," Thomas contended, "compel the conclusion that federal courts should not recognize private rights of action for violations of international law beyond the three historical torts identified in *Sosa*." Allowing additional claims under the ATS, he argued, "invariably gives rise to foreign-policy concerns."

Justice Gorsuch wrote separately to express the view that (1) domestic corporations should not have any special immunity from ATS liability, but that (2) courts also should not be creating any new causes of action under the ATS, whether against corporations or any other defendant. "However vigilant the doorkeeper," said Gorsuch, "the truth is that this is a door that *Sosa* should not have cracked." He was joined on the first point by Justices Alito and Kavanaugh and on the second point only by Justice Kavanaugh.

Justice Sotomayor, joined by Justices Breyer and Kagan, concurred in part and concurred in the judgment. She agreed that the suit here was impermissibly extraterritorial, but she disagreed with Justice Thomas that ATS suits should be limited to the three historic torts referenced in *Sosa*. As for potential foreign policy problems that could be created by allowing ATS suits, Sotomayor contended that completely disallowing any new causes of action under the statute "is a gross overreaction to a manageable (and largely hypothetical) problem."

The only dissent came from Justice Alito, who explained that he "would hold that if a particular claim may be brought under the ATS against a natural person who is a United States citizen, a similar claim may be brought against a domestic corporation," and he would remand for further proceedings to address the other issues in the case.

Two features of the voting lineup are noteworthy. First, the Court was nearly unanimous in strictly applying *Kiobel*'s extraterritoriality limitation. Second, a majority of the Justices appeared to believe that domestic corporations should be subject to suit under the ATS to the same extent as private individuals (which, to be sure, is not very much under *Kiobel*).

5.   BIBLIOGRAPHY

For discussions of corporate liability under the ATS prior to *Jesner*, see Curtis A. Bradley, State Action and Corporate Human Rights Liability, 85 Notre Dame L. Rev. 1823 (2010); Doug Cassel, Corporate Aiding and Abetting of Human Rights Violations: Confusion in the Courts, 6 Nw. U. J. Int'l Hum. Rts. 304 (2008); Chimene Keitner, Conceptualizing Complicity in Alien Tort Cases, 60 Hastings L.J. 61 (2008); Julian G. Ku, The Curious Case of Corporate Liability Under the Alien Tort Statute: A Flawed System of Judicial Lawmaking, 51 Va. J. Int'l L. 353 (2011); Michael D. Ramsey, International Law Limits on Investor Liability in Human Rights Litigation, 50 Harv. Int'l L.J. 271 (2009); Alan O. Sykes, Corporate Liability for Extraterritorial Torts Under the Alien Tort Statute and Beyond: An Economic Analysis, 100 Geo. L.J. 2161 (2012).

Kiobel generated significant commentary. For an effort to situate ATS litigation "within the traditional federal-courts framework of implied rights of action and federal common law," see Ernest A. Young, Universal Jurisdiction, the Alien Tort Statute, and Transnational Public Law Litigation After *Kiobel*, 64 Duke L.J. 1023 (2015). Young contends that this framework supports the Supreme Court's disallowance in *Kiobel* of "universal jurisdiction" under the ATS. For additional discussion of the decision and its implications, see the Symposium articles in Volume 89, Issue 4 of the Notre Dame Law Review: Roger P. Alford, The Future of Human Rights Litigation After *Kiobel*, 89 Notre Dame L. Rev. 749 (2014); Anthony J. Bellia, Jr. & Bradford R. Clark, Two Myths About the Alien Tort Statute, 89 Notre Dame L. Rev. 1609 (2014); William R. Casto, The ATS Cause of Action is *Sui Generis*, 89 Notre Dame L. Rev. 1545 (2014); Doug Cassell, Suing Americans for Human Rights Torts Overseas: The Supreme Court Leaves the Door Open, 89 Notre Dame L. Rev. 1773 (2014); William S. Dodge, Alien Tort Statute Litigation: The Road Not Taken, 89 Notre Dame L. Rev. 1577 (2014); Eugene Kontorovich, *Kiobel* Surprise: Unexpected by Scholars but Consistent with International Trends, 89 Notre Dame L. Rev. 1671 (2014); Thomas H. Lee, Three Lives of the Alien Tort Statute: The Evolving Role of the Judiciary in U.S. Foreign Relations, 89 Notre Dame L. Rev. 1645 (2014); Ralph G. Steinhardt, Determining Which Human Rights Claims "Touch and Concern" the United States: Justice Kennedy's *Filartiga*, 89 Notre Dame L. Rev. 1695 (2014); Beth Stephens, The Curious History of the Alien Tort Statute, 89 Notre Dame L. Rev. 1467 (2014); Carlos M. Vázquez, Things We Do with Presumptions: Reflections on *Kiobel v. Royal Dutch Petroleum*, 89 Notre Dame L. Rev. 1719 (2014). See also Roger P. Alford, Human Rights After *Kiobel*: Choice of Law and the Rise of Transnational Tort Litigation, 63 Emory L.J. 1089 (2014);

Seth Davis & Christopher A. Whytock, State Remedies for Human Rights, 98 B.U. L. Rev. 397 (2018).

CHAPTER III

JUDICIAL REVIEW AND JUSTICIABILITY

SECTION 2. STANDING

SUBSECTION A. CONSTITUTIONAL CORE

Page 305, add a new Note after Note 3:

3A. REDRESSABILITY AND MOOTNESS: *UZUEGBUNAM V. PRECZEWSKI*

Redressability is usually an afterthought in the law of standing. Yet in Uzuegbunam v. Preczewski, 592 U.S. ___, 141 S.Ct. 792 (2021), redressability surfaced in a context that might have been called mootness.

Uzuegbunam and another student wanting to proselytize fellow students at Georgia Gwinnett College, a public institution, ran afoul of highly restrictive rules on such activities. When Uzuegbunam sued, the college abandoned the challenged policies and sought to have the suit dismissed as moot. The only surviving issue was the plaintiffs' claim for nominal damages. The District Court and the Eleventh Circuit held that a claim merely for nominal damages failed to establish redressability for purposes of standing, but the Supreme Court disagreed.

Speaking through Justice Thomas, a nearly unanimous Court said that it was well established at common law "that a party whose rights are invaded can always recover nominal damages . . . ." "Nominal damages," said the Court, "are not a consolation prize for the plaintiff who pleads, but fails to prove, compensatory damages. They are instead the damages awarded by default until the plaintiff establishes entitlement to some other form of damages, such as compensatory or statutory damages." As the default, or ordinary, remedy for violation of a legal right, nominal damages satisfied the redressability element of standing.

Only Chief Justice Roberts dissented. The plaintiffs had graduated, the objectionable rules were no longer in force, and that, said the Chief Justice, made the case moot, nominal damages notwithstanding: "[A]n award of nominal damages does not alleviate the harms suffered by a plaintiff, and is not intended to. If nominal damages can preserve a live controversy, then federal courts will be required to give advisory opinions whenever a plaintiff tacks on a request for a dollar. Because I would place a higher value on Article III, I respectfully dissent."

Justice Kavanaugh concurred to say that he agreed with the Court's historical analysis but also asserted—in line with a suggestion separately made by the Chief Justice—"that a defendant should be able to accept the entry of a judgment for nominal damages against it and thereby end the litigation without a resolution of the merits." The Court did not pronounce on the sufficiency of this maneuver. If allowed, it might mean that the redress-ability issue resolved in *Uzuegbunam* will mean relatively little. That likely would depend on the application of Farrar v. Hobby, 506 U.S. 103 (1992), which held that, at least in some circumstances, judgment for nominal dam-ages does not support an award of attorney's fees.

Page 306, add a footnote at the end of the last paragraph:

c   For a critique of the "one-plaintiff rule" pursuant to which the Supreme Court and the lower federal courts have felt free in multiple-plaintiff cases to resolve the merits with respect to all of the plaintiffs as long as they find that at least one plaintiff has standing, see Aaron-Andrew P. Bruhl, One Good Plaintiff is Not Enough, 67 Duke L.J. 481 (2017).

Page 307, add at the end of Note 5:

James E. Pfander, Standing, Litigable Interests, and Article III's Case-or-Controversy Requirement, 65 UCLA L. Rev. 170 (2018), explains that, "in the late eighteenth and early nineteenth century, federal courts were rou-tinely exercising judicial power over claims of right that did not seek to rem-edy any injury (factual or otherwise) and did not necessitate the joinder of adverse parties" and that "[f]ederal courts continue to hear such matters to-day." Pfander contends that "[t]he ongoing willingness of Congress to pro-vide—and of the federal courts to accept—assignments of noncontentious ju-risdiction makes it very hard to see how an across-the-board injury-in-fact or adverse-party requirement could be understood as a historically compelled element of the right of an individual to invoke the judicial power of the United States."

Finally, a 2019 symposium in the Notre Dame Law Review addressed the increasingly prominent question of state standing. Articles include Tara Leigh Grove, Foreword: Some Puzzles of State Standing, 94 Notre Dame L. Rev. 1883 (2019); Ernest A. Young, State Standing and Cooperative Feder-alism, 94 Notre Dame L. Rev. 1893 (2019); F. Andrew Hessick, Quasi-Sover-eign Standing, 94 Notre Dame L. Rev. 1927 (2019); Bradford Mank & Mi-chael E. Solimine, State Standing and National Injunctions, 94 Notre Dame L. Rev. 1955 (2019); Jonathan Remy Nash, State Standing for Nationwide Injunctions Against the Federal Government, 94 Notre Dame L. Rev. 1985 (2019); Ann Woolhandler & Michael G. Collins, Reining in State Standing, 94 Notre Dame L. Rev. 2015 (2019); Robert A. Mikos, Standing for Nothing, 94 Notre Dame L. Rev. 2033 (2019); Katherine Mims Crocker, An Organiza-tional Account of State Standing, 94 Notre Dame L. Rev. 2057 (2019); Seth Davis, The Private Rights of Public Governments, 94 Notre Dame L. Rev. 2091 (2019); Aziz Z. Huq, State Standing's Uncertain Stakes, 94 Notre Dame L. Rev. 2127 (2019). For a related article published elsewhere, see Seth Da-vis, The New Public Law Standing, 71 Stan. L. Rev. 1229 (2019).

SUBSECTION B. STATUTORY STANDING

Page 325, add at the end of Note 6:

For an argument that Justice Thomas's proposed approach in *Spokeo* "is plausible and generally consistent with history and doctrine, and it provides an actual attempt at a way forward," see William Baude, Standing in the Shadow of Congress, 2016 Sup. Ct. Rev. 197, 229. For criticism of *Spokeo*'s concern with tangible, as distinct from intangible, harm, see Rachel Bayef-sky, Constitutional Injury and Tangibility, 59 Wm. & Mary L. Rev. 2285 (2018).

Page 325, add a new Note:

6A. *TRANSUNION LLC V. RAMIREZ*

TransUnion LLC v. Ramirez, 594 U.S. ___, 141 S.Ct. 2190 (2021), follows closely on *Spokeo*, but with an interesting change in the line-up. TransUnion was a major credit-reporting agency. In addition to standard credit reports, it offered an add-on product called Name Screen Alert. This service compared first and last names (and only first and last names) to a government list of "specially designated nationals" who pose a threat to national security. If a person's first and last name matched that of someone on the list, the credit report marked the individual as a "potential match" to a name on the list. Not surprisingly, this process generated many false positives. Plaintiff Ramirez discovered that he was one of them when a Nissan dealer refused to sell him a car because his name was on the "terrorist list."

Ramirez brought a class action under the Fair Credit Reporting Act, 15 U.S.C. § 1681 et seq., claiming, among other things, that TransUnion had violated the statutory requirement to "follow reasonable procedures to assure maximum possible accuracy." The District Court certified a class and ultimately rendered judgment on behalf of 8,185 persons who had been included in the Name Screen Alert. Of that number, only 1,853 persons (including Mr. Ramirez) had had their reports distributed to potential creditors during the relevant period. The District Court nonetheless ruled that all 8,185 persons who had been flagged in TransUnion's computers had standing, and the Ninth Circuit affirmed.

The Supreme Court reversed, holding that only the 1,853 persons whose names had been distributed to creditors had standing to sue (resulting in a reduced award of damages). Everyone agreed that the Fair Credit Reporting Act created a cause of action for, and authorized damages actions by, all persons subject to a failure to follow reasonable procedures, even if there were no practical consequences. The Justices disagreed on whether this statutory authorization sufficed to create standing in the face of Article III.

Justice Kavanaugh, speaking on behalf of himself, Chief Justice Roberts, and Justices Alito, Gorsuch, and Barrett, said that the class members whose names had not been reported to anyone lacked "concrete" injury:

> [A]n important difference exists between (i) a plaintiff's statutory cause of action to sue a defendant over the defendant's violation of federal law, and (ii) a plaintiff's suffering concrete harm because of the defendant's violation of federal law. Congress may enact legal prohibitions and obligations. And Congress may create causes of action for plaintiffs to sue defendants who violate those legal prohibitions or obligations. But under Article III, an injury in law is not an injury in fact. Only those plaintiffs who have been *concretely harmed* by a defendant's statutory violation may sue that private defendant over that violation of federal law. . . .

As to these plaintiffs, the Court said that "[t]he mere presence of an inaccuracy in an internal credit file, if it is not disclosed to a third party, causes no concrete harm. . . . No concrete harm, no standing."

The principal dissent was authored by Justice Thomas and joined by Justices Breyer, Sotomayor, and Kagan. The dissent did not rest on narrow grounds. On the contrary, Thomas disputed the necessity for requiring "injury in fact." He quoted Cohens v. Virginia, 19 U.S. (6 Wheat.) 264, 405 (1821), to the effect that the judicial power extends only "to 'a case in law or equity,' in which a *right*, under such law, is asserted":

> Key to the scope of the judicial power, then, is whether an individual asserts his or her own rights. At the time of the founding, whether a court possessed judicial power over an action with no showing of actual damages depended on whether the plaintiff sought to enforce a right held privately by an individual or a duty owed broadly to the community [citing Thomas's concurrence in *Spokeo*]. Where an individual sought to sue someone for a violation of his private rights, such as trespass on his land, the plaintiff needed to allege only the violation. Courts typically did not require any showing of actual damages. But where an individual sued based on the violation of a duty owed broadly to the whole community, such as the overgrazing of public lands, courts required 'not only *injuria* [legal injury] but also *damnum* [damage]" [quoting his *Spokeo* concurrence]. . . .
>
> The principle that the violation of an individual right gives rise to an actionable harm was widespread at the founding, in early American history, and in many modern cases. See Uzuegbunam v. Preczewski, 592 U.S. ___ (2021);[c] Havens Realty Corp. v. Coleman, 45 U.S. 363, 373 (1982) ("[T]he actual or threatened injury required by Art. III may exist solely by virtue of statutes creating legal rights, the invasion of which created standing."). And this understanding accords proper respect for the power of Congress and other legislatures to define legal rights. . . . In light of this history, tradition, and common practice, our test should be clear: So long as a "statute fixes a minimum of recovery . . . , there would seem to be no doubt of the right of one who establishes a technical ground of action to recover this minimum sum without any specific showing of loss." T. Cooley, Law of Torts *271. While the Court today discusses the supposed failure to show "injury in fact," courts for centuries held that injury in law to a private right was enough to create a case or controversy.

Critical to Thomas's reasoning was the distinction between private and public rights: "A statute that creates a public right plus a citizen-suit cause

---

c   *Uzuegbunam* was a nearly unanimous decision (only Chief Justice Roberts dissenting) upholding the sufficiency of a claim for merely nominal damages to keep a case from becoming moot. The lower court found that a claim for only nominal damages did not satisfy the redressability component of standing, but the Court disagreed, finding that nominal damages were the ordinary remedy for violation of a legal right. *Uzuegbunam* is discussed elsewhere in this Supplement.—[Footnote by eds.]

of action is insufficient by itself to establish standing. Lujan v. Defenders of Wildlife, 504 U.S. 555 (1992). A statute that creates a private right and a cause of action, however, *does* give plaintiffs an adequate interest in vindicating their private rights in federal court."

A second dissent was filed by Justice Kagan on behalf of herself and Justices Breyer and Sotomayor. That opinion made clear that the three "liberal" Justices did not entirely agree with Thomas's analysis. Their view depended less on a distinction between private and public rights and more on deference to Congress. Kagan said:

> I differ with Justice Thomas on just one matter, unlikely to make much difference in practice. In his view, any "violation of an individual right" created by Congress gives rise to Article III standing. But in *Spokeo*, this Court held that "Article III requires a concrete injury even in the context of a statute violation." 578 U.S. at 341. I continue to adhere to that view, but think it should lead to the same result as Justice Thomas's approach in all but highly unusual cases. As *Spokeo* recognized, "Congress is well positioned to identify [both tangible and] intangible harms" meeting Article III standards. Ibid. Article III requires for concreteness only a "real harm" (that is, a harm that "actually exist[s]") or a "risk of real harm." Ibid. And as today's decision definitively proves, Congress is better suited than courts to determine when something causes a harm or risk of harm in the real world. For that reason, courts should give deference to these congressional judgments. Overriding an authorization to sue is appropriate when but only when Congress could not reasonably have thought that a suit will contribute to compensating or preventing the harm at issue.

Page 326, add a new Note after Note 7:

7A. STANDING ISSUES IN LITIGATION OVER THE 2020 PRESIDENTIAL ELECTION

Before and after the 2020 presidential election, supporters of President Trump filed numerous lawsuits in state and federal courts, challenging the counting and certification of votes in multiple states. Although elections are primarily regulated by state law, these suits alleged violations of various federal constitutional provisions, including the Elections Clause (delegating to state legislatures the authority to regulate the "Times, Places and Manner of holding Elections for Senators and Representatives"), the Electors Clause ("Each State shall appoint, in such Manner as the Legislature thereof may direct, a Number of Electors. . . ."), and the Fourteenth Amendment's protection of due process and equal protection of the law. The courts rejected essentially all of these challenges, and the dismissals in federal court were often based on a lack of standing.[d] The following decisions are illustrative.

---

[d] On the night of January 6, 2021, Congress counted the electoral votes and certified the election of President Biden, despite a delay caused by a violent mob entering the Capitol, thereby effectively mooting any pending election challenges.

(i)   Bognet v. Sec'y of Pennsylvania, 980 F.3d 336 (3d Cir. 2020)

During the COVID-19 pandemic, the Pennsylvania Supreme Court held that, because of delays in the delivery of mail, all Pennsylvania ballots postmarked by 8:00 P.M. on Election Day (November 3) and received by 5:00 P.M. on the Friday after Election Day (November 6), would be considered timely and counted (a "Deadline Extension and Presumption of Timeliness"). The U.S. Supreme Court, by a four–four vote, declined to stay the Pennsylvania Supreme Court's decision. Four registered voters in Pennsylvania and a Pennsylvania congressional candidate, Jim Bognet, subsequently sued state election officials, seeking to enjoin them from counting ballots received after November 3. In rejecting this challenge, the Third Circuit first concluded that the plaintiffs lacked standing to sue under the Elections Clause and the Electors Clause:

> Federal courts are not venues for plaintiffs to assert a bare right "to have the Government act in accordance with law." Allen v. Wright, 468 U.S. 737, 754 (1984). When the alleged injury is undifferentiated and common to all members of the public, courts routinely dismiss such cases as "generalized grievances" that cannot support standing. United States v. Richardson, 418 U.S. 166, 173–75 (1974). Such is the case here insofar as Plaintiffs, and specifically candidate Bognet, theorize their harm as the right to have government administered in compliance with the Elections Clause and Electors Clause. . . .

The court also held that the plaintiffs could not assert third-party standing to litigate the rights of the Pennsylvania General Assembly:

> Because Plaintiffs are not the General Assembly, nor do they bear any conceivable relationship to state lawmaking processes, they lack standing to sue over the alleged usurpation of the General Assembly's rights under the Elections and Electors Clauses. No member of the General Assembly is a party to this lawsuit. That said, prudential standing can suspend Article III's general prohibition on a litigant's raising another person's legal rights. Yet Plaintiffs don't fit the bill. A plaintiff may assert the rights of another if he or she "has a 'close' relationship with the person who possesses the right" and "there is a 'hindrance' to the possessor's ability to protect his own interests." Kowalski v. Tesmer, 543 U.S. 125, 130 (2004). Plaintiffs cannot invoke this exception to the rule against raising the rights of third parties because they enjoy no close relationship with the General Assembly, nor have they alleged any hindrance to the General Assembly's ability to protect its own interests. . . .

Finally, the court held that the plaintiffs lacked standing to sue under the Equal Protection Clause of the Fourteenth Amendment:

> The Voter Plaintiffs claim that Defendants' implementation of the Deadline Extension violates the Equal Protection Clause because "unlawfully" counting ballots received within three days of Election Day dilutes their votes. But the source of this purported

illegality is necessarily a matter of state law, which makes any alleged harm abstract for purposes of the Equal Protection Clause. And the purported vote dilution is also not concrete because it would occur in equal proportion without the alleged procedural illegality—that is, had the General Assembly enacted the Deadline Extension, which the Voter Plaintiffs do not challenge substantively. . . . The opposite of a "particularized" injury is a "generalized grievance," where "the impact on plaintiff is plainly undifferentiated and common to all members of the public." The District Court correctly held that the Voter Plaintiffs' "dilution" claim is a "paradigmatic generalized grievance that cannot support standing." The Deadline Extension and Presumption of Timeliness, assuming they operate to allow the illegal counting of unlawful votes, "dilute" the influence of all voters in Pennsylvania equally and in an "undifferentiated" manner and do not dilute a certain group of voters particularly.

(ii) *Wood v. Raffensperger, 981 F.3d 1307 (11th Cir. 2020)*

In this case, a Georgia voter, Lin Wood, sued state election officials, seeking to enjoin certification of the state's election results. Wood alleged that the state's absentee ballot and recount procedures (which had been adopted as part of a settlement agreement in earlier litigation) violated Georgia law, and that these state law violations amounted to violations of the Elections and Electors Clauses as well as his due process and equal protection rights under the Fourteenth Amendment. The Eleventh Circuit held that he lacked standing, reasoning as follows:

> Georgia law makes clear that post-election litigation may proceed in a state court. But Wood chose to sue in federal court. In doing so, he had to prove that his suit presents a justiciable controversy under Article III of the Constitution. . . . He failed to satisfy this burden. . . . Wood lacks standing because he fails to allege the "first and foremost of standing's three elements": an injury in fact. Spokeo, Inc. v. Robins, 136 S. Ct. 1540, 1547 (2016). An injury in fact is "an invasion of a legally protected interest that is both concrete and particularized and actual or imminent, not conjectural or hypothetical." Trichell v. Midland Credit Mgmt., Inc., 964 F.3d 990, 996 (11th Cir. 2020). Wood's injury is not particularized. Wood asserts only a generalized grievance. A particularized injury is one that "affect[s] the plaintiff in a personal and individual way." Spokeo, 136 S. Ct. at 1548. For example, if Wood were a political candidate harmed by the recount, he would satisfy this requirement because he could assert a personal, distinct injury. But Wood bases his standing on his interest in "ensur[ing that] . . . only lawful ballots are counted." An injury to the right "to require that the government be administered according to the law" is a generalized grievance. And the Supreme Court has made clear that a generalized grievance, "no matter how sincere," cannot support standing. Hollingsworth v. Perry, 570 U.S. 693, 706 (2013). A generalized

grievance is "undifferentiated and common to all members of the public." *Lujan v. Defenders of Wildlife*, 504 U.S. 555, 575 (1992). Wood cannot explain how his interest in compliance with state election laws is different from that of any other person. Indeed, he admits that any Georgia voter could bring an identical suit. But the logic of his argument sweeps past even that boundary. All Americans, whether they voted in this election or whether they reside in Georgia, could be said to share Wood's interest in "ensur[ing] that [a presidential election] is properly administered."

(iii) Texas v. Pennsylvania, 592 U.S. ___, 141 S.Ct. 1230 (2020)

This case was filed by the state of Texas directly in the Supreme Court, invoking the Court's original jurisdiction over suits between states. Texas alleged that there had been voting irregularities in Georgia, Michigan, Pennsylvania, and Wisconsin. These irregularities, Texas contended, "violate one or more of the federal requirements for elections (i.e., equal protection, due process, and the Electors Clause) and thus arise under federal law." Texas sought to have the Court enjoin the defendant states from certifying presidential electors. The Supreme Court denied Texas's motion for leave to file a complaint, concluding that Texas lacked Article III standing. The Court explained that "Texas has not demonstrated a judicially cognizable interest in the manner in which another State conducts its elections." Justice Alito included a separate statement, which Justice Thomas joined, expressing the view that "we do not have discretion to deny the filing of a bill of complaint in a case that falls within our original jurisdiction," and that he "would therefore grant the motion to file the bill of complaint but would not grant other relief, and I express no view on any other issue."

Page 326, add to Note 8:

Randy Beck, Qui Tam Litigation Against Government Officials: Constitutional Implications of a Neglected History, 93 Notre Dame L. Rev. 1235, 1238 (2018) (relying on the Anglo-American tradition of using qui tam litigation to regulate public officials to "challenge[ ] *Lujan*'s conclusion that only the President or his subordinates may litigate generalized grievances about executive lawlessness"); Thomas B. Bennett, The Paradox of Exclusive State-Court Jurisdiction over Federal Claims, 105 Minn. L. Rev. 1211, 1213 (2021) (discussing how the Supreme Court's requirement of a concrete injury for Article III standing may mean that some federal statutory claims can be heard only in state courts, a result that the author describes as "at best bizarre and at worst harmful to the integrity of federal law").

SUBSECTION D. LEGISLATIVE AND GOVERNMENTAL STANDING

Page 360, add at the end of Note 3:

For a critical analysis of the allowance of legislative standing in *Arizona State Legislature* and other claims of "institutional injury," see Tara Leigh Grove, Government Standing and the Fallacy of Institutional Injury, 167 U. Pa. L. Rev. 611 (2019).

Page 360, add a new Note:

3A. *VIRGINIA HOUSE OF DELEGATES V. BETHUNE-HILL*

In 2011, after the 2010 census, the State of Virginia redrew legislative districts for its Senate and House of Delegates. Voters in 12 of the impacted House districts sued two Virginia state agencies and four election officials, arguing that the redrawn districts were racially gerrymandered in violation of the Fourteenth Amendment's Equal Protection Clause. The Virginia House of Delegates (controlled by Republicans) and its Speaker (collectively "the House") intervened as defendants and defended the constitutionality of the challenged districts. A three-judge federal district court held that there had been unconstitutional racial gerrymandering in 11 of the districts and enjoined Virginia from conducting elections in the challenged districts until a new redistricting plan was adopted. A few weeks after the three-judge district court's ruling, Virginia's Attorney General (a Democrat) announced that the State would not pursue an appeal to the Supreme Court. The House, however, filed an appeal, which the defendants argued should be dismissed for lack of standing.

In Virginia House of Delegates v. Bethune-Hill, 587 U.S. ___, 139 S.Ct. 1945 (2019), the Court held, in a five–four decision, that the House lacked standing to appeal. The lineup was unusual. The majority opinion was authored by Justice Ginsburg and was joined by Justices Thomas, Sotomayor, Kagan, and Gorsuch. Justice Alito dissented, joined by Chief Justice Roberts and Justices Breyer and Kavanaugh.

The majority first rejected the argument that the House had standing to represent the interests of the State of Virginia on appeal. Under Virginia law, the majority found, "[a]uthority and responsibility for representing the State's interests in civil litigation . . . rest exclusively with the State's Attorney General." The dissent did not address this issue.

Next, the majority held that the House lacked standing in its own right to defend the challenged districts. On this issue, the majority began by observing:

> To support standing, an injury must be "legally and judicially cognizable." Raines v. Byrd, 521 U.S. 811, 819 (1997). This Court has never held that a judicial decision invalidating a state law as unconstitutional inflicts a discrete, cognizable injury on each organ of government that participated in the law's passage. The Court's precedent thus lends no support for the notion that one House of a bicameral legislature, resting solely on its role in the legislative process, may appeal on its own behalf a judgment invalidating a state enactment.

The majority also noted that the Virginia constitution vests power over districting in the entire state legislature, not just the House. The fact that only the House was seeking to defend the legislature's prerogatives here, reasoned the majority, distinguished this case from *Arizona State Legislature*:

In [*Arizona State Legislature*], . . . the Court recognized the standing of the Arizona House and Senate—*acting together*—to challenge a referendum that gave redistricting authority exclusively to an independent commission, thereby allegedly usurping the legislature's authority under the Federal Constitution over congressional redistricting. In contrast to this case, in *Arizona State Legislature* there was no mismatch between the body seeking to litigate and the body to which the relevant constitutional provision allegedly assigned exclusive redistricting authority. Just as individual members lack standing to assert the institutional interests of a legislature, see *Raines v. Byrd*, a single House of a bicameral legislature lacks capacity to assert interests belonging to the legislature as a whole.

The majority further distinguished *Arizona State Legislature* on the ground that the referendum in that case "was assailed on the ground that it permanently deprived the legislative plaintiffs of their role in the redistricting process. Here, by contrast, the challenged order does not alter the General Assembly's dominant initiating and ongoing role in redistricting." Nor did *Coleman v. Miller* support standing in this case, reasoned the majority, because "this case does not concern the results of a legislative chamber's poll or the validity of any counted or uncounted vote. At issue here, instead, is the constitutionality of a concededly enacted redistricting plan."

The majority then proceeded to reject the House's argument that it had standing because altered districts would affect its membership. In support of this argument, the House had relied on Sixty-seventh Minnesota State Senate v. Beens, 406 U.S. 187 (1972) (per curiam), in which the Court had allowed the Minnesota Senate to challenge a district court order concerning malapportionment that reduced the Senate's size from 67 to 35 members. The majority first observed that *Beens* predated decisions by the Court making clear that intervenor status is insufficient for standing to appeal, and it noted that "[w]hether *Beens* established law on the question of standing, as distinct from intervention, is thus less than pellucid." In any event, the majority said, *Beens* was distinguishable because "[c]utting the size of a legislative chamber in half would necessarily alter its day-to-day operations," whereas here the redistricting would only affect the identity of the members and "the House as an institution has no cognizable interest in the identity of its members."

Finally, the majority rejected the House's contention that it was harmed because a court order causing legislators to seek reelection in districts different from those that they currently represent would affect the House's representational nature. The majority noted that:

> [L]egislative districts change frequently—indeed, after every decennial census—and the Virginia Constitution resolves any confusion over which district is being represented. It provides that delegates continue to represent the districts that elected them, even if their reelection campaigns will be waged in different districts. Va. Const., Art. 2, § 6 ("A member in office at the time that a decennial redistricting law is enacted shall complete his term of office and

shall continue to represent the district from which he was elected for the duration of such term of office . . . ."). We see little reason why the same would not hold true after districting changes caused by judicial decisions, and we thus foresee no representational confusion. And if harms centered on costlier or more difficult election campaigns are cognizable—a question that . . . we need not decide today—those harms would be suffered by individual legislators or candidates, not by the House as a body.

The majority concluded: "In short, Virginia would rather stop than fight on. One House of its bicameral legislature cannot alone continue the litigation against the will of its partners in the legislative process."

Justice Alito's dissent argued that redistricting would cause concrete harm to the House that should be sufficient to give it standing:

> A legislative districting plan powerfully affects a legislative body's output of work. Each legislator represents a particular district, and each district contains a particular set of constituents with particular interests and views. The interests and views of these constituents generally have an important effect on everything that a legislator does—meeting with the representatives of organizations and groups seeking the legislator's help in one way or another, drafting and sponsoring bills, pushing for and participating in hearings, writing or approving reports, and of course, voting. When the boundaries of a district are changed, the constituents and communities of interest present within the district are altered, and this is likely to change the way in which the district's representative does his or her work. And while every individual voter will end up being represented by a legislator no matter which districting plan is ultimately used, it matters a lot how voters with shared interests and views are concentrated or split up. The cumulative effects of all the decisions that go into a districting plan have an important impact on the overall work of the body. . . .

> It seems obvious that any group consisting of members who must work together to achieve the group's aims has a keen interest in the identity of its members, and it follows that the group also has a strong interest in how its members are selected. And what is more important to such a group than the content of its work? Apply what the Court says to a group other than a legislative body and it is immediately obvious that the Court is wrong. Does a string quartet have an interest in the identity of its cellist? Does a basketball team have an interest in the identity of its point guard? Does a board of directors have an interest in the identity of its chairperson? Does it matter to these groups how their members are selected? Do these groups care if the selection method affects their performance? Of course.

On this point, the majority specifically responded to the dissent, arguing:

> [G]roups like the string quartet and basketball team posited by the dissent select their own members. . . . In stark contrast, the

House does not select its own members. Instead, it is a representative body composed of members chosen by the people. Changes to its membership brought about by the voting public thus inflict no cognizable injury on the House.

Justice Alito concluded his dissent by suggesting that the majority was improperly influenced in its analysis by its views of the proper separation of powers structure at the federal level. He acknowledged that "[a]n interest asserted by a Member of Congress or by one or both Houses of Congress that is inconsistent with that structure may not be judicially cognizable," but he said that he did not "see how we can say anything similar about the standing of state legislators or state legislative bodies."

Page 361, add at the end of Note 4:

For a review of possible approaches to state standing, which concludes that "it is possible to recognize state standing in cases where a state suffers a significant injury without permitting every conceivable state suit against the federal government," see Bradford C. Mank, State Standing in *United States v. Texas*: Opening the Floodgates to States Challenging the Federal Government, or Proper Federalism?, 2018 U. Ill. L. Rev. 211, 233.

Page 361, add new Notes after Note 4:

4A. *DEPARTMENT OF COMMERCE V. NEW YORK*

In Department of Commerce v. New York, 588 U.S. ___, 139 S.Ct. 2551 (2019), the Supreme Court considered constitutional and statutory challenges to a decision by the Secretary of Commerce to include a question about citizenship on the 2020 census. There were two groups of challengers. One group consisted of 18 States, the District of Columbia, various counties and cities, and the United States Conference of Mayors. The second group consisted of non-governmental organizations that work with immigrant and minority communities. The challengers argued that including a citizenship question would depress the census response rate by non-citizens and that this would in turn cause the challengers a variety of injuries, such as diminishment of political representation, loss of federal funds, degradation of census data, and diversion of resources.

Although the Court was divided on the merits, it unanimously agreed that at least some of the challengers—who were the respondents before the Supreme Court—had Article III standing. In an opinion by Chief Justice Roberts, the Court said:

> Several state respondents here have shown that if noncitizen households are undercounted by as little as 2%—lower than the District Court's 5.8% prediction—they will lose out on federal funds that are distributed on the basis of state population. That is a sufficiently concrete and imminent injury to satisfy Article III, and there is no dispute that a ruling in favor of respondents would redress that harm.

In answer to the government's argument that any harm to the respondents would not be fairly traceable to the reinstatement of the census question because it would depend on the actions of third parties choosing not to respond to the census, the Court responded:

> [W]e are satisfied that, in these circumstances, respondents have met their burden of showing that third parties will likely react in predictable ways to the citizenship question, even if they do so unlawfully and despite the requirement that the Government keep individual answers confidential. The evidence at trial established that noncitizen households have historically responded to the census at lower rates than other groups, and the District Court did not clearly err in crediting the Census Bureau's theory that the discrepancy is likely attributable at least in part to noncitizens' reluctance to answer a citizenship question. Respondents' theory of standing thus does not rest on mere speculation about the decisions of third parties; it relies instead on the predictable effect of Government action on the decisions of third parties.

A majority of the Court then proceeded to uphold a decision by the District Court conditionally to eliminate the citizenship question and to remand the issue back to the Commerce Department because "the evidence tells a story that does not match the explanation the Secretary gave for his decision."

4B. *CALIFORNIA V. TEXAS*

The Affordable Care Act returned to the Supreme Court for a third time in California v. Texas, 593 U.S. ___, 141 S.Ct. 2104 (2021). In National Federation of Independent Business v. Sebelius, 567 U.S. 519 (2012), the Court held that the individual mandate (minimum health insurance coverage for individuals) could not be justified as an exercise of national power under the Commerce Clause, but that the financial penalties levied to enforce that provision fell within Congress's power to tax. It was as an exercise of the taxing power that the statute was upheld, five to four. Subsequently, Congress reduced the individual mandate penalty to zero. Texas (and other states) then returned to court, claiming that eliminating the penalty eliminated the "tax" and eliminated the taxing power as a justification for its passage. The statute should now be struck down as beyond Congress's power under the Commerce Clause. In *California v. Texas*, the Court refused to address that claim, holding instead that the plaintiffs lacked standing.[d]

In the view of Justice Alito, joined by Justice Gorsuch, in dissent, the states' standing was clear. Texas showed direct financial injury from various reporting requirements of the ACA. These reporting requirements were not in themselves unconstitutional, but they were imposed under a statute another part of which (the individual mandate) was unconstitutional. As Justice Thomas put it in his concurrence: "[T]he plaintiffs assert that the mandate is unconstitutional because it no longer imposes financial consequences and thus cannot be justified as a tax. And given that the mandate is

---

[d]   The odd style of the case arose from the fact that the Trump Administration declined to defend the constitutionality of the statute. California and other states intervened to do so and were styled as parties for that purpose.

unconstitutional, *other* portions of the Act that actually harm the plaintiffs must fall with it."

This argument depends on the claim that the statute is inseverable, that is, that invalidating part requires invalidating the whole. If the plaintiffs were right about inseverability, then they arguably would have had injury (the cost of complying with the reporting requirements) fairly traceable to the government's unlawful conduct (maintaining the individual mandate with zero penalty for non-compliance) and redressable by striking down the entire statute.

Justice Thomas termed this argument "standing-through-inseverability." He joined the majority in declining to address this theory on the ground that it had not been raised sufficiently clearly below.

Given the refusal to address severability, the majority, speaking through Justice Breyer, only had to show that the individual mandate itself, shorn of any enforcement penalty, caused plaintiffs no harm. This was easily done. The prospect that the toothless individual mandate would cause many citizens to enroll in state programs (and thus drive up costs) was too speculative. The significant direct costs of the reporting requirements did not count, as they did not arise from the specific provision that was allegedly unconstitutional.[e]

Because of its enormous political prominence, *California v. Texas* has the feel of an important decision. And perhaps it is. But the Court's refusal to address standing-through-inseverability, as Justice Thomas called it, means that that avenue remains open. Presumably, Texas could file a new suit tomorrow, stating clearly the argument that the dissent accepted and that the majority declined to address and forcing the courts to consider the constitutionality of the ACA yet again.

[e] There were also two individual plaintiffs, also found to lack standing. Basically, the Court reasoned that with zero penalty for non-compliance, the statute no longer caused individual plaintiffs an injury in forcing them to buy unwanted insurance.

Page 362, add at the end of the carryover paragraph:

For an argument that Congress lacks standing to enforce a congressional subpoena, see Amandeep S. Grewal, Congressional Subpoenas in Court, 98 N.C. L. Rev. 1043 (2020).

Page 391, add at the end of the first sentence in Note 3:

For a more recent article by the same author, see Ryan W. Scott, Circumventing Standing to Appeal, 72 Fla. L. Rev. 741 (2020). Scott examines possible rationales for the requirement of standing to appeal and concludes that it is best understood as reflecting the expiration of the underlying case or controversy once judgment becomes final: "When the time to file an appeal has expired, and no party whose injury forms part of the case or controversy has requested further review, the judicial department has finally resolved the case," and its power ceases. The problem of politically motivated attorneys general declining to defend defensible laws, Scott argues, could be solved by Congress creating special mechanisms to transfer selected cases for appellate review, perhaps at the suggestion of the trial judge, despite the absence of appeal by a party.

SECTION 3. RELATED DOCTRINES

SUBSECTION A. THIRD-PARTY STANDING

Page 403, add a new Note:

5A. *JUNE MEDICAL SERVICES LLC V. RUSSO*

In 2014, Louisiana enacted a law requiring that abortion providers in the state have admitting privileges at a nearby hospital. The law was almost identical to a Texas law that the Supreme Court held unconstitutional in Whole Woman's Health v. Hellerstedt, 579 U.S. ___, 136 S.Ct. 2292 (2016). *Whole Woman's Health* was a five–four decision. One of the Justices in the majority (Justice Kennedy) later retired from the Court and was replaced by Justice Kavanaugh. In June Medical Services LLC v. Russo, 591 U.S. ___, 140 S.Ct. 2103 (2020), the Supreme Court held that the Louisiana law was unconstitutional because, like the Texas law, it imposed an undue burden on the ability of women to obtain an abortion. This decision was also 5–4. Although Chief Justice Roberts had dissented in *Whole Woman's Health*, he provided the fifth vote for a majority in this case. He concurred in the judgment, citing considerations of stare decisis.

Like the challenge in *Whole Woman's Health*, the challenge in *June Medical Services* was brought by abortion providers, not by women seeking abortions. The Supreme Court has often allowed abortion providers to challenge abortion restrictions on the ground that such restrictions violate the abortion rights of actual or potential patients. Louisiana did not challenge standing while the case was being litigated in the lower courts. In fact, it appeared expressly to concede standing early in the litigation. But when the case reached the Supreme Court, Louisiana argued for the first time that the abortion providers should not have been allowed to bring suit.

The plurality opinion, authored by Justice Breyer, rejected Louisiana's argument. Because restrictions on third-party standing are merely prudential, the plurality reasoned, they can be waived or forfeited. The conclusion was that this had happened here. The plurality also emphasized that the restriction on third-party standing is "hardly absolute," and it noted that the Court had long allowed similar challenges by abortion providers. Citing a number of prior decisions, the plurality further observed that "we have generally permitted plaintiffs to assert third-party rights in cases where the 'enforcement of the challenged restriction *against the litigant* would result indirectly in the violation of third parties' rights' " (quoting Kowalski v. Tesmer, 543 U.S. 125, 130 (2004)) (emphasis in original). Finally, the plurality said that, because the plaintiffs are "the parties who must actually go through the process of applying for and maintaining admitting privileges, they are far better positioned than their patients to address the burdens of compliance." Chief Justice Roberts said in a footnote in his concurrence in the judgment that he agreed with the plurality's reasoning on standing.

Justice Thomas dissented, arguing that the limitation on third-party standing should be understood as stemming from Article III's "case or controversy" requirement rather than merely from prudential considerations.

He further contended that, "[b]ecause [the abortion] right belongs to the woman making that choice, not to those who provide abortions, plaintiffs cannot establish a personal legal injury by asserting that this right has been violated." Justice Alito also dissented and, in his discussion of third-party standing, was joined by Justices Thomas and Gorsuch. Alito argued that Louisiana should not be deemed to have waived objections to standing and that third-party standing should not be allowed where, as here, there is a potential conflict of interest between the plaintiffs and the third-party rights holders:

> This case features a blatant conflict of interest between an abortion provider and its patients. Like any other regulated entity, an abortion provider has a financial interest in avoiding burdensome regulations such as [Louisiana's] admitting privileges requirement. Applying for privileges takes time and energy, and maintaining privileges may impose additional burdens. Women seeking abortions, on the other hand, have an interest in the preservation of regulations that protect their health. The conflict inherent in such a situation is glaring.

In support of this proposition, Alito cited Elk Grove Unified School Dist. v. Newdow, 542 U.S. 1 (2004), where the Court had concluded that a father lacked standing to argue that a requirement in his daughter's school of reciting the words "under God" in the Pledge of Allegiance violated his daughter's First Amendment rights, in part because the father's and daughter's interests were potentially in conflict. Alito further argued that the abortion providers had not shown that they have a close relationship with their patients or that the patients face obstacles to bringing claims on their own behalf, and thus he concluded that the providers had failed to satisfy "the two prongs of our third-party standing doctrine." Justice Gorsuch similarly argued in a separate dissent that third-party standing should be allowed only in "narrow circumstances," and he complained that the traditional requirements for such standing had not been met. Justice Kavanaugh dissented on the merits but did not discuss standing.

Page 404, add at the end of footnote a:

For an effort to "unpack" third-party standing by more sharply distinguishing it from situations involving first-party standing and by separately considering the standing of (a) parties who are directly regulated, (b) parties who suffer collateral injuries, and (c) representative parties, see Curtis A. Bradley and Ernest A. Young, Unpacking Third-Party Standing, 131 Yale L.J. (forthcoming 2021). The authors argue, among other things, that limitations on third-party standing are properly thought of as prudential in nature, that a permissive approach to third-party standing makes sense in situations in which the litigant is subject to the law they are challenging, and that a stricter approach is warranted in other settings.

SUBSECTION B. RIPENESS

Page 417, add at the end of Note 6:

For a recent decision in which there was considerable overlap between standing and ripeness, see Trump v. New York, 592 U.S. ___, 141 S.Ct. 530 (2020). Several states, local governments, organizations, and individuals challenged the Trump administration's decision to exclude undocumented immigrants from the census, alleging that the exclusion violated both the

Enumeration Clause of the Constitution and a federal statutory requirement that the President "transmit to the Congress a statement showing the whole number of persons in each State," 2 U.S.C. § 2a(a). The state and local government plaintiffs claimed a "legally cognizable injury" because the unlawful apportionment threatened to undermine their congressional representation and federal funding. The Court held that the case did not satisfy Article III standing or ripeness requirements, because it was "riddled with contingencies and speculation that impede judicial review." Although the President had "made clear his desire to exclude aliens without lawful status from the apportionment base," he "qualified his directive by providing that the [Commerce] Secretary should gather information 'to the extent practicable' and that aliens should be excluded 'to the extent feasible.' " Accordingly, "[a]ny prediction how the Executive Branch might eventually implement this general statement of policy is 'no more than conjecture' at this time." The Court concluded: "At the end of the day, the standing and ripeness inquiries both lead to the conclusion that judicial resolution of this dispute is premature." Justice Breyer, joined by Justices Sotomayor and Kagan, dissented and asserted: "The Government does not deny that, if carried out, the policy [to exclude aliens without lawful status] will harm the plaintiffs. Nor does it deny that it will implement that policy imminently (to the extent it is able to do so). Under a straightforward application of our precedents, the plaintiffs have standing to sue. The question is ripe for resolution."

Page 420, omit footnote c.

[Explanation: The *Williamson* case was overruled in Knick v. Township of Scott, Pennsylvania, 588 U.S. ___, 139 S.Ct. 2162 (2019).]

SUBSECTION C. MOOTNESS

Page 421, delete the remainder of Note 2 after the words "that the wrong will be repeated" at the end of the first full paragraph and substitute:

For a fairly conventional application of this rule, see Already, LLC v. Nike, Inc., 568 U.S. 85 (2013). Nike sued Already for infringement of a trademark shoe design. Already counterclaimed for a declaration of trademark invalidity. After some preliminary proceedings, Nike apparently saw the handwriting on the wall, because it then moved to have its claims against Already dismissed with prejudice and eventually covenanted "unconditionally and irrevocably" to refrain from making any claims or demands of Already or its distributors for the allegedly infringing shoes or for "any colorable imitations thereof." Already nevertheless wanted to press its attack on Nike's trademark, but the Supreme Court found the case moot. The test was whether "the allegedly wrongful behavior [could] reasonably be expected to recur," and in light of the breadth and content of Nike's covenant, the answer was "no."

For two situations where the Court found this test unsatisfied, see City of Mesquite v. Aladdin's Castle, Inc., 455 U.S. 283 (1982), and Northeastern Florida Chapter of Associated General Contractors v. City of Jacksonville, 508 U.S. 656 (1993). In *Aladdin's Castle*, a municipal ordinance was declared unconstitutionally vague after it had been repealed. The Supreme Court noted that if the decision below were vacated, the municipality would be free to reenact the same ordinance. Accordingly, the case was not moot.

In *Associated General Contractors*, the contractors challenged Jacksonville's minority set-aside program as unconstitutional. After the Supreme Court granted certiorari, the city repealed the set-aside ordinance and enacted a more carefully constructed replacement. Speaking through Justice Thomas, the Court said the case was not moot: "There is no mere risk that Jacksonville will repeat its allegedly wrongful conduct; it has already done so." That the new ordinance differed from the old one did not matter: "[I]f that were the rule, a defendant could moot a case by repealing the challenged statute and replacing it with one that differs only in some insignificant respect."

Justice O'Connor, joined by Justice Blackmun, dissented. She argued that *Aladdin's Castle* stated an exceptional rule for those rare cases "where circumstances demonstrate that the legislature will likely reinstate the old law." Other precedents established that, "where a challenged statute is replaced with more narrowly drawn legislation pending our review, and the plaintiff seeks only prospective relief, we generally should decline to decide the case. The controversy with respect to the old statute is moot, because a declaration of its invalidity or an injunction against the law's future enforcement would not benefit the plaintiff."

Who has the better of this argument? Should the courts assume that a repealed ordinance will be reenacted or that other allegedly illegal activity will be resumed? In making that assumption, are the courts reaching to adjudicate mere hypotheticals? Or is this stance necessary to prevent the kind of cat-and-mouse game described by Justice Thomas? Is it possible for a court to assess, on a case-by-case basis, the defendant's good faith?

A more controversial situation arose in New York State Rifle & Pistol Ass'n, Inc. v. City of New York, 590 U.S. ___, 140 S.Ct. 1525 (2020). The city of New York passed an ordinance allowing the use of handguns at only seven firing ranges located within the city. Relying on District of Columbia v. Heller, 554 U.S. 570 (2008), which held that the Second Amendment protects the right of ordinary citizens to possess firearms, the plaintiffs asserted the right to take their guns to second homes or firing ranges located elsewhere. Both the District Court and the Second Circuit rejected this challenge.

When the Supreme Court granted review, the city amended the ordinance to allow the plaintiffs the right to engage in the conduct that was the subject of their complaint. The state of New York also amended its firearms licensing law to disallow local ordinances with restrictions like the ones challenged in this case. The city then sought dismissal on grounds of mootness.

The Court, speaking per curiam, decided the case was moot. It vacated the judgment below and remanded to the lower courts to consider such subsidiary issues as whether the amended ordinance allowed stops for coffee and whether a late-arising claim for damages could be added.

Justice Alito dissented, joined by Justice Gorsuch and in part by Justice Thomas. Alito said that the decision "permits our docket to be manipulated in a way that should not be countenanced":

> One might have thought that the City, having convinced the lower courts that the law was consistent with *Heller*, would have been willing to defend its victory in this Court. But once we granted certiorari, both the City and the State of New York sprang into action to prevent us from deciding this case. Although the City had previously insisted that its ordinance served important public safety purposes, our grant of review apparently led to an epiphany of sorts, and the City quickly changed its ordinance. And for good measure the State enacted a law making the old New York City ordinance illegal.

Five senators had filed a noteworthy amicus brief, alleging that the suit had been ginned up by the National Rifle Association and its allies after "a multimillion dollar advertising campaign to shape this Court's composition, no less, and an industrial-strength influence campaign aimed at this Court." Brief of Senator Sheldon Whitehouse et al. as Amici Curiae. The reference was to the disputed confirmation of Justice Kavanaugh, which, the amici alleged, was intended to "break the tie" in Second Amendment cases. After various intimations of judicial partisanship, the brief concluded with a thinly veiled threat:

> The Supreme Court is not well. And the people know it. Perhaps the Court can heal itself before the public demands it be "restructured in order to reduce the influence of politics" [quoting a question from a Quinnipiac Poll]. Particularly on the urgent issues of gun control, a nation desperately needs it to heal.

Justice Alito mentioned this brief in his dissent, implicitly suggesting that the majority may have been responding to political pressure.

Aside from the political fireworks regarding gun control, *New York State Rifle & Pistol Ass'n* is difficult to categorize doctrinally. Almost all instances of laws amended while under attack present the opportunity to avoid difficult and perhaps unnecessary decisions, but at the cost of postponing or evading decisions on the merits. In a sense, the dissenters' position in *New York State Rifle & Pistol Ass'n* was reminiscent of the opinion of Chief Justice Rehnquist, speaking only for himself, in Honig v. Doe, 484 U.S. 305 (1988), discussed in Note 4 below.

SECTION 4. THE POLITICAL QUESTION

Page 470, add at the end of Note 1:

Consider the argument in John Harrison, The Political Question Doctrines, 67 Am. U. L. Rev. 457 (2017):

> *Nixon v. United States* found substantial non-judicial finality under the political question rubric. Most likely the case means that Senate impeachments are absolutely conclusive as far as the courts are concerned, but the opinion can be read more narrowly. Each of

the three leading cases in which the Court has relied on the political question doctrine—*Luther, Coleman,* and *Nixon v. United States*—rests on non-judicial finality. In all three, the Court found that the judiciary was absolutely bound by a political actor's decision that applied legal rules to specific facts.

Harrison notes that while there is Supreme Court "dicta that the political question doctrine limits the power of Article III courts to decide certain cases," there are several ways in which the doctrine has been employed in the cases, "none of which involves a lack of jurisdiction under Article III." One, for example, is a requirement that the Court accept an earlier political decision as a merits resolution of the dispute. Another is a bar on judicial relief that would interfere with a political decision. He concludes that the doctrine is a limit "on the judicial power but not on the cases Article III courts may decide." It "tells courts how to decide cases." Is there a practical difference between saying that a court is powerless to grant relief and saying that it is powerless to hear the case? In any event, has Harrison read *Nixon* correctly? Do the other political question cases in these materials fit this description?

A related question that could be asked is this: suppose a dispute that the federal courts cannot hear because of the political question doctrine was initiated in a state court. Would the state court be free to address the merits of federal questions raised in the suit independently of the political question doctrine? If it did so, would its judgment be reviewable by the Supreme Court?

For a response to these questions, see Scott Dodson, Article III and the Political-Question Doctrine, 116 Northwestern U.L. Rev. (forthcoming 2021). One of the implications of treating the political-question doctrine as a justiciability requirement arising from Article III is that it would not apply in state courts. "How odd would it be," asks Dodson, "to learn that while the political-question doctrine prevents the U.S. Supreme Court from reviewing the propriety of an impeachment trial of the President of the United States, the doctrine does not bar a state judge—perhaps from a state whose population and government officials strongly support the President—from doing so?" For this and other reasons, Dodson argues that the political-question doctrine should not be viewed as "sourced" in Article III but rather as a matter of the substantive law on the question raised. In his view, "It is the Guarantee Clause itself (or the Impeachment Clause itself . . .) that makes something nonjusticiable," thus in every case pushing the question of judicial resolution back to the underlying substantive law.

Page 472, delete Note 3 on Political Gerrymandering and substitute the following:

Rucho v. Common Cause

Supreme Court of the United States, 2019.
588 U.S. ___, 139 S.Ct. 2484.

■ CHIEF JUSTICE ROBERTS delivered the opinion of the Court.

Voters and other plaintiffs in North Carolina and Maryland challenged their States' congressional districting maps as unconstitutional partisan gerrymanders. The North Carolina plaintiffs complained that the State's districting plan discriminated against Democrats; the Maryland plaintiffs complained that their State's plan discriminated against Republicans. The plaintiffs alleged that the gerrymandering violated the First Amendment, the Equal Protection Clause of the Fourteenth Amendment, the Elections Clause, and Article I, § 2, of the Constitution. The District Courts in both cases ruled in favor of the plaintiffs, and the defendants appealed directly to this Court.

These cases require us to consider once again whether claims of excessive partisanship in districting are "justiciable"—that is, properly suited for resolution by the federal courts. This Court has not previously struck down a districting plan as an unconstitutional partisan gerrymander, and has struggled without success over the past several decades to discern judicially manageable standards for deciding such claims. The districting plans at issue here are highly partisan, by any measure. The question is whether the courts below appropriately exercised judicial power when they found them unconstitutional as well.

I

[In Part I, the Court summarized the facts and the litigation history of the decisions reported as Rucho v. Common Cause, 318 F. Supp. 3d 777 (M.D.N.C. 2018), and Lamone v. Benisek, 348 F. Supp. 3d 493 (Md. 2018). Both cases showed energetic efforts to draw congressional districts so as to gain partisan advantage, for Republicans in North Carolina and for Democrats in Maryland.]

II

A

. . . Chief Justice Marshall famously wrote that it is "the province and duty of the judicial department to say what the law is." Marbury v. Madison, 5 U.S. (1 Cranch) 137, 177 (1803). Sometimes, however, "the law is that the judicial department has no business entertaining the claim of unlawfulness—because the question is entrusted to one of the political branches or involves no judicially enforceable rights." Vieth v. Jubelirer, 541 U.S. 267, 277 (2004) (plurality opinion). In such a case the claim is said to present a "political question" and to be nonjusticiable—outside the courts' competence and therefore beyond the courts' jurisdiction. Baker v. Carr, 369 U.S. 186, 217 (1962). Among the political question cases the Court has identified are those that lack "judicially discoverable and manageable standards for resolving [them]." Id.

Last Term in Gill v. Whitford, 585 U.S. ___, 138 S.Ct. 1916 (2018), we reviewed our partisan gerrymandering cases and concluded that those cases "leave unresolved whether such claims may be brought." . . . The question here . . . is whether there is an "appropriate role for the Federal Judiciary" in remedying the problem of partisan gerrymandering—whether such claims are claims of legal right, resolvable according to legal principles, or political questions that must find their resolution elsewhere.

B

Partisan gerrymandering is nothing new. Nor is frustration with it. . . . In 1812, Governor of Massachusetts and future Vice President Elbridge Gerry notoriously approved congressional districts that the legislature had drawn to aid the Democratic-Republican Party. The moniker "gerrymander" was born when an outraged Federalist newspaper observed that one of the misshapen districts resembled a salamander. See *Vieth*, 541 U.S., at 274 (plurality opinion); Elmer C. Griffith, The Rise and Development of the Gerrymander 17–19 (1907). "By 1840, the gerrymander was a recognized force in party politics and was generally attempted in all legislation enacted for the formation of election districts. It was generally conceded that each party would attempt to gain power which was not proportionate to its numerical strength." Id. at 123.

The Framers addressed the election of Representatives to Congress in the Elections Clause. Art. I, § 4, cl. 1. That provision assigns to state legislatures the power to prescribe the "Times, Places and Manner of holding Elections" for Members of Congress, while giving Congress the power to "make or alter" any such regulations. . . .

Congress has regularly exercised its Elections Clause power, including to address partisan gerrymandering. The Apportionment Act of 1842, which required single member districts for the first time, specified that those districts be "composed of contiguous territory," Act of June 25, 1842, ch. 47, 5 Stat. 491, in "an attempt to forbid the practice of the gerrymander," *Griffith*, supra, at 12. Later statutes added requirements of compactness and equality of population. (Only the single member district requirement remains in place today. 2 U.S.C. § 2c.) . . .

Appellants suggest that, through the Elections Clause, the Framers set aside electoral issues such as the one before us as questions that only Congress can resolve. See *Baker*, 369 U.S. at 217. We do not agree. In two areas—one-person, one-vote and racial gerrymandering—our cases have held that there is a role for the courts with respect to at least some issues that could arise from a State's drawing of congressional districts. See Wesberry v. Sanders, 376 U.S. 1 (1964); Shaw v. Reno, 509 U.S. 630 (1993) (*Shaw I*).

But the history is not irrelevant. The Framers were aware of electoral districting problems and considered what to do about them. They settled on a characteristic approach, assigning the issue to the state legislatures, expressly checked and balanced by the Federal Congress. . . . At no point was there a suggestion that the federal courts had a role to play. Nor was there any indication that the Framers had ever heard of courts doing such a thing.

C

Courts have nevertheless been called upon to resolve a variety of questions surrounding districting. Early on, doubts were raised about the competence of the federal courts to resolve those questions. See Wood v. Broom, 287 U.S. 1 (1932); Colegrove v. Green, 328 U.S. 549 (1946).

In the leading case of *Baker v. Carr*, supra, voters in Tennessee complained that the State's districting plan for state representatives "debase[d]" their votes, because the plan was predicated on a 60-year-old census that no longer reflected the distribution of population in the State. The plaintiffs argued that votes of people in overpopulated districts held less value than those of people in less populated districts, and that this inequality violated the Equal Protection Clause of the Fourteenth Amendment. The District Court dismissed the action on the ground that the claim was not justiciable, relying on this Court's precedents, including *Colegrove*. This Court reversed. It identified various considerations relevant to determining whether a claim is a nonjusticiable political question, including whether there is "a lack of judicially discoverable and manageable standards for resolving it." 369 U.S. at 217. The Court concluded that the claim of population inequality among districts did not fall into that category, because such a claim could be decided under basic equal protection principles. Id. at 226. In *Wesberry v. Sanders*, the Court extended its ruling to malapportionment of congressional districts, holding that Article I, § 2, required that "one man's vote in a congressional election is to be worth as much as another's." 376 U.S. at 8.

Another line of challenges to districting plans has focused on race. Laws that explicitly discriminate on the basis of race, as well as those that are race neutral on their face but are unexplainable on grounds other than race, are of course presumptively invalid. The Court applied those principles to electoral boundaries in Gomillion v. Lightfoot, 364 U.S. 339 (1960), concluding that a challenge to an "uncouth twenty-eight sided" municipal boundary line that excluded black voters from city elections stated a constitutional claim. In Wright v. Rockefeller, 376 U.S. 52 (1964), the Court extended the reasoning of *Gomillion* to congressional districting.

Partisan gerrymandering claims have proved far more difficult to adjudicate. The basic reason is that, while it is illegal for a jurisdiction to depart from the one-person, one-vote rule, or to engage in racial discrimination in districting, "a jurisdiction may engage in constitutional political gerrymandering." Hunt v. Cromartie, 526 U.S. 541, 551 (1999). See also Gaffney v. Cummings, 412 U.S. 735, 753 (1973) (recognizing that "[p]olitics and political considerations are inseparable from districting and apportionment").

To hold that legislators cannot take partisan interests into account when drawing district lines would essentially countermand the Framers' decision to entrust districting to political entities. The "central problem" is not determining whether a jurisdiction has engaged in partisan gerrymandering. It is "determining when political gerrymandering has gone too far." *Vieth*, 541 U.S. at 296 (plurality opinion). See League of United Latin American Citizens v. Perry, 548 U.S. 399, 420 (2006) (*LULAC*) (opinion of Kennedy, J.) (difficulty is "providing a standard for deciding how much partisan dominance is too much"). . . .

[I]n Davis v. Bandemer, 478 U.S. 109, 116–17 (1986) (plurality opinion), we addressed a claim that Indiana Republicans had cracked and packed Democrats in violation of the Equal Protection Clause. A majority of the Court agreed that the case was justiciable, but the Court splintered over the proper standard to apply. Four Justices would have required proof of "intentional discrimination against an identifiable political group and an actual discriminatory effect on that group." Id. at 127. Two Justices would have focused on "whether the boundaries of the voting districts have been distorted deliberately and arbitrarily to achieve illegitimate ends." Id. at 165 (Powell, J., concurring in part and dissenting in part). Three Justices, meanwhile, would have held that the Equal Protection Clause simply "does not supply judicially manageable standards for resolving purely political gerrymandering claims." Id. at 147 (O'Connor, J., concurring in judgment). At the end of the day, there was 'no 'Court' for a standard that properly should be applied in determining whether a challenged redistricting plan is an unconstitutional partisan political gerrymander." Id. at 185 n.25 (opinion of Powell, J.). In any event, the Court held that the plaintiffs had failed to show that the plan violated the Constitution.

Eighteen years later, in *Vieth*, the plaintiffs complained that Pennsylvania's legislature "ignored all traditional redistricting criteria, including the preservation of local government boundaries," in order to benefit Republican congressional candidates. 541 U.S. at 272–73 (plurality opinion) (brackets omitted). Justice Scalia wrote for a four-Justice plurality. He would have held that the plaintiffs' claims were nonjusticiable because there was no "judicially discernible and manageable standard" for deciding them. Id. at 306. Justice Kennedy, concurring in the judgment, noted "the lack of comprehensive and neutral principles for drawing electoral boundaries [and] the absence of rules to limit and confine judicial intervention." Id. at 306–07. He nonetheless left open the possibility that "in another case a standard might emerge." Id. at 312. Four Justices dissented.

In *LULAC*, the plaintiffs challenged a mid-decade redistricting map approved by the Texas Legislature. Once again a majority of the Court could not find a justiciable standard for resolving the plaintiffs' partisan gerrymandering claims. See 548 U.S. at 414. . . .

III

A

In considering whether partisan gerrymandering claims are justiciable, we are mindful of Justice Kennedy's counsel in *Vieth*: Any standard for resolving such claims must be grounded in a "limited and precise rationale" and be "clear, manageable, and politically neutral." 541 U.S. at 306–08 (opinion concurring in judgment). An important reason for those careful constraints is that, as a Justice with extensive experience in state and local politics put it,"[t]he opportunity to control the drawing of electoral boundaries through the legislative process of apportionment is a critical and traditional part of politics in the United States." *Bandemer*, 478 U.S. at 145 (opinion of O'Connor, J.). An expansive standard requiring "the correction of all election district lines drawn for partisan reasons would commit federal and state courts to unprecedented intervention in the American political process," *Vieth*, 541 U.S. at 306 (opinion of Kennedy, J.).

As noted, the question is one of degree: How to "provid[e] a standard for deciding how much partisan dominance is too much." *LULAC*, 548 U.S. at 420 (opinion of Kennedy, J.). And it is vital in such circumstances that the Court act only in accord with especially clear standards: "With uncertain limits, intervening courts—even when proceeding with best intentions—would risk assuming political, not legal, responsibility for a process that often produces ill will and distrust." *Vieth*, 541 U.S. at 307 (opinion of Kennedy, J.). If federal courts are to "inject [themselves] into the most heated partisan issues" by adjudicating partisan gerrymandering claims, *Bandemer*, 478 U.S. at 145 (opinion of O'Connor, J.), they must be armed with a standard that can reliably differentiate unconstitutional from "constitutional political gerrymandering." Hunt v. Cromartie, 526 U.S. 541, 551 (1999).

B

Partisan gerrymandering claims rest on an instinct that groups with a certain level of political support should enjoy a commensurate level of political power and influence. Explicitly or implicitly, a districting map is alleged to be unconstitutional because it makes it too difficult for one party to translate statewide support into seats in the legislature. But such a claim is based on a "norm that does not exist" in our electoral system—"statewide elections for representatives along party lines." *Bandemer*, 478 U.S. at 159 (opinion of O'Connor, J.).

Partisan gerrymandering claims invariably sound in a desire for proportional representation. As Justice O'Connor put it, such claims are based on "a conviction that the greater the departure from proportionality, the more suspect an apportionment plan becomes." Id. "Our cases, however, clearly foreclose any claim that the Constitution requires proportional representation or that legislatures in reapportioning must draw district lines to come as near as possible to allocating seats to the contending parties in proportion to what their anticipated statewide vote will be." Id. at 130 (plurality opinion).

The Founders certainly did not think proportional representation was required. For more than 50 years after ratification of the Constitution, many States elected their congressional representatives through at-large or "general ticket" elections. Such States typically sent single-party delegations to Congress. That meant that a party could garner nearly half of the vote statewide and wind up without any seats in the congressional delegation. . . .

Unable to claim that the Constitution requires proportional representation outright, plaintiffs inevitably ask the courts to make their own political judgment about how much representation particular political parties *deserve*—based on the votes of their supporters—and to rearrange the challenged districts to achieve that end. But federal courts are not equipped to apportion political power as a matter of fairness, nor is there any basis for concluding that they were authorized to do so. As Justice Scalia put it for the plurality in *Vieth*, 541 U.S. at 291:

> "Fairness" does not seem to us a judicially manageable standard. . . . Some criterion more solid and more demonstrably met than that seems to us necessary to enable the state legislatures to discern the limits of their districting discretion, to meaningfully constrain the discretion of the courts, and to win public acceptance for the courts' intrusion into a process that is the very foundation of democratic decisionmaking.

The initial difficulty in settling on a "clear, manageable and politically neutral" test for fairness is that it is not even clear what fairness looks like in this context. There is a large measure of "unfairness" in any winner-take-all system. Fairness may mean a greater number of competitive districts. Such a claim seeks to undo packing and cracking so that supporters of the disadvantaged party have a better shot at electing their preferred candidates. But making as many districts as possible more competitive could be a recipe for disaster for the disadvantaged party. As Justice White has pointed out, "[i]f all or most of the districts are competitive . . . even a narrow statewide preference for either party would produce an overwhelming majority for the winning party in the state legislature." *Bandemer*, 478 U.S. at 130 (plurality opinion).

On the other hand, perhaps the ultimate objective of a "fairer" share of seats in the congressional delegation is most readily achieved by yielding to the gravitational pull of proportionality and engaging in cracking and packing, to ensure each party its "appropriate" share of "safe" seats. Such an approach, however, comes at the expense of competitive districts and of individuals in districts allocated to the opposing party.

Or perhaps fairness should be measured by adherence to "traditional" districting criteria, such as maintaining political subdivisions, keeping communities of interest together, and protecting incumbents. See Brief for Bipartisan Group of Current and Former Members of the House of Representatives as Amici Curiae. But protecting incumbents, for example, enshrines a particular partisan distribution. And the "natural political geography" of a State—such as the fact that urban electoral districts are often dominated by one political party—can itself lead to inherently packed districts. As Justice Kennedy has explained, traditional criteria such as compactness and contiguity "cannot promise political neutrality . . . ." *Vieth*, 541 U.S. at 308–09 (opinion concurring in judgment).

Deciding among just these different visions of fairness (you can imagine many others) poses basic questions that are political, not legal. There are no legal standards discernible in the Constitution for making such judgments, let alone limited and precise standards that are clear, manageable, and politically neutral. Any judicial decision on what is "fair" in this context would be an "unmoored determination" of the sort characteristic of a political question beyond the competence of the federal courts.

And it is only after determining how to define fairness that you can even begin to answer the determinative question: "How much is too much?" At what point does permissible partisanship become unconstitutional? If compliance with traditional districting criteria is the fairness touchstone, for example, how much deviation from those criteria is constitutionally acceptable and how should mapdrawers prioritize competing criteria? Should a court "reverse gerrymander" other parts of a State to counteract "natural" gerrymandering caused, for example, by the urban concentration of one party? If a districting plan protected half of the incumbents but redistricted the rest into head to head races, would that be constitutional? A court would have to rank the relative importance of those traditional criteria and weigh how much deviation from each to allow.

If a court instead focused on the respective number of seats in the legislature, it would have to decide the ideal number of seats for each party and determine at what point deviation from that balance went too far. If a five–three allocation corresponds most closely to statewide vote totals, is a six–two allocation permissible, given that legislatures have the authority to engage in a certain degree of partisan gerrymandering? Which seats should be packed and which cracked? Or if the goal is as many competitive districts as possible, how close does the split need to be for the district to be considered competitive? Presumably not all districts could qualify, so how to choose? Even assuming the court knew which version of fairness to be looking for, there are no discernible and manageable standards for deciding whether there has been a violation. The questions are "unguided and ill suited to the development of judicial standards," *Vieth*, 541 U.S. at 296 (plurality opinion), and "results from one gerrymandering case to the next would likely be disparate and inconsistent," id. at 308 (opinion of Kennedy, J.).

Appellees contend that if we can adjudicate one-person, one-vote claims, we can also assess partisan gerrymandering claims. But the one-person, one-vote rule is relatively easy to administer as a matter of math. The same cannot be said of partisan gerrymandering claims, because the Constitution supplies no objective measure for assessing whether a districting map treats a political party fairly. . . .

More fundamentally, "vote dilution" in the one-person, one-vote cases refers to the idea that each vote must carry equal weight. In other words, each representative must be accountable to (approximately) the same number of constituents. That requirement does not extend to political parties. It does not mean that each party must be influential in proportion to its number of supporters. As we stated unanimously in *Gill*, "this Court is not responsible for vindicating generalized partisan preferences. The Court's constitutionally prescribed role is to vindicate the individual rights of the people appearing before it." 585 U.S. at ___, 138 S.Ct. at 1933.*

Nor do our racial gerrymandering cases provide an appropriate standard for assessing partisan gerrymandering. "[N]othing in our case law compels the conclusion that racial and political gerrymanders are subject to precisely the same constitutional scrutiny. In fact, our country's long and persistent history of racial discrimination in voting—as well as our Fourteenth Amendment jurisprudence, which always has reserved the strictest scrutiny for discrimination on the basis of race—would seem to compel the opposite conclusion." *Shaw I*, 509 U.S. at 650 (citation omitted). Unlike partisan gerrymandering claims, a racial gerrymandering claim does not ask for a fair share of political power and influence, with all the justiciability conundrums that entails. It asks instead for the elimination of a racial classification. A partisan gerrymandering claim cannot ask for the elimination of partisanship.

IV

Appellees and the dissent propose a number of "tests" for evaluating partisan gerrymandering claims, but none meets the need for a limited and precise standard that is judicially discernible and manageable. And none provides a solid grounding for judges to take the extraordinary step of reallocating power and influence between political parties.

A

The *Common Cause* District Court concluded that all but one of the districts in North Carolina's 2016 Plan [the districting plan challenged

---

*   The dissent's observation that the Framers viewed political parties "with deep suspicion, as fomenters of factionalism and symptoms of disease in the body politic" is exactly right. Its inference from that fact is exactly wrong. The Framers would have been amazed at a constitutional theory that guarantees a certain degree of representation to political parties.

in the litigation] violated the Equal Protection Clause by intentionally diluting the voting strength of Democrats. In reaching that result the court first required the plaintiffs to prove "that a legislative mapdrawer's predominant purpose in drawing the lines of a particular district was to 'subordinate adherents of one political party and entrench a rival party in power.' " The District Court next required a showing "that the dilution of the votes of supporters of a disfavored party in a particular district— by virtue of cracking or packing—is likely to persist in subsequent elections such that an elected representative from the favored party in the district will not feel a need to be responsive to constituents who support the disfavored party." Finally, after a prima facie showing of partisan vote dilution, the District Court shifted the burden to the defendants to prove that the discriminatory effects are "attributable to a legitimate state interest or other neutral explanation."

The District Court's "predominant intent" prong is borrowed from the racial gerrymandering context. In racial gerrymandering cases, we rely on a "predominant intent" inquiry to determine whether race was, in fact, the reason particular district boundaries were drawn the way they were. If district lines were drawn for the purpose of separating racial groups, then they are subject to strict scrutiny because "race-based decisionmaking is inherently suspect." Miller v. Johnson, 515 U.S. 900, 915 (1995). But determining that lines were drawn on the basis of partisanship does not indicate that the districting was improper. A permissible intent—securing partisan advantage—does not become constitutionally impermissible, like racial discrimination, when that permissible intent "predominates."

The District Court tried to limit the reach of its test by requiring plaintiffs to show, in addition to predominant partisan intent, that vote dilution "is likely to persist" to such a degree that the elected representative will feel free to ignore the concerns of the supporters of the minority party. But "[t]o allow district courts to strike down apportionment plans on the basis of their prognostications as to the outcome of future elections . . . invites 'findings' on matters as to which neither judges nor anyone else can have any confidence." *Bandemer*, 478 U.S. at 160 (opinion of O'Connor, J.). . . .

Experience proves that accurately predicting electoral outcomes is not so simple, either because the plans are based on flawed assumptions about voter preferences and behavior or because demographics and priorities change over time. In our two leading partisan gerrymandering cases themselves, the predictions of durability proved to be dramatically wrong. In 1981, Republicans controlled both houses of the Indiana Legislature as well as the governorship. Democrats challenged the state legislature districting map enacted by the Republicans. This Court in *Bandemer* rejected that challenge, and just months later the Democrats increased their share of House seats in the 1986 elections. Two years later the House was split 50–50 between Democrats and Republicans, and the Democrats took control of the chamber in 1990. Democrats also challenged the Pennsylvania congressional districting plan at issue in *Vieth*. Two years after that challenge failed, they gained four seats in the delegation, going from a 12–7 minority to an 11–8 majority. At the next election, they flipped another Republican seat.

Even the most sophisticated districting maps cannot reliably account for some of the reasons voters prefer one candidate over another, or why their preferences may change. Voters elect individual candidates in individual districts, and their selections depend on the issues that matter to them, the quality of the candidates, the tone of the candidates' campaigns, the performance of an incumbent, national events or local issues that drive voter turnout, and other considerations. Many voters split their tickets. Others never register with a political party, and vote for candidates from both major parties at different points during their lifetimes. For all of those reasons, asking judges to predict how a particular districting map will perform in future elections risks basing constitutional holdings on unstable ground outside judicial expertise.

It is hard to see what the District Court's third prong—providing the defendant an opportunity to show that the discriminatory effects were due to a "legitimate redistricting objective"—adds to the inquiry. The first prong already requires the plaintiff to prove that partisan advantage predominates. Asking whether a legitimate purpose other than partisanship was the motivation for a particular districting map just restates the question.

B

The District Courts also found partisan gerrymandering claims justiciable under the First Amendment, coalescing around a basic three-part test: proof of intent to burden individuals based on their voting history or party affiliation; an actual burden on political speech or associational rights; and a causal link between the invidious intent and actual burden. Both District Courts concluded that the districting plans at issue violated the plaintiffs' First Amendment right to association. The District Court in North Carolina relied on testimony that, after the 2016 Plan was put in place, the plaintiffs faced "difficulty raising money, attracting candidates, and mobilizing voters to support the political causes and issues such Plaintiffs sought to advance." Similarly, the District Court in Maryland . . . concluded that Republicans in the Sixth District "were burdened in fundraising, attracting volunteers, campaigning, and generating interest in voting."

To begin, there are no restrictions on speech, association, or any other First Amendment activities in the districting plans at issue. The plaintiffs are free to engage in those activities no matter what the effect of a plan may be on their district.

The plaintiffs' argument is that partisanship in districting should be regarded as simple discrimination against supporters of the opposing party on the basis of political viewpoint. Under that theory, any level of partisanship in districting would constitute an infringement of their First Amendment rights. . . . It provides no standard for determining when partisan activity goes too far.

As for actual burden, the slight anecdotal evidence found sufficient by the District Courts in these cases shows that this too is not a serious standard for separating constitutional from unconstitutional partisan gerrymandering. The District Courts relied on testimony about difficulty drumming up volunteers and enthusiasm. How much of a decline in voter engagement is enough to constitute a First Amendment burden? How many door knocks must go unanswered? How many petitions unsigned? How many calls for volunteers unheeded? . . .

These cases involve blatant examples of partisanship driving districting decisions. But the First Amendment analysis below offers no "clear" and "manageable" way of distinguishing permissible from impermissible partisan motivation. The *Common Cause* court embraced that conclusion, observing that "a judicially manageable framework for evaluating partisan gerrymandering claims need not distinguish an 'acceptable' level of partisan gerrymandering from 'excessive' partisan gerrymandering" because "the Constitution does not authorize state redistricting bodies to engage in such partisan gerrymandering." The decisions below prove the prediction of the *Vieth* plurality that "a First Amendment claim, if it were sustained, would render unlawful *all* consideration of political affiliation in districting," 541 U.S. at 294, contrary to our established precedent.

C

The dissent proposes using a State's own districting criteria as a neutral baseline from which to measure how extreme a partisan gerrymander is. The dissent would have us line up all the possible maps drawn using those criteria according to the partisan distribution they would produce. Distance from the "median" map would indicate whether a particular districting plan harms supporters of one party to an unconstitutional extent.

As an initial matter, it does not make sense to use criteria that will vary from State to State and year to year as the baseline for determining whether a gerrymander violates the Federal Constitution. The degree of partisan advantage that the Constitution tolerates should not turn on criteria offered by the gerrymanderers themselves. . . .

Even if we were to accept the dissent's proposed baseline, it would return us to "the original unanswerable question (How much political motivation and effect is too much?)." *Vieth*, 541 U.S. at 296–97 (plurality opinion). Would twenty percent away from the median map be okay? Forty percent? Sixty percent? Why or why not? (We appreciate that the dissent finds all the unanswerable questions annoying, but it seems a useful way to make the point.) The dissent's answer says it all: "This much is too much." That is not even trying to articulate a standard or rule.

The dissent argues that there are other instances in law where matters of degree are left to the courts. True enough. But those instances typically involve constitutional or statutory provisions or common law confining and guiding the exercise of judicial discretion. . . . Here, on the other hand, the Constitution provides no basis whatever to guide the exercise of judicial discretion. Common experience gives content to terms such as "substantial risk" or "substantial harm," but the same cannot be said of substantial deviation from a median map. There is no way to tell whether the prohibited deviation from that map should kick in at 25 percent or 75 percent or some other point. The only provision in the Constitution that specifically addresses the matter assigns it to the political branches. See Art. I, § 4, cl. 1.

D

The North Carolina District Court further concluded that the 2016 Plan violated the Elections Clause and Article I, § 2. We are unconvinced by that novel approach.

Article I, § 2, provides that "[t]he House of Representatives shall be composed of Members chosen every second Year by the People of the several States." The Elections Clause provides that "[t]he Times, Places and Manner of holding Elections for Senators and Representatives, shall be prescribed in each State by the Legislature thereof; but the Congress may at any time by Law make or alter such Regulations, except as to the Places of chusing Senators." Art. I, § 4, cl. 1.

The District Court concluded that the 2016 Plan exceeded the North Carolina General Assembly's Elections Clause authority because, among other reasons, "the Elections Clause did not empower State legislatures to disfavor the interests of supporters of a particular candidate or party in drawing congressional districts." The court further held that partisan gerrymandering infringes the right of "the People" to select their representatives. Before the District Court's decision, no court had reached a similar conclusion. In fact, the plurality in *Vieth* concluded—without objection from any other Justice—that neither § 2 nor § 4 of Article I "provides a judicially enforceable limit on the political considerations that the States and Congress may take into account when districting." 541 U.S. at 305.

The District Court nevertheless asserted that partisan gerrymanders violate "the core principle of [our] republican government" preserved in Art. I, § 2, "namely, that the voters should choose their representatives, not the other way around." That seems like an objection more properly grounded in the Guarantee Clause of Article IV, § 4, which "guarantee[s] to every State in [the] Union a Republican Form of Government." This Court has several times concluded, however, that the

Guarantee Clause does not provide the basis for a justiciable claim. See, e.g., Pacific States Telephone & Telegraph Co. v. Oregon, 223 U.S. 118 (1912).

V

Excessive partisanship in districting leads to results that reasonably seem unjust. But the fact that such gerrymandering is "incompatible with democratic principles," Arizona State Legislature v. Arizona Independent Redistricting Commission, 576 U.S. 787, 791, 135 S.Ct. 2652, 2658 (2015), does not mean that the solution lies with the federal judiciary. We conclude that partisan gerrymandering claims present political questions beyond the reach of the federal courts. Federal judges have no license to reallocate political power between the two major political parties, with no plausible grant of authority in the Constitution, and no legal standards to limit and direct their decisions. "[J]udicial action must be governed by *standard*, by *rule*," and must be "principled, rational, and based upon reasoned distinctions" found in the Constitution or laws. *Vieth*, 541 U.S. at 278, 279 (plurality opinion). Judicial review of partisan gerrymandering does not meet those basic requirements.

Today the dissent essentially embraces the argument that the Court unanimously rejected in *Gill*: "this Court can address the problem of partisan gerrymandering because it *must*." 585 U.S. at ___, 138 S.Ct. at 1929. That is not the test of our authority under the Constitution; that document instead "confines the federal courts to a properly judicial role." Town of Chester v. Laroe Estates, Inc., 581 U.S. ___, ___, 137 S.Ct. 1645, 1650 (2017).

What the appellees and dissent seek is an unprecedented expansion of judicial power. We have never struck down a partisan gerrymander as unconstitutional—despite various requests over the past 45 years. The expansion of judicial authority would not be into just any area of controversy, but into one of the most intensely partisan aspects of American political life. That intervention would be unlimited in scope and duration—it would recur over and over again around the country with each new round of districting, for state as well as federal representatives. Consideration of the impact of today's ruling on democratic principles cannot ignore the effect of the unelected and politically unaccountable branch of the Federal Government assuming such an extraordinary and unprecedented role.

Our conclusion does not condone excessive partisan gerrymandering. Nor does our conclusion condemn complaints about districting to echo into a void. The States, for example, are actively addressing the issue on a number of fronts. In 2015, the Supreme Court of Florida struck down that State's congressional districting plan as a violation of the Fair Districts Amendment to the Florida Constitution. League of Women Voters of Florida v. Detzner, 172 So. 3d 363 (2015). The dissent wonders why we can't do the same. The answer is that there is no "Fair Districts Amendment" to the Federal Constitution. Provisions in state statutes and state constitutions can provide standards and guidance for state courts to apply. . . . [N]umerous other States are restricting partisan considerations in districting through legislation. One way they are doing so is by placing power to draw electoral districts in the hands of independent commissions. . . .

Other States have mandated at least some of the traditional districting criteria for their mapmakers. Some have outright prohibited partisan favoritism in redistricting. . . .

As noted, the Framers gave Congress the power to do something about partisan gerrymandering in the Elections Clause. The first bill introduced in the 116th Congress would require States to create 15-member independent commissions to draw congressional districts and would establish certain redistricting criteria, including protection for communities of interest, and ban partisan gerrymandering. H.R. 1, 116th Cong., 1st Sess., §§ 2401, 2411 (2019).

Dozens of other bills have been introduced to limit reliance on political considerations in redistricting. . . .

[An] example is the Fairness and Independence in Redistricting Act, which was introduced in 2005 and has been reintroduced in every Congress since. That bill would require every State to establish an independent commission to adopt redistricting plans. The bill also set forth criteria for the independent commissions to use, such as compactness, contiguity, and population equality. It would prohibit consideration of voting history, political party affiliation, or incumbent Representative's residence. H.R. 2642, 109th Cong., 1st Sess., § 4 (referred to subcommittee).

We express no view on any of these pending proposals. We simply note that the avenue for reform established by the Framers, and used by Congress in the past, remains open.

* * *

No one can accuse this Court of having a crabbed view of the reach of its competence. But we have no commission to allocate political power and influence in the absence of a constitutional directive or legal standards to guide us in the exercise of such authority. "It is emphatically the province and duty of the judicial department to say what the law is." *Marbury v. Madison*, 10 U.S. at 177. In this rare circumstance, that means our duty is to say "this is not law."

The [judgments below] are vacated, and the cases are remanded with instructions to dismiss for lack of jurisdiction.

■ JUSTICE KAGAN, with whom JUSTICE GINSBURG, JUSTICE BREYER, and JUSTICE SOTOMAYOR join, dissenting.

For the first time ever, this Court refuses to remedy a constitutional violation because it thinks the task beyond judicial capabilities.

And not just any constitutional violation. The partisan gerrymanders in these cases deprived citizens of the most fundamental of their constitutional rights: the rights to participate equally in the political process, to join with others to advance political beliefs, and to choose their political representatives. In so doing, the partisan gerrymanders here debased and dishonored our democracy, turning upside-down the core American idea that all governmental power derives from the people. These gerrymanders enabled politicians to entrench themselves in office as against voters' preferences. They promoted partisanship above respect for the popular will. They encouraged a politics of polarization and dysfunction. If left unchecked, gerrymanders like the ones here may irreparably damage our system of government.

And checking them is *not* beyond the courts. The majority's abdication comes just when courts across the country, including those below, have coalesced around manageable judicial standards to resolve partisan gerrymandering claims. Those standards satisfy the majority's own benchmarks. They do not require—indeed, they do not permit—courts to rely on their own ideas of electoral fairness, whether proportional representation or any other. And they limit courts to correcting only egregious gerrymanders, so judges do not become omnipresent players in the political process. But yes, the standards used here do allow as well they should—judicial intervention in the worst-of-the-worst cases of democratic subversion, causing blatant constitutional harms. In other words, they allow courts to undo partisan gerrymanders of the kind we face today from North Carolina and Maryland. In giving such gerrymanders a pass from judicial review, the majority goes tragically wrong.

I

Maybe the majority errs in these cases because it pays so little attention to the constitutional harms at their core. After dutifully reciting each case's facts, the majority leaves them forever behind, instead immersing itself in everything that could conceivably go amiss if courts became involved. [At this point and in Part I-A, Justice Kagan reviewed the facts in more detail than the Court had provided. Her point was to show that naked partisan political advantage motivated the redistricting decisions. She began her recitation of the details: "As I relate what happened in those two States, ask yourself: Is this how American democracy is supposed to work?"]

B

Now back to the question I asked before: Is that how American democracy is supposed to work? I have yet to meet the person who thinks so.

"Governments," the Declaration of Independence states, "deriv[e] their just Powers from the Consent of the Governed." The Constitution begins: "We the People of the United States." The Gettysburg Address (almost) ends: "[G]overnment of the people, by the people, for the people." If there is a single idea that made our Nation (and that our Nation commended to the world), it is this one: The people are sovereign. The "power," James Madison wrote, "is in the people over the Government, and not in the Government over the people." 4 Annals of Cong. 934 (1794).

Free and fair and periodic elections are the key to that vision. The people get to choose their representatives. And then they get to decide, at regular intervals, whether to keep them. . . . Election day—next year, and two years later, and two years after that—is what links the people to their representatives, and gives the people their sovereign power. That day is the foundation of democratic governance.

And partisan gerrymandering can make it meaningless. At its most extreme—as in North Carolina and Maryland—the practice amounts to "rigging elections." Vieth v. Jubelirer, 541 U.S. 267, 317 (2004) (Kennedy, J., concurring in judgment) (internal quotation marks omitted). By drawing districts to maximize the power of some voters and minimize the power of others, a party in office at the right time can entrench itself there for a decade or more, no matter what the voters would prefer. [P]oliticians can cherry-pick voters to ensure their reelection. . . .

The majority disputes none of this. I think it important to underscore that fact: The majority disputes none of what I have said (or will say) about how gerrymanders undermine democracy. Indeed, the majority concedes (really, how could it not?) that gerrymandering is "incompatible with democratic principles" (quoting Arizona State Legislature v. Arizona Independent Redistricting Commission, 576 U.S. ___, ___, 135 S.Ct. 2652, 2658 (2015)). And therefore what? That recognition would seem to demand a response. The majority offers two ideas that might qualify as such. One is that the political process can deal with the problem—a proposition so dubious on its face that I feel secure in delaying my answer for some time. The other is that political gerrymanders have always been with us. To its credit, the majority does not frame that point as an originalist constitutional argument. After all (as the majority rightly notes), racial and residential gerrymanders were also once with us, but the Court has done something about that fact. The majority's idea instead seems to be that if we have lived with partisan gerrymanders so long, we will survive.

That complacency has no cause. Yes, partisan gerrymandering goes back to the Republic's earliest days. (As does vociferous opposition to it.) But big data and modern technology—of just the kind that the mapmakers in North Carolina and Maryland used—make today's gerrymandering altogether different from the crude linedrawing of the past. Old-time efforts, based on little more than guesses, sometimes led to so-called dummymanders—gerrymanders that went spectacularly wrong. Not likely in today's world. Mapmakers now have access to more granular data about party preference and voting behavior than ever before. County-level voting data has given way to precinct-level or city-block-level data; and increasingly, mapmakers avail themselves of data sets providing wideranging information about even individual voters. Just as important, advancements in computing technology have enabled map-makers to put that information to use with unprecedented efficiency and precision. While bygone mapmakers may have drafted three or four al-ternative districting plans, today's mapmakers can generate thousands of possibilities at the touch of a key—and then choose the one giving their party maximum advantage (usually while still meeting traditional dis-tricting requirements). The effect is to make gerrymanders far more ef-fective and durable than before, insulating politicians against all but the most titanic shifts in the political tides. These are not your grandfa-ther's—let alone the Framers'—gerrymanders. . . .

C

Partisan gerrymandering of the kind before us not only subverts de-mocracy (as if that weren't bad enough). It violates individuals' constitu-tional rights as well. That statement is not the lonesome cry of a dissent-ing Justice. This Court has recognized extreme partisan gerrymandering as such a violation for many years.

Partisan gerrymandering operates through vote dilution—the deval-uation of one citizen's vote as compared to others. A mapmaker draws district lines to "pack" and "crack" voters likely to support the disfavored party. He packs supermajorities of those voters into a relatively few dis-tricts, in numbers far greater than needed for their preferred candidates to prevail. Then he cracks the rest across many more districts, spreading them so thin that their candidates will not be able to win. Whether the person is packed or cracked, his vote carries less weight—has less conse-quence—than it would under a neutrally drawn (non-partisan) map. In short, the mapmaker has made some votes count for less, because they are likely to go for the other party.

That practice implicates the Fourteenth Amendment's Equal Protec-tion Clause. The Fourteenth Amendment, we long ago recognized, "guar-antees the opportunity for equal participation by all voters in the elec-tion" of legislators. Reynolds v. Sims, 377 U.S. 533, 566 (1964). And that opportunity "can be denied by a debasement or dilution of the weight of a citizen's vote just as effectively as by wholly prohibiting the free exer-cise of the franchise." Id. at 555. Based on that principle, this Court in its one-person-one-vote decisions prohibited creating districts with signifi-cantly different populations. A State could not, we explained, thus "di-lut[e] the weight of votes because of place of residence." Id. at 566. The constitutional injury in a partisan gerrymandering case is much the same, except that the dilution is based on party affiliation. In such a case, too, the districters have set out to reduce the weight of certain citizens' votes, and thereby deprive them of their capacity to "full[y] and effec-tive[ly] participat[e] in the political process[ ]." Id. at 565. As Justice Ken-nedy (in a controlling opinion) once hypothesized: If districters declared that they were drawing a map "so as most to burden [the votes of] Party X's" supporters, it would violate the Equal Protection Clause. Vieth, 541 U.S. at 312. For (in the language of the one-person-one-vote decisions) it would infringe those voters' rights to "equal [electoral] participation." *Reynolds*, 377 U.S. at 566.

And partisan gerrymandering implicates the First Amendment too. That Amendment gives its greatest protection to political beliefs, speech, and association. Yet partisan gerrymanders subject certain voters to "disfavored treatment"—again, counting their votes for less—precisely because of "their voting history [and] their expression of political views." *Vieth*, 541 U.S. at 314 (opinion of Kennedy, J.). And added to that strictly personal harm is an associational one. Representative democracy is "unimaginable without the ability of citizens to band together in [support of] candidates who espouse their political views." California Democratic Party v. Jones, 530 U.S. 567, 574 (2000). By diluting the votes of certain citizens, the State frustrates their efforts to translate those affiliations into political effectiveness. In both those ways, partisan gerrymanders of the kind we confront here undermine the protections of "democracy embodied in the First Amendment." Elrod v. Burns, 427 U.S. 347, 357 (1976) (internal quotation marks omitted).

Though different Justices have described the constitutional harm in diverse ways, nearly all have agreed on this much: Extreme partisan gerrymandering (as happened in North Carolina and Maryland) violates the Constitution. Once again, the majority never disagrees; it appears to accept the "principle that each person must have an equal say in the election of representatives." And indeed, without this settled and shared understanding that cases like these inflict constitutional injury, the question of whether there are judicially manageable standards for resolving them would never come up.

II

So the only way to understand the majority's opinion is as follows: In the face of grievous harm to democratic governance and flagrant infringements on individuals' rights—in the face of escalating partisan manipulation whose compatibility with this Nation's values and law no one defends—the majority declines to provide any remedy. For the first time in this Nation's history, the majority declares that it can do nothing about an acknowledged constitutional violation because it has searched high and low and cannot find a workable legal standard to apply.

The majority gives two reasons for thinking that the adjudication of partisan gerrymandering claims is beyond judicial capabilities. First and foremost, the majority says, it cannot find a neutral baseline—one not based on contestable notions of political fairness—from which to measure injury. According to the majority, "[p]artisan gerrymandering claims invariably sound in a desire for proportional representation." But the Constitution does not mandate proportional representation. So, the majority contends, resolving those claims "inevitably" would require courts to decide what is "fair" in the context of districting. They would have "to make their own political judgment about how much representation particular political parties *deserve*" and "to rearrange the challenged districts to achieve that end." And second, the majority argues that even after establishing a baseline, a court would have no way to answer "the determinative question: 'How much is too much?' " No "discernible and manageable" standard is available, the majority claims—and so courts could willy-nilly become embroiled in fixing every districting plan.

I'll give the majority this one—and important—thing: It identifies some dangers everyone should want to avoid. Judges should not be apportioning political power based on their own vision of electoral fairness, whether proportional representation or any other. And judges should not be striking down maps left, right, and center, on the view that every smidgen of politics is a smidgen too much. Respect for state legislative processes—and restraint in the exercise of judicial authority—counsels intervention in only egregious cases.

But in throwing up its hands, the majority misses something under its nose: What it says can't be done *has* been done. Over the past several years, federal courts across the country—including, but not exclusively, in the decisions below—have largely converged on a standard for adjudicating partisan gerrymandering claims (striking down both Democratic and Republican districting plans in the process). And that standard does what the majority says is impossible. The standard does not use any judge-made conception of electoral fairness—either proportional representation or any other; instead, it takes as its baseline a State's own criteria of fairness, apart from partisan gain. And by requiring plaintiffs to make difficult showings relating to both purpose and effects, the standard invalidates the most extreme, but only the most extreme, partisan gerrymanders. . . .

A

Start with the standard the lower courts used. . . . Both courts focused on the harm of vote dilution, though the North Carolina court mostly grounded its analysis in the Fourteenth Amendment and the Maryland court in the First. And both courts (like others around the country) used basically the same three-part test to decide whether the plaintiffs had made out a vote dilution claim. As many legal standards do, that test has three parts: (1) intent; (2) effects; and (3) causation. First, the plaintiffs challenging a districting plan must prove that state officials' "predominant purpose" in drawing a district's lines was to "entrench [their party] in power" by diluting the votes of citizens favoring its rival. Second, the plaintiffs must establish that the lines drawn in fact have the intended effect by "substantially" diluting their votes. And third, if the plaintiffs make those showings, the State must come up with a legitimate, non-partisan justification to save its map. If you are a lawyer, you know that this test looks utterly ordinary. It is the sort of thing courts work with every day.

Turn now to the test's application. First, did the North Carolina and Maryland districters have the predominant purpose of entrenching their own party in power? Here, the two District Courts catalogued the over-whelming direct evidence that they did. . . .

The majority's response to the District Courts' purpose analysis is discomfiting. The majority does not contest the lower courts' findings; how could it? Instead, the majority says that state officials' intent to en-trench their party in power is perfectly "permissible," even when it is the predominant factor in drawing district lines. But that is wrong. True enough, that the intent to inject "political considerations" into districting may not raise any constitutional concerns. In Gaffney v. Cummings, 412 U.S. 735 (1973), for example, we thought it nonproblematic when state officials used political data to ensure rough proportional representation between the two parties. And true enough that even the naked purpose to gain partisan advantage may not rise to the level of constitutional no-tice when it is not the driving force in mapmaking or when the intended gain is slight. See *Vieth*, 541 U.S. at 286 (plurality opinion). But when political actors have a specific and predominant intent to entrench them-selves in power by manipulating district lines, that goes too far. . . .

On to the second step of the analysis, where the plaintiffs must prove that the districting plan substantially dilutes their votes. The majority fails to discuss most of the evidence the District Courts relied on to find that the plaintiffs had done so. But that evidence—particularly from North Carolina—is the key to understanding both the problem these cases present and the solution to it they offer. The evidence reveals just how bad the two gerrymanders were (in case you had any doubts). And it shows how the same technologies and data that today facilitate extreme partisan gerrymanders also enable courts to discover them, by exposing just how much they dilute votes.

Consider the sort of evidence used in North Carolina first. There, the plaintiffs demonstrated the districting plan's effects mostly by relying on what might be called the "extreme outlier approach." (Here's a spoiler: the State's plan was one.) The approach—which also has recently been used in Michigan and Ohio litigation—begins by using advanced compu-ting technology to randomly generate a large collection of districting plans that incorporate the State's physical and political geography and meet its declared districting criteria, except for partisan gain. For each of those maps, the method then uses actual precinct-level votes from past elections to determine a partisan outcome (i.e., the number of Democratic and Republican seats that map produces). Suppose we now have 1,000 maps, each with a partisan outcome attached to it. We can line up those maps on a continuum—the most favorable to Republicans on one end, the most favorable to Democrats on the other. We can then find the median outcome—that is, the outcome smack dab in the center—in a world with no partisan manipulation. And we can see where the State's actual plan falls on the spectrum—at or near the median or way out on one of the tails? The further out on the tail, the more extreme the partisan distor-tion and the more significant the vote dilution.

Using that approach, the North Carolina plaintiffs offered a boatload of alternative districting plans—all showing that the State's map was an out-out-out-outlier. One expert produced 3,000 maps, adhering in the way described above to the districting criteria that the North Carolina redistricting committee had used, other than partisan advantage. To calculate the partisan outcome of those maps, the expert also used the same election data (a composite of seven elections) that [had been] employed when devising the North Carolina plan in the first instance. The results were, shall we say, striking. Every single one of the 3,000 maps would have produced at least one more Democratic House Member than the State's actual map, and 77% would have elected three or four more. A second expert obtained essentially the same results with maps conforming to more generic districting criteria (e.g., compactness and contiguity of districts). Over 99% of that expert's 24,518 simulations would have led to the election of at least one more Democrat, and over 70% would have led to two or three more. Based on those and other findings, the District Court determined that the North Carolina plan substantially dilutes the plaintiffs' votes.

Because the Maryland gerrymander involved just one district, the evidence in that case was far simpler—but no less powerful for that. . . .

The majority claims all these findings are mere "prognostications" about the future, in which no one "can have any confidence." But the courts below did not gaze into crystal balls, as the majority tries to suggest. Their findings about these gerrymanders' effects on voters—both in the past and predictably in the future—were evidence-based, data-based, statistics-based. Knowledge-based, one might say. The courts did what anyone would want a decisionmaker to do when so much hangs in the balance. They looked hard at the facts, and they went where the facts led them. They availed themselves of all the information that mapmakers . . . and politicians . . . work so hard to amass and then use to make every districting decision. They refused to content themselves with unsupported and out-of-date musings about the unpredictability of the American voter. They did not bet America's future—as today the majority does—on the idea that maps constructed with so much expertise and care to make electoral outcomes impervious to voting would somehow or other come apart. They looked at the evidence—at the facts about how these districts operated—and they could reach only one conclusion. By substantially diluting the votes of citizens favoring their rivals, the politicians of one party had succeeded in entrenching themselves in office. They had beat democracy.

B

The majority's broadest claim, as I've noted, is that this is a price we must pay because judicial oversight of partisan gerrymandering cannot be "politically neutral" or "manageable." Courts, the majority argues, will have to choose among contested notions of electoral fairness. (Should they take as the ideal mode of districting proportional representation, many competitive seats, adherence to traditional districting criteria, or so forth?) And even once courts have chosen, the majority continues, they will have to decide "[h]ow much is too much?"—that is, how much deviation from the chosen "touchstone" to allow? In answering that question, the majority surmises, they will likely go far too far. So the whole thing is impossible, the majority concludes. To prove its point, the majority throws a bevy of question marks on the page. (I count nine in just two paragraphs.) But it never tries to analyze the serious question presented here—whether the kind of standard developed below falls prey to those objections, or instead allows for neutral and manageable oversight. The answer, as you've already heard enough to know, is the latter. That kind of oversight is not only possible; it's been done.

Consider neutrality first. Contrary to the majority's suggestion, the District Courts did not have to—and in fact did not—choose among competing visions of electoral fairness. That is because they did not try to compare the State's actual map to an "ideally fair" one (whether based on proportional representation or some other criterion). Instead, they looked at the difference between what the State did and what the State would have done if politicians hadn't been intent on partisan gain. Or put differently, the comparator (or baseline or touchstone) is the result not of a judge's philosophizing but of the State's own characteristics and judgments. . . . All the courts did was determine how far the State had gone off that track because of its politicians' effort to entrench themselves in office.

The North Carolina litigation well illustrates the point. The thousands of randomly generated maps I've mentioned formed the core of the plaintiffs' case that the North Carolina plan was an "extreme[ ] outlier." Those maps took the State's political landscape as a given. In North Carolina, for example, Democratic voters are highly concentrated in cities. That fact was built into all the maps; it became part of the baseline. On top of that, the maps took the State's legal landscape as a given. They incorporated the State's districting priorities, excluding partisanship. So in North Carolina, for example, all the maps adhered to the traditional criteria of contiguity and compactness. But the comparator maps in another State would have incorporated different objectives—say, the emphasis Arizona places on competitive districts or the requirement Iowa imposes that counties remain whole. The point is that the assemblage of maps, reflecting the characteristics and judgments of the State itself, creates a neutral baseline from which to assess whether partisanship has run amok. Extreme outlier as to what? As to the other maps the State could have produced given its unique political geography and its chosen districting criteria. *Not* as to the maps a judge, with his own view of electoral fairness, could have dreamed up. . . .

The majority's sole response misses the point. According to the majority, "it does not make sense to use" a State's own (non-partisan) districting criteria as the baseline from which to measure partisan gerrymandering because those criteria "will vary from State to State and year to year." But that is a virtue, not a vice—a feature, not a bug. Using the criteria the State itself has chosen at the relevant time prevents any judicial predilections from affecting the analysis—exactly what the majority claims it wants. At the same time, using those criteria enables a court to measure just what it should: the extent to which the pursuit of partisan advantage—by these legislators at this moment—has distorted the State's districting decisions. Sure, different non-partisan criteria could result, as the majority notes, in different partisan distributions to serve as the baseline. But that in itself raises no issue: Everyone agrees that state officials using non-partisan criteria (e.g., must counties be kept together? should districts be compact?) have wide latitude in districting. The problem arises only when legislators or mapmakers substantially deviate from the baseline distribution by manipulating district lines for partisan gain. So once again, the majority's analysis falters because it equates the demand to eliminate partisan gerrymandering with a demand for a single partisan distribution—the one reflecting proportional representation. But those two demands are different, and only the former is at issue here.

The majority's "how much is too much" critique fares no better than its neutrality argument. How about the following for a first-cut answer: This much is too much. By any measure, a map that produces a greater partisan skew than any of 3,000 randomly generated maps (all with the State's political geography and districting criteria built in) reflects "too much" partisanship. Think about what I just said: The absolute worst of 3,001 possible maps. . . . Even the majority acknowledges that "[t]hese cases involve blatant examples of partisanship driving districting decisions." If the majority had done nothing else, it could have set the line here. How much is too much? At the least, any gerrymanders as bad as these.

And if the majority thought that approach too case-specific, it could have used the lower courts' general standard—focusing on "predominant" purpose and "substantial" effects—without fear of indeterminacy. I do not take even the majority to claim that courts are incapable of investigating whether legislators mainly intended to seek partisan advantage. That is for good reason. Although purpose inquiries carry certain hazards (which courts must attend to), they are a common form of analysis in constitutional cases. See, e.g., Miller v. Johnson, 515 U.S. 900, 916 (1995); Church of Lukumi Babalu Aye, Inc. v. Hialeah, 508 U.S. 520, 533 (1993); Washington v. Davis, 426 U.S. 229, 239 (1976). Those inquiries would be no harder here than in other contexts.

Nor is there any reason to doubt, as the majority does, the competence of courts to determine whether a district map "substantially" dilutes the votes of a rival party's supporters from the everything-but-partisanship baseline described above. . . . As this Court recently noted, "the law is full of instances" where a judge's decision rests on "estimating rightly . . . some matter of degree"—including the "substantial[ity]" of risk or harm. Johnson v. United States, 576 U.S. ___, ___, 135 S.Ct. 2551, 2561 (2015) (internal quotation marks omitted). . . . [C]ourts all the time make judgments about the substantiality of harm without reducing them to particular percentages. If courts are no longer competent to do so, they will have to relinquish, well, substantial portions of their docket.

And the combined inquiry used in these cases set the bar high, so that courts could intervene in the worst partisan gerrymanders, but no others. Or to say the same thing, so that courts could intervene in the kind of extreme gerrymanders that nearly every Justice for decades has thought to violate the Constitution. Illicit purpose was simple to show here only because politicians and mapmakers thought their actions could not be attacked in court. They therefore felt free to openly proclaim their intent to entrench their party in office. But if the Court today had declared that behavior justiciable, such smoking guns would all but disappear. Even assuming some officials continued to try implementing extreme partisan gerrymanders, they would not brag about their efforts. So plaintiffs would have to prove the intent to entrench through circumstantial evidence—essentially showing that no other explanation (no geographic feature or non-partisan districting objective) could explain the districting plan's vote dilutive effects. And that would be impossible unless those effects were even more than substantial—unless mapmakers had packed and cracked with abandon in unprecedented ways. As again, they did here. That the two courts below found constitutional violations does not mean their tests were unrigorous; it means that the conduct they confronted was constitutionally appalling—by even the strictest measure, inordinately partisan.

The majority, in the end, fails to understand both the plaintiffs' claims and the decisions below. Everything in today's opinion assumes that these cases grew out of a "desire for proportional representation" or, more generally phrased, a "fair share of political power." And everything in it assumes that the courts below had to (and did) decide what that fair share would be. But that is not so. The plaintiffs objected to one specific practice—the extreme manipulation of district lines for partisan gain. Elimination of that practice could have led to proportional representation. Or it could have led to nothing close. What was left after the practice's removal could have been fair, or could have been unfair, by any number of measures. That was not the crux of this suit. The plaintiffs asked only that the courts bar politicians from entrenching themselves in power by diluting the votes of their rivals' supporters. And the courts, using neutral and manageable—and eminently legal—standards, provided that (and only that) relief. This Court should have cheered, not overturned, that restoration of the people's power to vote.

III

This Court has long understood that it has a special responsibility to remedy violations of constitutional rights resulting from politicians' districting decisions. . . . [T]he need for judicial review is at its most urgent in cases like these. "For here, politicians' incentives conflict with voters' interests, leaving citizens without any political remedy for their constitutional harms." *Gill*, 585 U.S. at ___, 138 S.Ct. at 1941 (Kagan, J., concurring). Those harms arise because politicians want to stay in office. No one can look to them for effective relief.

The majority disagrees, concluding its opinion with a paean to congressional bills limiting partisan gerrymanders. "Dozens of [those] bills have been introduced," the majority says. One was "introduced in 2005 and has been reintroduced in every Congress since." And might be reintroduced until the end of time. Because what all these bills have in common is that they are not laws. The politicians who benefit from partisan gerrymandering are unlikely to change partisan gerrymandering. And because those politicians maintain themselves in office through partisan gerrymandering, the chances for legislative reform are slight.

No worries, the majority says; it has another idea. The majority notes that voters themselves have recently approved ballot initiatives to put power over districting in the hands of independent commissions or other nonpartisan actors. . . . Fewer than half the States offer voters an opportunity to put initiatives to direct vote; in all the rest (including North Carolina and Maryland), voters are dependent on legislators to make electoral changes (which for all the reasons already given, they are unlikely to do). . . .

The majority's most perplexing "solution" is to look to state courts. . . . But what do those courts know that this Court does not? If they can develop and apply neutral and manageable standards to identify unconstitutional gerrymanders, why couldn't we?

We could have, and we should have. The gerrymanders here—and they are typical of many—violated the constitutional rights of many hundreds of thousands of American citizens. Those voters (Republicans in the one case, Democrats in the other) did not have an equal opportunity to participate in the political process. Their votes counted for far less than they should have because of their partisan affiliation. When faced with such constitutional wrongs, courts must intervene: "It is emphatically the province and duty of the judicial department to say what the law is." Marbury v. Madison, 10 U.S. (1 Cranch) 137, 177 (1803). That is what the courts below did. Their decisions are worth a read. They (and others that have recently remedied similar violations) are detailed, thorough, painstaking. They evaluated with immense care the factual evidence and legal arguments the parties presented. They used neutral and manageable and strict standards. They had not a shred of politics about them. Contra the majority, this *was* law.

That is not to deny, of course, that these cases have great political consequence. They do. Among the amicus briefs here is one from a bipartisan group of current and former Members of the House of Representatives. They describe all the ways partisan gerrymandering harms our political system—what they call "a cascade of negative results." These artificially drawn districts shift influence from swing voters to party-base voters who participate in primaries; make bipartisanship and pragmatic compromise politically difficult or impossible; and drive voters away from an ever more dysfunctional political process. Last year, we heard much the same from current and former state legislators. In their view, partisan gerrymandering has "sounded the death-knell of bipartisanship," creating a legislative environment that is "toxic" and "tribal." Brief as Amicus Curiae in *Gill v. Whitford*, O.T. 2016, No.16–1161, pp. 6, 25. Gerrymandering, in short, helps create the polarized political system so many Americans loathe. . . .

Of all times to abandon the Court's duty to declare the law, this was not the one. The practices challenged in these cases imperil our system of government. Part of the Court's role in that system is to defend its foundations. None is more important than free and fair elections. With respect but deep sadness, I dissent.

NOTES ON *RUCHO V. COMMON CAUSE*

In *Rucho*, the majority concludes that "partisan gerrymandering claims present political questions beyond the reach of the federal courts." But did the majority in effect decide that partisan gerrymandering is constitutional? It reasons, for example, that the Constitution does not require proportional representation and that there are "no legal standards discernible in the Constitution" for making judgments about fairness in this context. What is added (or subtracted) by calling this a political question? Is the majority's contention that its holding "does not condone excessive partisan gerrymandering" persuasive?

Kagan's dissent argues that there are judicially manageable standards for addressing the worst cases of partisan gerrymandering. Is she right? She emphasizes in particular the approach that had been used in the North Carolina litigation, which she calls the "extreme outlier approach." What reasons does the majority give for rejecting that approach? Is Justice Kagan's response effective?

What impact, if any, does *Rucho* have on the ability of state courts to hear challenges to partisan gerrymandering? Given that state courts are not bound by the limitations of Article III, could they adjudicate federal constitutional challenges to partisan gerrymandering that cannot be adjudicated in the federal courts? Or is the Court's analysis based on more than just the limits of Article III? In any event, can state courts hear challenges to partisan gerrymandering based on *state* constitutional law?

Finally, consider the lineup. The Court was presented with challenges to partisan gerrymandering by both Democrats (in Maryland) and Republicans (in North Carolina). Why was the Court divided along traditional ideological lines?

For commentary on *Rucho*, see Michael R. Dimino, You've Got (Political) Questions? We've Got No Answers, 71 Mercer L. Rev. 719 (2020); G. Michael

Parsons, Gerrymandering and Justiciability: The Political Question Doctrine after *Rucho v. Common Cause*, 95 Ind. L.J. 1295 (2020).

Page 486, add at the end of Note 6:

For a wide-ranging effort to rethink the political question doctrine, by reference to what the author calls the "ultra vires conundrum," see Richard H. Fallon Jr., Political Questions and the Ultra Vires Conundrum, 87 U. Chi. L. Rev. 1481 (2020). Fallon argues that "[t]he political question doctrine marks some questions as ultra vires, or beyond the jurisdiction of courts to resolve," but that "[e]ven after denominating a question as political . . . courts typically retain a responsibility to check actions by other institutions that overreach the outer limits of those institutions' authority." "As a result," he contends, "denomination of a question as a political question marks a less categorical commitment to judicial nonintervention than many and perhaps most commentators have imagined." Fallon also suggests that one reason that the Supreme Court only rarely invokes the doctrine is that "the arguments that would support identifying a question as political frequently overlap indistinguishably with arguments for upholding a challenged action on the merits."

CHAPTER IV

CONGRESSIONAL CONTROL OF THE FEDERAL COURTS

SECTION 1. POWER TO LIMIT FEDERAL COURT JURISDICTION

Page 507, add a footnote at the end of the carryover paragraph at the top of the page:

j   A federal immigration statute provides for expedited removal from the United States of certain non-citizens seeking asylum but does not apply to persons who can show that they face a "credible fear of persecution" if they are denied asylum. By statute, a determination by immigration officials that an asylum applicant lacks a credible fear of persecution is not reviewable by the courts, including in a petition for a writ of habeas corpus. See 8 U.S.C. § 1252(a)(2)(A)(iii). In Department of Homeland Security v. Thuraissigiam, 591 U.S. ___, 140 S.Ct. 1959 (2020), the Supreme Court held that the habeas restriction is constitutional. In an opinion by Justice Alito, the Court reasoned that the Suspension Clause protects only the ability to challenge the lawfulness of detention, not the ability to enter or remain in the country. The Court also concluded that, as applied in this case, the restriction does not violate the Due Process Clause. Justice Breyer concurred in the judgment, joined by Justice Ginsburg. Justice Sotomayor, joined by Justice Kagan, dissented. See also Lee Kovarsky, Habeas Privilege Origination and *DHS v. Thuraissigiam*, 121 Colum. L. Rev. F. 23 (2021).

Page 508, add at the end of footnote c:

For a wide-ranging discussion of the continued relevance of the dialogue presented in Hart's famous article, see Henry P. Monaghan, Jurisdiction Stripping Circa 2020: What *The Dialogue* (Still) Has to Teach Us, 69 Duke L.J. 1 (2010).

Page 515, add at the end of Note 8:

The "rise of federal courts and apparent fall of state courts" is elaborately considered in Diego A. Zambrano, Federal Expansion and the Decay of State Courts, 86 U. Chi. L. Rev. 2101 (2019). Zambrano divides judicial federalism into three broad historical periods, each with "distinctive philosophies toward the allocation of cases between the two judicial systems." The "defining feature" of the first era was that "state judiciaries were the primary trial courts for federal claims because federal courts did not have plenary federal question jurisdiction." The second era began in 1875 and extended into the 1980s. It was marked by the expansion of federal question jurisdiction and attacks on diversity jurisdiction. The attack on diversity jurisdiction "reached its peak in 1978, when the House [of Representatives] overwhelmingly adopted a bipartisan bill that endeavored to wholly eliminate federal diversity jurisdiction."q The current era developed in the 1980s and 1990s when "for the first time in the nation's history, the government became committed to the expansion of *both* diversity and federal question jurisdiction." This " 'federal expansion' . . . (1) aggressively federalized areas previously governed by state law, including state class action claims; (2) promoted the concentration of monetarily significant claims in federal court; and (3) unintentionally contributed to the decay of state courts." In "the heart of the article," he then draws on political economy literature to explore the effects of these changes on state courts. In the end, he attributes these changes to "large institutional defendants" and calls for "increasing the financial resources and vibrancy of state courts." His summary of "benefits and costs to the system" include:

> On the negative side of the ledger, state procedures are increasingly drifting toward plaintiff preferences and federal courts toward defendants; this may cause further federalization and forum shopping. Large business defendants are also now seemingly divorced from the well-being of their local judiciaries, perhaps weakening the financial base of those systems. Finally, state courts have a diminished ability to shape certain areas of the common law. On the positive side of the ledger, however, federal courts have efficiently exploited economies of scale and the "federal franchise," and have better-aligned court competency with outcomes.[r]

> [q]   "[A]n impressive array of institutions and interests had lined up behind the effort: President Jimmy Carter, Attorney General Griffin Bell, Chief Justice Burger, the Judicial Conference, and the National Conference of State Chief Justices (claiming to be 'ready' for cases to return where they rightfully belonged). The bill even had the backing of the NAACP and the ACLU." Senator Ted Kennedy opened the debate on the Senate floor in 1979 in support of the bill, but "the floor vote never arrived."

> [r]   In Michael E. Solimine, The Political Economy of Judicial Federalism, U. Chi. L. Rev. Online 1 (2019), three main concerns with the Zambrano article are advanced: "it (1) overstates the 'decay' of state courts; (2) is not clear on the causal link between federal aggrandizement and the decay of state courts; and (3) overstates the scope of the aggrandizement." These criticisms nonetheless do not, Solimine concludes, "undermine his insights and their implications."—[Footnote by eds.]

Page 515, add a new Note after Note 8:

8A. PROPOSALS TO REFORM THE SUPREME COURT

Supreme Court reform has become an increasingly salient topic. Proposed reforms include, but extend beyond, efforts to restrict the Court's appellate jurisdiction. Some observers advocate limiting the terms of Supreme Court Justices by statute, imposing a supermajority requirement on any effort to strike down federal (and possibly state) legislation, or—most commonly—expanding the size of the Supreme Court, a measure that is often described as "court packing." In April 2021, a group of House and Senate Democrats introduced legislation to increase the size of the Court from nine to thirteen members. Such a proposal is notable, in part because it presses against a strong bipartisan norm against "court packing" that dates from the mid-twentieth century. Congress has not seriously considered a proposal to expand the size of the Supreme Court since President Franklin Roosevelt's failed effort in 1937. See Curtis A. Bradley and Neil S. Siegel, Historical Gloss, Constitutional Conventions, and the Judicial Separation of Powers, 105 Geo. L.J. 255 (2017); Tara Leigh Grove, The Origins (and Fragility) of Judicial Independence, 71 Vand. L. Rev. 465 (2018).

Also in April 2021, President Biden established a Presidential Commission on the Supreme Court of the United States. See Exec. Order 14023 (April 9, 2021). In an accompanying press release, the Biden administration described the Commission as a "bipartisan group of experts" that will analyze "the principal arguments in the contemporary public debate for and against Supreme Court reform. . . . The topics it will examine include the genesis of the reform debate; the Court's role in the Constitutional system; the length of service and turnover of justices on the Court; the membership and size of the Court; and the Court's case selection, rules, and practices." The Commission is expected to produce a report in November 2021.

For a sample of the literature exploring recent reform proposals, see Joshua Braver, Court-Packing: An American Tradition?, 61 Boston College L. Rev. 2748 (2020); Ryan D. Doerfler and Samuel Moyn, Democratizing the Supreme Court, 109 Cal. L. Rev. (forthcoming 2021); Daniel Epps & Ganesh Sitaraman, How to Save the Supreme Court, 129 Yale L.J. 148 (2019); Stephen E. Sachs, Supreme Court as Superweapon: A Response to Epps & Sitaraman, 129 Yale L.J. Forum 93 (2019); Suzanna Sherry & Christopher Sunby, Term Limits and Turmoil: *Roe v. Wade*'s Whiplash, 98 Texas L. Rev. 121 (2019); Christopher John Sprigman, Congress's Article III Power and the Process of Constitutional Change, 95 N.Y.U. L. Rev. 1778 (2020). For an argument that threats to judicial independence stem from the constitutional design itself, see Aziz Z. Huq, Why Judicial Independence Fails, 115 Nw. U. L. Rev. 1055 (2021).

Page 515, add as the first citation in the first paragraph of Note 9:

Daniel D. Birk, The Common-Law Exceptions Clause: Congressional Control of Supreme Court Appellate Jurisdiction in Light of British Precedent, 63 Vill. L. Rev. 189 (2018);

Page 515, add at the end of the first paragraph in Note 9:

For a recent endorsement of the view that Congress has plenary power over federal jurisdiction, see Christopher John Sprigman, Congress's Article III Power and the Process of Constitutional Change, 95 N.Y.U. L. Rev. 1778 (2020) (arguing that this congressional power can "help reconcile constitutionalism with democracy and, perhaps counterintuitively, help preserve the legitimacy of courts as enforcers of constitutional rules"). For a consideration of Congress's power to strip *state* courts of jurisdiction to hear federal claims, and a conclusion that, although Congress has broad power to do so in many instances, it lacks the authority to "simultaneously close both state and federal courts to federal constitutional challenges to state laws," see Michael C. Dorf, Congressional Power to Strip State Courts of Jurisdiction, 97 Tex. L. Rev. 1 (2018).

SECTION 2. POWER TO REGULATE FEDERAL RULES OF DECISION AND JUDGMENTS

Page 547, add a new Note:

10A. *PATCHAK V. ZINKE*

The Court again considered a congressional intervention into pending litigation in Patchak v. Zinke, 583 U.S. ___, 138 S.Ct. 897 (2018). In that case, the federal government had taken into trust a parcel of land in Michigan known as the "Bradley Property" for the benefit of an Indian tribe, so that the tribe could operate a casino there. In doing so, the government relied on statutory authority conferred in the 1934 Indian Reorganization Act. A neighboring landowner, David Patchak, sued the Secretary of the Interior, arguing that the government lacked authority under the Act to take the property into trust because the Indian tribe in question had not been formally recognized by the government until long after the Act was passed. The case made its way up to the Supreme Court, and the Court held that Patchak had standing to bring the suit and that the suit fell within a statutory exception to the government's sovereign immunity. The Court remanded for further proceedings.

While the case was pending on remand in the District Court, Congress passed the Gun Lake Act, 128 Stat. 1913. Section 2(a) of the Act provides that the Bradley Property "is reaffirmed as trust land, and the actions of the Secretary of the Interior in taking that land into trust are ratified and confirmed." Section 2(b) provides: "Notwithstanding any other provision of law, an action (including an action pending in a Federal court as of the date of enactment of this Act) relating to the land described in subsection (a) shall not be filed or maintained in a Federal court and shall be promptly dismissed." Based on this Act, the District Court dismissed the case, and the Court of Appeals affirmed.

In a splintered decision, the Supreme Court affirmed, rejecting Patchak's argument that Section 2(b) of the Act violated Article III of the Constitution. Justice Thomas, writing for himself and Justices Breyer, Alito, and Kagan, reasoned that Congress has broad authority both to strip federal court jurisdiction and to change the statutory law applicable to a pending case:

> Section 2(b) changes the law. Specifically, it strips federal courts of jurisdiction over actions "relating to" the Bradley Property. Before the Gun Lake Act, federal courts had jurisdiction to hear these actions. See 28 U.S.C. § 1331. Now they do not. This kind of legal change is well within Congress's authority and does not violate Article III. . . .

> Statutes that strip jurisdiction "chang[e] the law" for the purpose of Article III, [Plaut v. Spenthrift Farm, Inc., 514 U.S. 211, 218 (1995)], just as much as other exercises of Congress's legislative authority. Article I permits Congress "[t]o constitute Tribunals inferior to the supreme Court," § 8, and Article III vests the judicial power "in one supreme Court, and in such inferior Courts as the Congress may from time to time ordain and establish," § 1. These provisions reflect the so-called Madisonian Compromise, which resolved the Framers' disagreement about creating lower federal courts by leaving that decision to Congress. . . . Congress's greater power to create lower federal courts includes its lesser power to "limit the jurisdiction of those Courts." United States v. Hudson, 11 U.S. (7 Cranch) 32, 33 (1812). So long as Congress does not violate other constitutional provisions, its "control over the jurisdiction of the federal courts" is "plenary." Trainmen v. Toledo, P. & W. R. Co., 321 U.S. 50, 63–64 (1944).

Relying on *Ex parte McCardle*, Thomas also noted that "this Court has held that Congress generally does not violate Article III when it strips federal jurisdiction over a class of cases." While acknowledging that the Court in *McCardle* observed that another avenue of Supreme Court review remained available, Thomas contended that the Court was making that observation to address a potential problem under the Habeas Suspension Clause, not a potential problem under Article III. Thomas further argued that the present case was distinguishable from *United States v. Klein* because in *Klein* "Congress had no authority to declare that pardons are not evidence of loyalty, so it could not achieve the same result by stripping jurisdiction whenever claimants cited pardons as evidence of loyalty. Nor could Congress confer jurisdiction to a federal court but then strip jurisdiction from that same court once the court concluded that a pardoned claimant should prevail under the statute." Section 2(b) of the Gun Lake Act, by contrast, "does not attempt to exercise a power that the Constitution vests in another branch. And unlike the selective jurisdiction-stripping statute in *Klein*, § 2(b) strips jurisdiction over every suit relating to the Bradley Property." Quoting from *Bank Markazi*, Thomas observed that "a statute does not impinge on judicial power when it directs courts to apply a new legal standard to undisputed facts."

Finally, Thomas rejected the argument that Section 2(b) of the Act interfered with the federal judicial power in violation of *Plaut v. Spendthrift Farm, Inc.* Unlike in *Plaut*, the litigation in this case had not been concluded when Congress acted. "As this Court emphasized in *Plaut*," Justice Thomas noted, "Article III does not prohibit Congress from enacting new laws that apply to pending civil cases. . . . This principle applies equally to statutes that strip jurisdiction." In answer to the dissent's concern that Congress had targeted a specific case and directed its outcome, Thomas doubted that this presented a constitutional problem, and, in any event, he disagreed with this characterization of what Congress had done: "Nothing on the face of § 2(b) is limited to Patchak's case, or even to his challenge under the Indian Reorganization Act. Instead, the text extends to all suits 'relating to' the Bradley Property."

Justice Breyer added a separate concurrence to emphasize that Section 2(a) of the Act, the validity of which was not challenged, makes clear that the Secretary of the Interior had authority to keep the Bradley Property in trust, and that Section 2(b) merely supplements that provision: "The second part, the jurisdictional part, perhaps gilds the lily, perhaps simplifies judicial decisionmaking (the judge need only determine whether a lawsuit relates to the Bradley Property), but, read in context, it does no more than provide an alternative legal standard for courts to apply that seeks the same real-world result as does the first part: The Bradley Property shall remain in trust."

Joined by Justice Sotomayor, Justice Ginsburg concurred in the judgment but did not join Thomas's plurality opinion. Ginsburg reasoned that in this case Congress had simply retracted its waiver of sovereign immunity: "Just as it is Congress's prerogative to consent to suit, so too is it within Congress's authority to withdraw consent once given."

Justice Sotomayor also wrote separately to note that she agreed with a number of points in the dissent: "I agree with the dissent that Congress may not achieve through jurisdiction stripping what it cannot permissibly achieve outright, namely, directing entry of judgment for a particular party. I also agree that an Act that merely deprives federal courts of jurisdiction over a single proceeding is not enough to be considered a change in the law and that any statute that portends to do so should be viewed with great skepticism." She did not join the dissent, she explained, because she agreed with Justice Ginsburg that the Gun Lake Act "should not be read to strip the federal courts of jurisdiction but rather to restore the Federal Government's sovereign immunity."

Chief Justice Roberts dissented and was joined by Justices Kennedy and Gorsuch. Roberts contended that "Congress has previously approached the boundary between legislative and judicial power, but it has never gone so far as to target a single party for adverse treatment and direct the precise disposition of his pending case. Section 2(b)—remarkably—does just that." Unlike the plurality, Roberts said that he "would hold that Congress exercises the judicial power when it manipulates jurisdictional rules to decide the outcome of a particular pending case. Because the Legislature has no authority to direct entry of judgment for a party, it cannot achieve the same result by stripping jurisdiction over a particular proceeding." Roberts also argued that *McCardle* should not be "[r]ead for all it is worth" and that such an expansive reading would be inconsistent with *Klein*. Roberts concluded: "[A]lthough the stakes of this particular dispute may seem insignificant, the principle that the plurality would enshrine is of historic consequence. In no uncertain terms, the plurality disavows any limitations on Congress's power to determine judicial results, conferring on the Legislature a colonial-era authority to pick winners and losers in pending litigation as it pleases."

What does this decision suggest about the scope of Congress's authority to strip federal court jurisdiction over a pending case? Note that four of the Justices endorse some constitutional limits on jurisdiction-stripping: the three dissenters, and Justice Sotomayor. By contrast, the four Justices in the plurality appear to view Congress's authority to strip jurisdiction as essentially plenary. Justice Ginsburg's position on the issue is not clear. How easy would it be for courts to administer the proposed constitutional limitation articulated by the dissent? Is Justice Breyer right that, in any event, the case was effectively over as a result of Section 2(a) of the statute, given Congress's authority to change the statutory law applicable to a pending civil case?

For a critical analysis of the Court's approach in *Bank Markazi* and *Patchak*, see Ronald J. Krotoszynski, Jr. & Atticus DeProspo, Against Congressional Case Snatching, 62 Wm. & Mary L. Rev. 791 (2021). The authors argue that "the federal courts in general, and the Supreme Court in particular, should more zealously guard their institutional authority by more strictly enforcing the separation of powers doctrine when Congress attempts to usurp or transfer away pieces of the judicial power of the United States from the Article III courts." Part of their argument is that the constitutional text "disavows legislation with limited generality," such as that in *Bank Markazi* and *Patchak*. By contrast, Maggie Blackhawk, Equity Outside the

Courts, 120 Colum. L. Rev. 203 (2020), argues that the petition and private bill system of the nineteenth century suggests that, under our scheme of separated powers, the legislature may issue specific as well as general laws.

SECTION 4. POWER TO CREATE NON-ARTICLE III COURTS

Page 575, add a footnote at the end of Note 2:

[a] For an argument that *Palmore* is wrong and that "[t]he original meaning of the Constitution, longstanding historical practice and precedent, and functional concerns all show that Article III's judicial protections should apply to courts in the capital," see James Durling, The District of Columbia and Article III, 107 Geo. L.J. 1205 (2019).

Page 614, add a new Note after Note 3:

3A. REAFFIRMING THE PUBLIC RIGHTS DOCTRINE: *OIL STATES ENERGY SERVICES, LLC v. GREENE'S ENERGY GROUP, LLC*

The Patent and Trademark Office (PTO), an administrative agency, is responsible for issuing patents, based on a determination of whether the claims in the patent meet various statutory criteria. Since 1980, Congress has given the PTO the authority to conduct ex parte reexamination of patents it has issued. In 1999, Congress added a procedure called "inter partes reexamination," pursuant to which any person could file with the PTO a request for reexamination of a patent, and these requests would be resolved by the agency.

In 2012, Congress replaced inter partes reexamination with an adversarial process known as "inter partes review." Under this process, anyone other than the patent holder can petition for a review of the validity of patent claims. The decision whether to initiate the review is in the discretion of the Director of the PTO, but before doing so the Director must determine "that there is a reasonable likelihood that the petitioner would prevail with respect to at least 1 of the claims challenged."[a] Inter partes review proceedings are heard by the Patent Trial and Appeal Board, an adjudicatory body within the PTO that sits in three-member panels of administrative law patent judges. In the proceedings, the petitioner and the patent owner are entitled to certain discovery; to file affidavits, declarations, and written memoranda; and to receive an oral hearing before the Board. Appeals from Board decisions can be heard in the U.S. Court of Appeals for the Federal Circuit, an Article III court.

In 2001, Oil States Energy Services, LLC, an oilfield services company, obtained a patent relating to an apparatus and method for protecting wellhead equipment used in hydraulic fracturing. In 2012, it brought suit in a federal district court against a competing oilfield services company, Greene's Energy Group, LLC, for allegedly infringing the patent. While the case was pending, Greene's petitioned the PTO to institute inter partes review of the validity of two of Oil States' patent claims. The review was allowed to

---

[a] In SAS Institute Inc. v. Iancu, 584 U.S. ___, 138 S.Ct. 1348 (2018), the Supreme Court construed the relevant statute to require that, if the Director authorizes inter partes review, the review must extend to all claims raised by the petitioner.

proceed, and the Board held that Oil States' two patent claims were invalid. Oil States appealed that decision to the Federal Circuit, challenging not only the merits of the Board's decision but also arguing that the inter partes review process violated both Article III of the Constitution and the Seventh Amendment. The Federal Circuit rejected these arguments.

In Oil States Energy Services, LLC v. Greene's Energy Group, LLC, 584 U.S. ___, 138 S.Ct. 1365 (2018), the Supreme Court affirmed. In an opinion by Justice Thomas, the Court explained that its precedents "have given Congress significant latitude to assign adjudication of public rights to entities other than Article III courts." While acknowledging that its decisions have not always been clear or consistent about the distinction between public and private rights, the Court stated that "[i]nter partes review falls squarely within the public-rights doctrine."

It is undisputed, said the Court, that the decision whether to *grant* a patent is a matter involving public rights. Such a decision, the Court explained, "has the key features to fall within this Court's longstanding formulation of the public-rights doctrine." In particular, the Court noted that patents involve a grant of rights from the government, these rights did not exist at common law and instead arise from statutes, and Congress and the executive branch have the constitutional authority to make such a grant without a judicial determination. The Court reasoned that "[i]nter partes review is simply a reconsideration of that grant, and Congress has permissibly reserved the PTO's authority to conduct that reconsideration." This review, the Court further noted, "involves the same basic matter as the grant of a patent. So it, too, falls on the public-rights side of the line." As a result, said the Court, "[t]he Constitution does not prohibit the Board from resolving it outside of an Article III court."

As for the court-like powers exercised by the Board, the Court explained:

> [T]his Court has never adopted a "looks like" test to determine if an adjudication has improperly occurred outside of an Article III court. The fact that an agency uses court-like procedures does not necessarily mean it is exercising the judicial power. This Court has rejected the notion that a tribunal exercises Article III judicial power simply because it is "called a court and its decisions called judgments." Williams v. United States, 289 U.S. 553, 563 (1933). Nor does the fact that an administrative adjudication is final and binding on an individual who acquiesces in the result necessarily make it an exercise of the judicial power. See, e.g., Murray's Lessee v. Hoboken Land & Improvement Co., 59 U.S. 272, 280–81 (1856) (permitting the Treasury Department to conduct "final and binding" audits outside of an Article III court). Although inter partes review includes some of the features of adversarial litigation, it does not make any binding determination regarding "the liability of [Greene's Energy] to [Oil States] under the law as defined." Crowell v. Benson, 285 U.S. 22, 51 (1932). It remains a matter involving public rights, one "between the government and others,

which from [its] nature do[es] not require judicial determination."
Ex parte Bakelite Corp., 279 U.S. 438, 451 (1929).[5]

Its conclusion that the inter partes review process was consistent with
Article III was also sufficient, the Court explained, to dispose of the Seventh
Amendment challenge: "This Court's precedents establish that, when Congress properly assigns a matter to adjudication in a non-Article III tribunal,
'the Seventh Amendment poses no independent bar to the adjudication of
that action by a nonjury factfinder.' Granfinanciera, S. A. v. Nordberg, 492
U.S. 33, 53–54 (1989)."

The Court concluded by emphasizing the "narrowness" of its holding:

> We address the constitutionality of inter partes review only.
> We do not address whether other patent matters, such as infringe-
> ment actions, can be heard in a non-Article III forum. And because
> the Patent Act provides for judicial review by the Federal Circuit,
> we need not consider whether inter partes review would be consti-
> tutional "without any sort of intervention by a court at any stage of
> the proceedings," Atlas Roofing Co. v. Occupational Safety and
> Health Review Comm'n, 430 U.S. 442, 455 n.13 (1977). Moreover,
> we address only the precise constitutional challenges that Oil
> States raised here. Oil States does not challenge the retroactive ap-
> plication of inter partes review, even though that procedure was
> not in place when its patent issued. Nor has Oil States raised a due
> process challenge. Finally, our decision should not be misconstrued
> as suggesting that patents are not property for purposes of the Due
> Process Clause or the Takings Clause.

Justice Breyer, in a brief concurrence joined by Justices Ginsburg and
Sotomayor, insisted that "the Court's opinion should not be read to say that
matters involving private rights may never be adjudicated other than by Article III courts, say, sometimes by agencies. Our precedent is to the contrary."

Justice Gorsuch dissented and was joined by Chief Justice Roberts.
Based on a review of various historical materials, Gorsuch contended that
"only courts could hear patent challenges in England at the time of the founding," and he argued that this history should inform the interpretation of Article III. He also noted that, "from the time it established the American patent system in 1790 until about 1980, Congress left the job of invalidating
patents at the federal level to courts alone." He rejected the argument that,
because the grant of a patent is a public right, a decision to revoke a patent
can be reserved to non-Article III adjudicators: "Just because you give a gift
doesn't mean you forever enjoy the right to reclaim it." Gorsuch concluded:

> Today's decision may not represent a rout but it at least sig-
> nals a retreat from Article III's guarantees. Ceding to the political
> branches ground they wish to take in the name of efficient

---

[5]   Oil States also points out that inter partes review "is initiated by private parties and
implicates no waiver of sovereign immunity." Brief for Petitioner 30–31. But neither of those
features takes inter partes review outside of the public-rights doctrine. . . . Also, inter partes
review is not initiated by private parties in the way that a common-law cause of action is. To be
sure, a private party files the petition for review. But the decision to institute review is made
by the Director and committed to his unreviewable discretion.

government may seem like an act of judicial restraint. But enforcing Article III isn't about protecting judicial authority for its own sake. It's about ensuring the people today and tomorrow enjoy no fewer rights against governmental intrusion than those who came before. And the loss of the right to an independent judge is never a small thing. It's for that reason Hamilton warned the judiciary to take "all possible care . . . to defend itself against" intrusions by the other branches. The Federalist No. 78, at 466. It's for that reason I respectfully dissent.

3B. *ISSUES ARISING UNDER THE APPOINTMENTS CLAUSE*

Even if adjudication within the executive branch does not violate Article III, it can raise issues under the Appointments Clause. Art. II, § 2 of the Constitution defines the appointment powers of the President. Some senior appointments (federal court judges, cabinet officers, etc.) are made by the President with the advice and consent of the Senate. For "all other Officers of the United States," Congress "may by Law vest the Appointment of such inferior Officers, as they think proper, in the President alone, in the Courts of Law, or in the Heads of Departments."

Lucia v. Securities and Exchange Commission, 585 U.S. ___, 138 S.Ct. 2044 (2018), involved whether administrative law judges in the SEC are "Officers of the United States" within this description or whether they are mere "employees" of the federal government whose appointment is not controlled by any constitutional provision. The question arose in an administrative enforcement proceeding against the purveyor of a retirement savings plan called "Buckets of Money." The defendant objected to the administrative law judge (ALJ) assigned to hear the case on the ground that he had not been properly appointed. It was undisputed that the SEC is a "Head of Department" within the meaning of Art. II and thus eligible to be given the power of appointment, but the SEC commissioners did not choose the ALJ. Rather, they delegated that task to the staff. Hence, if the ALJ were found an "Officer of the United States," he had not been properly appointed and could not hear the case.

The D.C. Circuit upheld the SEC proceeding, then affirmed by an equally divided vote on rehearing en banc, but the Supreme Court reversed. Speaking through Justice Kagan, the Court found that the defining characteristics of an officer were that the individual (1) "occupy a 'continuing' position established by law" and (2) exercise "significant authority" under the laws of the United States. Applying these criteria and in close reliance on the earlier decision in Freytag v. Commissioner, 501 U.S. 868 (1991), the Court found that the ALJ was an officer and had to be appointed by the SEC itself rather than by its staff.

The concurrences and dissenting opinions revealed a wide range of disagreement. Justice Thomas, joined by Justice Gorsuch, concurred to suggest that "officer" should have a far broader definition than the Court approved. Relying chiefly on history, they argued that the Framers likely understood "Officers of the United States" to encompass "all federal civil officials who perform an ongoing, statutory duty—no matter how important or significant that duty." This formula would significantly expand the class of federal employees subject to the requirements of Art. II.

Justice Sotomayor, joined by Justice Ginsburg, dissented to propose a much narrower definition. They argued that the question should turn on whether the individual in question had "the ability to make final, binding decisions on behalf of the Government." This definition would have excluded the ALJ, because he had the power only to make an "initial decision," which would then be reviewed or at least allowed by the SEC.

Justice Breyer concurred in part and dissented in part (in which part he was joined by Justices Ginsburg and Sotomayor). Breyer based his concurrence on the Administrative Procedure Act and avoided the constitutional question altogether. He was motivated to do so by a fear that declaring ALJs "Officers of the United States" would imperil provisions protecting them from removal without cause. He derived this implication from the Court's decision in Free Enterprise Fund v. Public Company Accounting Oversight Board, 561 U.S. 477 (2010), which disapproved a scheme that provided two levels of insulation between the President and an executive officer. The *Free Enterprise Fund* Court's rejection of "multilevel protection from removal" was somewhat Delphic, and it is unclear what, if any, application it might have to other executive officers. The *Lucia* majority did not address the issue.

United States v. Arthrex, Inc., 594 U.S. ___, 141 S.Ct. 1970 (2021), involved an Appointments Clause challenge to the power of the Patent Trial and Appeal Board, the adjudicatory body at issue in the *Oil States* case discussed above in Note 3A. The Board consists of administrative patent judges (APJs) who are appointed by the Secretary of Commerce. After the Board invalidated Arthrex's patent for an orthopedic surgical device, the company challenged this appointment scheme as invalid. The APJs, the company asserted, were principal officers who must be appointed by the President with the advice and consent of the Senate. The federal government argued that the APJs were only inferior officers who could be appointed by the Secretary of Commerce, a "Head[ ] of Department[ ]" under Article II. (In contrast to *Lucia*, no one contended that the APJs might be mere "employees.")

In an opinion by Chief Justice Roberts, the Supreme Court held that the selection of the APJs violated the Appointments Clause. The Court emphasized that, although the APJs' decisions in inter partes review proceedings could be appealed to the Federal Circuit, they were not first reviewed by the Director of the Patent and Trademark Office (PTO) "or any other principal officer in the Executive Branch. . . . [T]he unreviewable authority wielded by APJs during inter partes review is incompatible with their appointment by the Secretary to an inferior office." The Chief Justice then articulated a modest remedy for this constitutional problem: "Decisions by APJs must be subject to review by the Director [of the PTO]." Specifically as to Arthrex, the Chief Justice stated that the "appropriate remedy is a remand to the Acting Director for him to decide whether to rehear" the dispute over the company's patent. "Because the source of the constitutional violation is the restraint on the review authority of the Director, rather than the appointment of APJs by the Secretary, Arthrex is not entitled to a hearing before a new panel of APJs."

Justice Thomas, joined by Justices Breyer, Sotomayor, and Kagan, dissented on the merits, asserting that the Director of the PTO already had ample power to supervise the APJs, and that they were therefore inferior officers and the existing appointments scheme was valid. Writing only for himself, Justice Thomas also rejected the Chief Justice's proposed remedy. Justice Thomas argued that, if there were in fact a constitutional problem with the composition of the Board, "then surely Arthrex is entitled to a new hearing before officers untainted by an appointments violation." Justice Breyer, joined by Justices Sotomayor and Kagan, filed a separate dissent, advocating a functional approach to the separation-of-powers question before the Court: "the Court should interpret the Appointments Clause as granting Congress a degree of leeway to establish and empower federal offices." Those three Justices did, however, accept the remedy offered by the Chief Justice.

Note the interesting line-up of Justices in *Arthrex*. The Chief Justice's opinion for the Court on the merits was joined by Justices Alito, Gorsuch, Kavanaugh, and Barrett. The remedial portion of the Chief Justice's opinion was joined by Justices Alito, Kavanaugh, and Barrett and separately accepted by Justices Breyer, Sotomayor, and Kagan. Justice Gorsuch joined the Chief Justice's decision on the merits but separately dissented as to remedy, reiterating concerns he had raised in what he called the Court's "wrong turn" in *Oil States*. Justice Thomas, the author of *Oil States*, dissented as to both merits and remedy in *Arthrex*.

3C. *ORTIZ V. UNITED STATES*

In Ortiz v. United States, 585 U.S. ___, 138 S.Ct. 2165 (2018), the Supreme Court held that it was constitutional for Congress to provide for Supreme Court review of decisions by the Court of Appeals for the Armed Forces (CAAF), a non-Article III military court. Although the parties had not questioned the Court's jurisdiction, a law professor, Aditya Bamzai, filed an amicus brief arguing that the Court lacked Article III authority to hear appeals from the CAAF. The Court gave significant attention to this argument but rejected it in a seven–two decision. Justice Kagan, writing for the Court, reasoned that the "essential character" of the military court system is judicial; that it is well established that the Supreme Court can review the decisions of state courts, territorial courts, and D.C. courts, even though they are, like the CAAF, not Article III tribunals; and that, even though the CAAF resides within the executive branch, it is a judicial entity created by Congress. Kagan observed, however, that "[i]f Congress were to grant us appellate jurisdiction over decisions of newer entities advancing an administrative (rather than judicial) mission, the question would be different—and the answer not found in this opinion." Justice Thomas concurred, explaining that he agreed fully with the Court's decision but was writing separately "to explain why that conclusion is consistent with the Founders' understanding of judicial power—specifically, the distinction they drew between public and private rights." Justice Alito dissented and was joined by Justice Gorsuch. Alito reasoned that the Supreme Court's Article III appellate jurisdiction extends only to "review[ing] one thing: the lawful exercise of *judicial* power," and that "Executive Branch officers . . . cannot lawfully exercise the judicial power of any sovereign, no matter how court-like their decisionmaking process might appear." Because the CAAF is "an agent of executive power to aid the Commander in Chief," said Alito, "[i]t follows that our appellate jurisdiction does not permit us to review its decisions directly."

Page 619, add at the end of Note 6:

For an argument that dismissals of cases from the federal courts on justiciability grounds should be viewed as "invitations to legislators to consider other pathways for adjudication," such as state courts, administrative agencies, and other non-Article III tribunals, see Zachary D. Clopton, Justiciability, Federalism, and the Administrative State, 103 Cornell L. Rev. 1431 (2018). For a challenge to the idea that the parties' consent should provide a constitutional basis for non-Article III adjudication, see F. Andrew Hessick, Consenting to Adjudication Outside the Article III Courts, 71 Vand. L. Rev. 715 (2018). For historical analysis of the public-rights doctrine, see John Harrison, Public Rights, Private Privileges, and Article III, 54 Ga. L. Rev. 143 (2019).

For an argument that the constitutionality of non-Article III tribunals should be assessed by reference to the power that the tribunal is exercising rather than by the process that it is using, and that this explains the constitutionality of certain longstanding categories of non-Article III adjudication, see William Baude, Adjudication Outside Article III, 133 Harv. L. Rev. 1511 (2020). Baude explains:

> [N]on-Article III tribunals can exercise one of three different kinds of power. Some exercise the judicial power, but not the judicial power of the United States. Rather, they exercise the judicial power of some other government. The obvious example is state courts, but the same logic explains adjudication by territorial courts, tribal courts, and foreign courts.
>
> Some exercise executive power, not judicial power. The main constitutional constraint on this form of executive power is the longstanding principle, codified by the Due Process Clause, that requires judicial process before one can be deprived of life, liberty, or property. This power, and this proviso, explains the administrative adjudication of public rights. Executive power also explains military courts, although they have a historically different relationship to due process.
>
> Finally, some adjudication is done in bodies that are vested with no governmental power at all. These bodies must derive their ability to adjudicate either from a nongovernmental source, such as the consent of the parties, or from their close relationship as an "adjunct" of a true court vested with judicial power.

Is it that simple? Or does this approach simply shift the debate to the content of the various labels and distinctions being invoked, such as "of the United States," executive vs. judicial, and "from a nongovernmental source"?

For essays discussing the history, importance, and current state of administrative agency adjudication, as part of a symposium issue commemorating the 75th anniversary of the Administrative Procedure Act, see Michael S. Greve, Why We Need Federal Administrative Courts, 28 Geo. Mason L. Rev. 765 (2021); Aaron L. Nielson, Three Wrong Turns in Agency Adjudication, 28 Geo. Mason L. Rev. 657 (2021); and Richard J. Pierce, Jr., Agency Adjudication: It Is Time to Hit the Rest Button, 28 Geo. Mason L. Rev. 463 (2021).

CHAPTER V

SUBJECT MATTER JURISDICTION

SECTION 1. FEDERAL QUESTION JURISDICTION

Page 647, add a footnote at the end of Note 1:

[b] Donald L. Doernberg, The Supreme Court's Cloaking Device: "[C]ongressional Judgment About the Sound Division of Labor Between State and Federal Courts," 50 U. Pac. L. Rev. 539 (2019), describes the evolution of the statutory meaning of federal question jurisdiction "as a carefully calibrated balancing" by a Supreme Court that "has fashioned an amorphous body of federal common law." He is no friend of this development. The "Court is now defining its own subject-matter jurisdiction." "Doing so," he adds, "raises serious questions of legitimacy." It "undermines separation of powers," which perhaps is "why the Court attempts to conceal its efforts by claiming, entirely without evidence, that it is all Congress's doing."

SECTION 2. DIVERSITY JURISDICTION

Page 700, add at the end of footnote a:

For an argument that discussion of the merits of diversity jurisdiction should be shifted "away from its myopic focus on out-of-state bias and toward considerations that are more meaningful for modern civil litigation," see Scott Dodson, Beyond Bias in Diversity Jurisdiction, 69 Duke L.J. 267 (2019).

Page 731, add a footnote at the end of the first paragraph of Note 4:

[h] In Home Depot U.S.A., Inc. v. Jackson, 587 U.S. ___, 139 S.Ct. 1743 (2019), the Court narrowly interpreted the removal provision in CAFA to preclude removal by a third-party counterclaim defendant. Citibank had filed a debt-collection action against Jackson in a North Carolina state court. Jackson then filed a counterclaim against Citibank and a third-party class action claim against Home Depot and another defendant. Citibank ultimately dismissed its claim against Jackson, after which Home Depot sought to remove the case to federal court under 28 U.S.C. §§ 1441(a) and 1453. The Court held that § 1441(a) "does not permit removal based on counterclaims at all" and that in § 1453 "Congress intended only to alter certain restrictions on removal, not expand the class of persons who can remove a class action."

An unusual feature of the decision is the lineup. Justice Thomas wrote for a Court that was divided five to four. Justice Alito wrote the dissent, joined by Chief Justice Roberts and Justices Gorsuch and Kavanaugh.

SECTION 3. THE SUBSTANCE/PROCEDURE PROBLEM

Page 757, add after the first full paragraph:

A. Benjamin Spencer, Substance, Procedure, and the Rules Enabling Act, 66 U.C.L.A. L. Rev. 654 (2019), concludes that "the Court's failure to provide a rigorous articulation of the contours of the [Rules Enabling Act] has . . . enabled some rules to escape being detected as ultra vires judicial regulation." In particular, Spencer argues that Rules 15(c)(1) (relation back of amendments), 4(k) (relating to personal jurisdiction), and 4(n) (relating to jurisdiction over property) are problematic under a proper interpretation of the Enabling Act. As to Rule 15(c)(1), Spencer concludes:

> Given that a statute of limitations period confers on defendants a substantive right "to be free of stale claims," a Federal Rule

that extinguishes that right for a person who was not sued on the same facts within the statutorily-prescribed period abridges that defendant's substantive rights. . . . The claimant's rights are enlarged by reviving an extinguished claim or by giving the claim a longer life than the state has prescribed; the defendant's rights are abridged by subjecting him to liability from which he would otherwise be protected. The transgression of the [Enabling Act] mandates, it would seem, could not be more clear.

As to Rule 4, he concludes that "Procedural rules must be confined to addressing the manner in which adjudication occurs. Jurisdictional rules address a court's power to entertain a matter at all. Congress—not the courts—has the authority to delineate the jurisdictional reach of the inferior federal courts."

SECTION 4. FINALITY AND APPELLATE REVIEW

SUBSECTION A. SUPREME COURT REVIEW OF STATE COURT DECISIONS

Page 768, add at the end of Note 1(*i*):

A similar result was reached on a different rationale in Atlantic Richfield Co. v. Christian, 590 U.S. ___, 140 S.Ct. 1335 (2020). Landowners in Montana sued Atlantic Richfield in a Montana state court seeking restoration damages for harms caused to their property by arsenic and lead deposits resulting from decades of copper mining. The land was already subject to a cleanup plan established by the EPA under federal Superfund legislation. The state trial court denied summary judgment and allowed the suit to proceed to trial in the face of several preemption arguments made by Atlantic Richfield. Atlantic Richfield then sought a "writ of supervisory control" in the Montana Supreme Court, arguing that allowing the suit to go forward was inconsistent with federal law. The Montana Supreme Court held that the suit could proceed to trial, and the U.S. Supreme Court granted certiorari.

The landowners argued that the Supreme Court lacked jurisdiction "because the Montana Supreme Court allowed the case to proceed to trial [and] its judgment was [therefore] not final." The Court responded:

> But the Montana Supreme Court exercised review in this case through a writ of supervisory control. Under Montana law, a supervisory writ proceeding is a self-contained case, not an interlocutory appeal. . . . When the Montana Supreme Court issues a writ of supervisory control, it initiates a separate lawsuit. It is the nature of the Montana proceeding . . . that establishes our jurisdiction.

The Court relied for this holding on Fisher v. District Court, 424 U.S. 382 (1976) (per curiam), where it had held in a footnote that the Montana writ of supervisory control "is available only in original proceedings in the Montana Supreme Court" and that it was "not equivalent to an appeal." It added that a "judgment that terminates original proceedings in a state appellate court, in which the only issue decided concerns the jurisdiction of a lower state court, is final, even if further proceedings are to be had in the lower court."

SUBSECTION B. CIRCUIT COURT REVIEW OF DISTRICT COURT DECISIONS

Page 800, add at the end of footnote c:

Rule 42(a)(2) provides that "[i]f actions before the court involve a common question of law or fact, the court may . . . consolidate the actions . . . ." *Gelboim* left open the question whether cases consolidated under Rule 42(a) were immediately appealable when one of them was disposed of by final order.

In a unanimous opinion by Chief Justice Roberts in Hall v. Hall, 584 U.S. ___, 138 S.Ct. 1118 (2018), the Court held that such a case was immediately appealable:

> The history against which Rule 42(a) was adopted resolves any ambiguity regarding the meaning of "consolidate" in subsection (a)(2). It makes clear that one of multiple cases consolidated under the Rule retains its independent character, at least to the extent it is appealable when finally resolved, regardless of any ongoing proceedings in the other cases. . . . [C]onstituent cases retain their separate identities at least to the extent that a final decision in one is immediately appealable by the losing party.

For consideration of *Hall* in the broader context of finality in general, see Bryan Lammon, Finality, Appealability, and the Scope of Interlocutory Review, 93 Wash. L. Rev. 1809 (2018). For a more focused view on *Hall* itself, see Bryan Lammon, *Hall v. Hall*: A Lose-Lose Case for Appellate Jurisdiction, 68 Emory L.J. Online 1001 (2018).

Page 805, add at the end of the first paragraph of Note 11:

For a comparison of the relative merits of permissive interlocutory appeals and the collateral order doctrine, see Michael E. Solimine, The Renaissance of Permissive Interlocutory Appeals and the Demise of the Collateral Order Doctrine, 53 Akron L. Rev. 607 (2019). Solimine observes that various factors have led to the "withering" of the collateral order doctrine and concludes that "more nuanced appeals under § 1292(b), or perhaps under new rule-making by the Supreme Court, are more appropriate vehicles for allowing interlocutory appeals, since unlike the collateral order doctrine, they permit more surgical precision in weighing the pros (avoiding hardship) and cons (disrupting the ordinary litigation process at the trial level) of interlocutory appeals in individual cases."

Page 806, add after the first full paragraph:

For more recent treatment of the finality question, see Bryan Lammon, Finality, Appealability, and the Scope of Interlocutory Review, 93 Wash. L. Rev. 1809 (2018). Lammon concludes that the

> federal courts have interpreted the term final decision in three contexts to create three kinds of rules: (1) rules about when district court proceedings have ended and parties can take the traditional, end-of-proceedings appeal on the merits; (2) rules about when litigants can appeal before the end of those proceedings; and (3) rules limiting or expanding the scope of review in those appeals. Though related, these contexts are distinct and involve unique issues and interests. The future of federal appellate jurisdiction—whether it comes from rulemaking or further judicial decisions—must reckon with these three distinct kinds of rules and the unique interests

that they entail. And successful reform must fill each of the roles that interpretations of the term "final decision" have played.

CHAPTER VI

ABSTENTION

SECTION 1. INTRODUCTION

Page 809, add a footnote at the end of the carryover paragraph at the top of the page:

d What about criminal cases that proceed separately in state and federal court based on the same facts? Res judicata principles would not preclude multiple prosecutions because the two cases would involve different prosecuting authorities, neither of which could be bound by the actions of the other.

The Court faced this issue in Gamble v. United States, 587 U.S. ___, 139 S.Ct. 1960 (2019). Gamble pleaded guilty to a violation of an Alabama law punishing felons who possess a firearm. He was sentenced to 10 years imprisonment, all but one year of which was suspended. He then was indicted for the same instance of possession that also violated a federal criminal law. He was convicted in federal court, and sentenced to almost three more years of imprisonment. In an opinion written by Justice Alito, the Court followed "170 years of precedent" and upheld the federal conviction based on the "dual sovereignty" doctrine, under which each sovereign is permitted to pursue violations of its own laws. The Double Jeopardy Clause, the Court said, "protects individuals from being twice put in jeopardy 'for the same *offence*, not the same *conduct* or *actions*." The original understanding, the Court continued, was that "an 'offence' is defined by a law, and each law is defined by a sovereign. So where there are two sovereigns, there are two laws, and two 'offences.' " The vote was seven to two. Justices Ginsburg and Gorsuch wrote separate dissents.

Dual prosecutions based on the same facts are rare. Typically, prosecutorial agreements result in one sovereign deferring to the other. After *Gamble*, one question to be asked is when a second prosecution would be justified following an acquittal or a conviction in the other forum.

SECTION 2. *YOUNGER* ABSTENTION

Page 827, add at the end of Note 6:

See also Fred O. Smith, Jr., Abstention in the Time of Ferguson, 131 Harv. L. Rev. 2283 (2018), which argues for a *Younger* exception in cases where there "are structural or systemic constitutional flaws built into a state's procedural apparatus."

SECTION 4. *PULLMAN* ABSTENTION

Page 872, add at the end of Note 6:

For an historical account of Justice Frankfurter's contribution to the modern law of judicial federalism, with a particular focus on abstention doctrines, see Lael Weinberger, Frankfurter, Abstention Doctrine, and the Development of Modern Federalism: A History and Three Futures, 87 U. Chi. L. Rev. 1737 (2020).

SECTION 6. INTERNATIONAL COMITY ABSTENTION

Page 906, add at the end of Note 8:

For a critique of judicial reliance on a general doctrine of international comity abstention and an argument that courts should "identify instead distinct bases for abstention in transnational cases—much as they have in domestic cases—that can then be distinctly analyzed," see Maggie Gardner, Abstention at the Border, 105 Va. L. Rev. 63, 69 (2019). For a defense of international comity-based abstention, and a proposed federal common law framework to govern it, see Samuel Estreicher and Thomas H. Lee, In Defense of International Comity, 93 S. Cal. L. Rev. 169 (2020).

CHAPTER VII

HABEAS CORPUS

SECTION 1. REVIEW OF STATE COURT DECISIONS ON THE MERITS: JUDICIAL LIMITATIONS

Page 926, add at the end of footnote c:

For an argument that the restrictions and obligations imposed on sex-offender registrants should qualify as "custody" for purposes of federal habeas corpus, see Wendy R. Calloway, Sex Offenders, Custody and Habeas, 92 St. John's Law Rev. 755 (2018).

Page 944, omit Subsection B, pages 944–62, and substitute the following:

SUBSECTION B: RETROACTIVE APPLICATION OF NEW CONSTITUTIONAL RIGHTS

INTRODUCTORY NOTE ON RETROACTIVE APPLICATION OF NEW CONSTITUTIONAL RIGHTS

Brown v. Allen opened the door to a vast potential for habeas relief. Taken literally, it meant that federal district and circuit courts could reexamine de novo on federal habeas corpus the merits of every federal constitutional issue raised in every state criminal case. The potential breadth of federal relief was significantly enlarged, moreover, as federal constitutional rights applicable to criminal cases were expanded and newly applied to the states, especially during the 1960s and thereafter. Cases like *Mapp*, *Miranda*, and many others created new possibilities for prisoners whose convictions had become final as they sought to take advantage of these new rules. Potentially, *all* substantive and procedural rights based on the federal Constitution—whether newly developed or not—could be invoked by anyone whose case was open to relitigation on habeas corpus, that is, anyone still in custody.

The potential for such broad habeas relief prompted both Congress and the Supreme Court to develop limitations. The most important congressional limitations are contained in the Antiterrorism and Effective Death Penalty Act of 1996 (AEDPA), which is dealt with in Section 2 of this Chapter. Even before AEDPA, the Supreme Court had independently developed various limiting doctrines. *Stone v. Powell* is an example. Other judicially adopted limitations are dealt with later in this Chapter. An important one is covered here.

An early pre-*Stone* series of decisions addressed the retroactive application of newly developed constitutional rights. The initial step came in Linkletter v. Walker, 381 U.S. 618 (1965). *Linkletter* held that the exclusionary rule developed in *Mapp v. Ohio* would not apply to convictions that became final before *Mapp* was decided.[a] The later decision in *Stone* effectively excluded *Mapp* issues from federal collateral attack altogether, but *Stone* has not been extended to other constitutional rights. *Linkletter*, in contrast, led to a complex and much more inclusive analysis that involved (in the words of the Court in *Linkletter*) "weigh[ing] the merits and demerits [of retroactivity] in each case by looking to the prior history of the rule in question, its purpose and effect, and whether retrospective operation will further or retard its operation."

In a series of cases, Justice Harlan argued for a more restrictive approach. He thought that new rules of constitutional law should continue to apply in all cases still open on direct review. But, he added, it is "sounder, in adjudicating habeas petitions, generally to apply the law prevailing at the time a conviction became final than it is to seek to dispose of [habeas] cases on the basis of intervening changes in constitutional interpretation." Mackey v. United States, 401 U.S. 667, 689 (1971) (opinion of Harlan, J.). Thus, for Harlan, retroactive application of constitutional criminal procedure rights did not depend on the right asserted but on the remedy sought.

With this as the starting point, Harlan proposed that newly recognized rights should not be applied retroactively on collateral review, with two exceptions. First, rules that placed "certain kinds of primary, private individual conduct beyond the power of the criminal law-making authority to proscribe" should be applied retroactively on habeas review. Second, "those procedures that . . . are 'implicit in the concept of ordered liberty,'" should also be applied retroactively on habeas review.

Harlan's approach was eventually embraced by the Court, beginning in Teague v. Lane, 489 U.S. 288 (1989). *Teague* was written by Justice O'Connor, who was joined in the relevant part of her opinion only by Chief Justice Rehnquist and Justices Scalia and Kennedy. The *Teague* plurality on retroactivity became a majority when Justice White added his vote to O'Connor's approach later that term in Penry v. Lynaugh, 492 U.S. 302 (1989). *Teague* then became embedded as a central tenet of federal habeas jurisprudence.

Under the analysis in *Teague*, the first question was whether the rule of decision in a Supreme Court case was "new." If it was merely a statement or restatement of law that existed when the events at issue were litigated, then it would be straightforwardly applied to all cases whether they arose on direct appeal or habeas corpus. If, on the other hand, the decision announced a "new" rule, it would be applied to cases still in the direct review pipeline but would not be applied retroactively to convictions that became final before the rule was announced.

But there were two exceptions, mirroring those suggested by Justice Harlan. New "substantive" rules—that is rules that precluded the state from criminally punishing identified conduct—would be applied retroactively no matter how or when the case arose. And new rules that established "watershed" procedures were also eligible for retroactive application. The next main case describes the content, the history, and the fate of this "watershed"

---

[a]   "Final" was defined as after direct review had concluded.

procedure exception. The Notes that follow elaborate on *Teague*'s exception for new "substantive" rules.

Edwards v. Vannoy

Supreme Court of the United States, 2021.
593 U.S. ___, 141 S.Ct. 1547.

■ JUSTICE KAVANAUGH delivered the opinion of the Court.

Last Term in Ramos v. Louisiana, 590 U.S. ___, 140 S.Ct. 1390 (2020), this Court held that a state jury must be unanimous to convict a criminal defendant of a serious offense. *Ramos* repudiated this Court's 1972 decision in Apodaca v. Oregon, 406 U.S. 404 (1972), which had allowed non-unanimous juries in state criminal trials. The question in this case is whether the new rule of criminal procedure announced in *Ramos* applies retroactively to overturn final convictions on federal collateral review. Under this Court's retroactivity precedents, the answer is no.

This Court has repeatedly stated that a decision announcing a new rule of criminal procedure ordinarily does not apply retroactively on federal collateral review. See Teague v. Lane, 489 U.S. 288, 310 (1989) (plurality opinion). Indeed, in the 32 years since *Teague* underscored that principle, this Court has announced many important new rules of criminal procedure. But the Court has not applied *any* of those new rules retroactively on federal collateral review. . . .

In light of the Court's well-settled retroactivity doctrine, we conclude that the *Ramos* jury-unanimity rule likewise does not apply retroactively on federal collateral review. . . .

I

On the night of May 13, 2006, in Baton Rouge, Louisiana, Thedrick Edwards and an accomplice kidnapped Ryan Eaton, a student at LSU. As Eaton was getting out of his car, Edwards and his accomplice confronted Eaton at gunpoint and forced him back into the car. Edwards and his accomplice then jumped into the car with Eaton. They drove with Eaton to an ATM where they hoped to withdraw money using Eaton's card. When they discovered that Eaton did not have any money in his account, they drove to Eaton's apartment. Once there, they bound and blindfolded Eaton, rummaged through his apartment, and took some of his belongings to Eaton's car.

After they were back in the car, Edwards and his accomplice coerced Eaton into arranging a meeting with Eaton's girlfriend. They then drove to the girlfriend's apartment and, at gunpoint, forced Eaton to knock on the door. When Eaton's girlfriend opened the door, Edwards and his accomplice rushed inside. Both Edwards and his accomplice were armed, and Edwards's accomplice had his gun drawn. Edwards and his accomplice instructed Eaton, Eaton's girlfriend, and two other women in the apartment to lie on the floor. Edwards then raped one of the women. His accomplice raped another woman. As they left, they grabbed some personal property from the apartment. Edwards and his accomplice hurried back into Eaton's car and drove around the corner. They then abandoned the car and fled. . . .

Edwards was indicted in Louisiana state court for armed robbery, kidnapping, and rape. Edwards pled not guilty and went to trial. . . . The jury convicted Edwards of five counts of armed robbery, two counts of kidnapping, and one count of rape. At the time, Louisiana law permitted guilty verdicts if at least 10 of the 12 jurors found the defendant guilty. The jury convicted Edwards by an 11-to-1 vote on one of the armed robbery counts, the two kidnapping counts, and the rape count. The jury convicted Edwards by a 10-to-2 vote on the four remaining armed robbery counts.

At sentencing, the trial judge stated: "I can say without hesitation that this is the most egregious case that I've had before me." The judge sentenced Edwards to life imprisonment without parole. The Louisiana First Circuit Court of Appeal affirmed the conviction and sentence. In March 2011, Edwards's conviction became final on direct review.

After his conviction became final, Edwards applied for state postconviction relief in the Louisiana courts. The Louisiana courts denied relief.

In 2015, Edwards filed a petition for a writ of habeas corpus in the U.S. District Court for the Middle District of Louisiana. He argued that the non-unanimous jury verdict violated his constitutional right to a unanimous jury. The District Court rejected that claim as foreclosed by this Court's 1972 decision in *Apodaca*. . . . The U.S. Court of Appeals for the Fifth Circuit denied a certificate of appealability. Edwards then petitioned for a writ of certiorari in this Court, arguing that the Constitution requires a unanimous jury in state criminal trials.

II

While Edwards's petition for certiorari was pending, this Court [held in] *Ramos* . . . that the Fourteenth Amendment incorporates the Sixth Amendment right to a unanimous jury against the States. Therefore, in state court as well as federal court, a jury must be unanimous to convict a defendant of a serious offense.

The Court's decision in *Ramos* directly affected Louisiana and Oregon, which were the only two States that still allowed non-unanimous juries. For those States, this Court's decision in *Ramos* immediately triggered a pressing question: Does *Ramos* apply retroactively to overturn final convictions on federal collateral review? We granted certiorari in Edwards's case to decide that question. . . .

A

A new rule of criminal procedure applies to cases on *direct* review, even if the defendant's trial has already concluded. See Griffith v.

Kentucky, 479 U.S. 314, 328 (1987). But under the habeas corpus statute as interpreted by this Court, a new rule of criminal procedure ordinarily does not apply retroactively to overturn final convictions on federal *collateral* review.[2]

In stating that new procedural rules ordinarily do not apply retroactively on federal collateral review, *Teague* reinforced what had already been the Court's regular practice for several decades under the retroactivity standard articulated in Linkletter v. Walker, 381 U.S. 618 (1965). *Linkletter* set forth a balancing test for determining retroactivity. But even under *Linkletter*, "new rules that constituted clear breaks with the past generally were not given retroactive effect," including on federal collateral review. *Teague*, 489 U.S. at 304 (plurality opinion).

As the Court has explained, applying "constitutional rules not in existence at the time a conviction became final seriously undermines the principle of finality which is essential to the operation of our criminal justice system." Id. at 309. Here, for example, applying *Ramos* retroactively would potentially overturn decades of convictions obtained in reliance on *Apodaca*. Moreover, conducting scores of retrials years after the crimes occurred would require significant state resources. And a State may not be able to retry some defendants at all because of "lost evidence, faulty memory, and missing witnesses." Allen v. Hardy, 478 U.S. 255, 260 (1986) (per curiam). When previously convicted perpetrators of violent crimes go free merely because the evidence needed to conduct a retrial has become stale or is no longer available, the public suffers, as do the victims. Even when the evidence can be reassembled, conducting retrials years later inflicts substantial pain on crime victims who must testify again and endure new trials. In this case, the victims of the robberies, kidnappings, and rapes would have to relive their trauma and testify again, 15 years after the crimes occurred.

Put simply, the "costs imposed upon the States by retroactive application of new rules of constitutional law on habeas corpus thus generally far outweigh the benefits of this application." Sawyer v. Smith, 497 U.S. 227, 242 (1990). For that reason, the Court has repeatedly stated that new rules of criminal procedure ordinarily do not apply retroactively on federal collateral review.

The Court has identified only one possible exception to that principle. The Court has stated that a new procedural rule will apply retroactively on federal collateral review only if it constitutes a "watershed" rule of criminal procedure. *Teague*, 489 U.S. at 311 (plurality opinion). But the *Teague* Court stated that it was "unlikely" that such watershed "components of basic due process have yet to emerge." And in the 32 years

---

[2]   Before Griffith v. Kentucky, 479 U.S. 314 (1987), the Court sometimes would decline to apply new procedural rules even to cases on *direct* review. See, e.g., Johnson v. New Jersey, 384 U.S. 719, 721 (1966) (rule announced in Miranda v. Arizona, 384 U.S. 436 (1966), applies only to cases in which the trial began after the date of the *Miranda* decision). *Griffith* ended that practice and declared that new rules apply to all cases on direct review.

since *Teague*, as we will explain, the Court has *never* found that any new procedural rule actually satisfies that purported exception.[3]

B

To determine whether *Ramos* applies retroactively on federal collateral review, we must answer two questions.

First, did *Ramos* announce a new rule of criminal procedure, as opposed to applying a settled rule? . . .

Second, if *Ramos* announced a new rule, does it fall within an exception for watershed rules of criminal procedure that apply retroactively on federal collateral review?

1

. . . A rule is new unless it was "*dictated* by precedent existing at the time the defendant's conviction became final." *Teague*, 489 U.S. at 301 (plurality opinion). In other words, a rule is new unless, at the time the conviction became final, the rule was already "apparent to all reasonable jurists." Lambrix v. Singletary, 520 U.S. 518, 528 (1997). The starkest example of a decision announcing a new rule is a decision that overrules an earlier case.

. . . Edwards responds that the Court's decision in *Ramos* must have applied a settled rule, not a new rule, because the decision adhered to the original meaning of the Sixth Amendment's right to a jury trial and the Fourteenth Amendment's incorporation of that right (and others) against the States. That argument conflates the merits question presented in *Ramos* with the retroactivity question presented here. On the merits question, the critical point, as the Court thoroughly explained in *Ramos*, is that the Constitution's text and history require a unanimous jury in state criminal trials. On the retroactivity question, the critical point is that reasonable jurists who considered the question before *Ramos* interpreted *Apodaca* to allow non-unanimous jury verdicts in state criminal trials.

By renouncing *Apodaca* and expressly requiring unanimous jury verdicts in state criminal trials, *Ramos* plainly announced a new rule for purposes of this Court's retroactivity doctrine. . . .

2

. . . This Court has stated that the watershed exception is "extremely narrow" and applies only when, among other things, the new rule alters "our understanding of the bedrock procedural elements essential to the fairness of a proceeding." Whorton v. Bockting, 549 U.S. 406, 417–18 (2007).

---

[3] By contrast, a new *substantive* rule—for example, a rule that particular conduct cannot constitutionally be criminalized—usually applies retroactively on federal collateral review. The parties here agree, as do we, that the rule announced in *Ramos* is procedural. The *Ramos* rule affects "only the manner of determining the defendant's culpability," not the "range of conduct or the class of persons that the law punishes." Schriro v. Summerlin, 542 U.S. 348, 353 (2004).

In the abstract, those various adjectives—watershed, narrow, bedrock, essential—do not tell us much about whether a particular decision of this Court qualifies for the watershed exception. In practice, the exception has been theoretical, not real. The Court has identified only one pre-*Teague* procedural rule as watershed: the right to counsel recognized in the Court's landmark decision in Gideon v. Wainwright, 372 U.S. 335 (1963). See *Whorton*, 549 U.S. at 419, 421. The Court has never identified any other pre-*Teague* or post-*Teague* rule as watershed. None. . . .

The list of cases declining to retroactively apply a new rule of criminal procedure extends back long before *Teague* to some of this Court's most historic criminal procedure decisions. For example, in *Johnson v. New Jersey* the Court declined to retroactively apply *Miranda* . . . . And in *Linkletter v. Walker* the Court refused to retroactively apply *Mapp v. Ohio*.

Edwards seeks to distinguish *Ramos* from the long line of cases where the Court has declined to retroactively apply new procedural rules. Edwards emphasizes three aspects of *Ramos*: (i) the significance of the jury-unanimity right; (ii) *Ramos*'s reliance on the original meaning of the Constitution; and (iii) the effect of *Ramos* in preventing racial discrimination in the jury process.

But Edwards's attempts to distinguish *Ramos* are unavailing because the Court has already considered and rejected those kinds of arguments in prior retroactivity cases.

First, Edwards emphasizes the significance of the jury-unanimity right for criminal defendants. But that argument for retroactivity cannot be squared with the Court's decisions in Duncan v. Louisiana, 391 U.S. 145 (1968), and DeStefano v. Woods, 392 U.S. 631, 635 (1968). In *Duncan*, the Court repudiated several precedents and ruled that a defendant has a constitutional right to a jury trial in a state criminal case. Notwithstanding the extraordinary significance of *Duncan* in guaranteeing a jury trial and expanding the rights of criminal defendants, the Court in *DeStefano* declined to retroactively apply the jury right. We cannot discern a principled basis for retroactively applying the subsidiary *Ramos* jury-unanimity right when the Court in *DeStefano* declined to retroactively apply the broader jury right itself.

Second, Edwards stresses that *Ramos* relied on the original meaning of the Sixth Amendment. But that argument for retroactivity is inconsistent with Crawford v. Washington, 541 U.S. 36 (2004), and Whorton v. Bockting, 549 U.S. 406. In *Crawford*, the Court relied on the original meaning of the Sixth Amendment's Confrontation Clause to overrule precedent and restrict the use of hearsay evidence against criminal defendants. Notwithstanding *Crawford*'s reliance on the original meaning of the Sixth Amendment, the Court in *Whorton* declined to retroactively apply *Crawford*.

Third, Edwards says that *Ramos* prevents racial discrimination by ensuring that the votes of all jurors, regardless of race, matter in the jury room. But that argument for retroactivity cannot prevail in light of Batson v. Kentucky, 476 U.S. 79 (1986), and *Allen v. Hardy.* In *Batson,* the Court overruled precedent and revolutionized day-to-day jury selection by holding that state prosecutors may not discriminate on the basis of race when exercising individual peremptory challenges. Nonetheless, the Court in *Allen* declined to retroactively apply *Batson.*

The Court's decisions in *Duncan, Crawford,* and *Batson* were momentous and consequential. All three decisions fundamentally reshaped criminal procedure throughout the United States and significantly expanded the constitutional rights of criminal defendants. . . . Yet the Court did not apply any of those decisions retroactively on federal collateral review. *Ramos* is likewise momentous and consequential. But we see no good rationale for treating *Ramos* differently from *Duncan, Crawford,* and *Batson.* Consistent with the Court's long line of retroactivity precedents, we hold that the *Ramos* jury-unanimity rule does not apply retroactively on federal collateral review.[6]

In so concluding, we recognize that the Court's many retroactivity precedents taken together raise a legitimate question: If landmark and historic criminal procedure decisions—including *Mapp, Miranda, Duncan, Crawford, Batson,* and now *Ramos*—do not apply retroactively on federal collateral review, how can any additional new rules of criminal procedure apply retroactively on federal collateral review? At this point, some 32 years after *Teague,* we think the only candid answer is that none can—that is, no new rules of criminal procedure can satisfy the watershed exception. We cannot responsibly continue to suggest otherwise to litigants and courts. [F]or decades, the Court has rejected watershed status for new procedural rule after new procedural rule, amply demonstrating that the purported exception has become an empty promise.

Continuing to articulate a theoretical exception that never actually applies in practice offers false hope to defendants, distorts the law, misleads judges, and wastes the resources of defense counsel, prosecutors, and courts. Moreover, no one can reasonably rely on an exception that is non-existent in practice, so no reliance interests can be affected by forthrightly acknowledging reality. It is time—probably long past time—to make explicit what has become increasingly apparent to bench and bar over the last 32 years: New procedural rules do not apply retroactively on federal collateral review. . . .

3

We respectfully offer four responses to the dissent.

---

[6]   The *Ramos* rule does not apply retroactively on *federal* collateral review. States remain free, if they choose, to retroactively apply the jury-unanimity rule as a matter of state law in state post-conviction proceedings. See Danforth v. Minnesota, 552 U.S. 264, 282 (2008).

First, in the dissent's view, if a right is important enough to justify overruling or repudiating precedent (as in *Ramos*), then it often is important enough to apply retroactively as a watershed rule of criminal procedure. But the Court's precedents say the opposite and demonstrate that the dissent's position erroneously inverts stare decisis and *Teague*. *Teague* recognized that the Court would occasionally announce new rules of criminal procedure by overruling or repudiating existing precedents. *Teague* further explained, however, that it was "unlikely" that such new procedural rules would apply retroactively on federal collateral review. In other words, under this Court's longstanding case law, it is easier to overrule or repudiate a precedent—as the Court did in *Mapp*, *Miranda*, *Duncan*, *Batson*, and *Crawford*, for example—than it is to apply the new procedural rule retroactively on federal collateral review—as demonstrated by the Court's corresponding non-retroactivity decisions in *Linkletter*, *Johnson*, *DeStefano*, *Allen*, and *Whorton*.

The *Ramos* Court fully understood all of this. Although *Ramos* stopped short of expressly deciding this retroactivity question (because it was not squarely presented), *Ramos* discussed retroactivity and plainly foreshadowed today's decision. The lead opinion in *Ramos*—which was joined in relevant part by two of today's dissenters [Justices Breyer and Sotomayor]. . . —explained that overruling or repudiating *Apodaca* was not likely to significantly affect Louisiana's and Oregon's reliance interests in preserving final convictions because *Ramos* was not likely to apply retroactively on federal collateral review. In particular, the lead opinion said that the States' "worries" about *Ramos* applying retroactively and overturning hundreds of final convictions outstripped "the facts" because "*Teague*'s test is a demanding one, so much so that this Court has yet to announce a new rule of criminal procedure capable of meeting it." The lead opinion added that *Teague* is "demanding by design, expressly calibrated to address the reliance interests States have in the finality of their criminal judgments." In light of that explicit language in *Ramos*, the Court's decision today can hardly come as a surprise. . . .

Second, the dissent suggests that the Court knows that *Ramos* should apply retroactively under the watershed exception, but wants to avoid applying *Ramos* retroactively, and for that reason has decided to just eliminate the watershed exception altogether. That suggestion is unfounded. *Ramos* was a momentous decision, and those of us who joined it continue to agree with it. But as we have explained, *Ramos* itself analyzed the Court's retroactivity precedents and foretold today's decision on retroactivity. We are simply following through on what *Ramos* (as well as the Court's many other precedents) already said about retroactivity to now squarely hold that *Ramos* does not apply retroactively on federal collateral review. . . . After reaching that conclusion, we then took account of the overall jurisprudential landscape of the last several decades in *Teague* cases and acknowledged what has become unmistakably clear: The purported watershed exception is moribund.

Third, on that last point, the dissent responds that *Teague* nominally identified a retroactivity exception for watershed procedural rules and that we should do so as well. But the problem, as we see it, is that *Teague* simultaneously said that it was "unlikely" that new procedural rules would qualify as watershed. So *Teague* took with one hand what it seemingly gave with the other. And in the 32 years since *Teague*, this Court has never once held that a new procedural rule qualifies for the purported watershed exception. What is more, the Court has regularly repeated that *Teague*'s watershed exception would likely never be satisfied. The Court today need not and does not overrule any post-*Teague* cases that held the watershed exception satisfied because there are no post-*Teague* cases that held the watershed exception satisfied.

As noted above, no stare decisis values would be served by continuing to indulge the fiction that *Teague*'s purported watershed exception endures. No one can reasonably rely on a supposed exception that has never operated in practice. And perpetuating what has become an illusory exception misleads litigants and judges, and needlessly expends the scarce resources of defense counsel, prosecutors, and courts. At this point, given that landmark cases like *Mapp*, *Miranda*, *Duncan*, *Batson*, *Crawford*, and now *Ramos* have not applied retroactively, we are simply acknowledging reality and stating the obvious: The purported watershed exception retains no vitality.

Fourth, the dissent asserts that the Court is not living up to the promise of *Ramos* for criminal defendants. To begin with, the dissent cannot reasonably charge the Court with failing to live up to *Ramos* given that *Ramos* itself explicitly forecast today's decision on retroactivity. Moreover, with respect, Justice Kagan dissented in *Ramos*. To be sure, the dissent's position on the jury-unanimity rule in *Ramos* was perfectly legitimate, as is the dissent's position on retroactivity in today's case. And it is of course fair for a dissent to vigorously critique the Court's analysis. But it is another thing altogether to dissent in *Ramos* and then to turn around and impugn today's majority for supposedly shortchanging criminal defendants. To properly assess the implications for criminal defendants, one should assess the implications of *Ramos* and today's ruling *together*. And criminal defendants as a group are better off under *Ramos* and today's decision, taken together, than they would have been if Justice Kagan's dissenting view had prevailed in *Ramos*. If the dissent's view had prevailed in *Ramos*, no defendant would ever be entitled to the jury-unanimity right—not on collateral review, not on direct review, and not in the future. By contrast, under the Court's holdings in *Ramos* and this case, criminal defendants whose cases are still on direct review or whose cases arise in the future will have the benefit of the jury-unanimity right announced in *Ramos*. The rhetoric in today's dissent is misdirected. Different Members of the Court have reached different conclusions in *Ramos* and in this case, but each Member of the Court has acted in good faith in deciding the difficult questions before us.

* * *

To summarize the Court's retroactivity principles: New substantive rules alter "the range of conduct or the class of persons that the law punishes." *Summerlin*, 542 U.S. at 353. Those new substantive rules apply to cases pending in trial courts and on direct review, and they also apply retroactively on federal collateral review. New procedural rules alter "only the manner of determining the defendant's culpability." Id. Those new procedural rules apply to cases pending in trial courts and on direct review. But new procedural rules do not apply retroactively on federal collateral review.

Ramos announced a new rule of criminal procedure. It does not apply retroactively on federal collateral review. We affirm the judgment of the U.S. Court of Appeals for the Fifth Circuit.

It is so ordered.

[The concurring opinions of Justice Thomas, joined by Justice Gorsuch, and Justice Gorsuch, joined by Justice Thomas, have been omitted.]

■ JUSTICE KAGAN, with whom JUSTICE BREYER and JUSTICE SOTOMAYOR join, dissenting.

. . . Citing centuries of history, the Court in *Ramos* termed the Sixth Amendment right to a unanimous jury "vital," "essential," "indispensable," and "fundamental" to the American legal system. The Court therefore saw fit to disregard stare decisis and overturn a 50-year-old precedent enabling States to convict criminal defendants based on non-unanimous verdicts.[1] And in taking that weighty step, the Court also vindicated core principles of racial justice. For in the Court's view, the state laws countenancing non-unanimous verdicts originated in white supremacism and continued in our own time to have racially discriminatory effects. Put all that together, and it is easy to see why the opinions in *Ramos* read as historic. Rarely does this Court make such a fundamental change in the rules thought necessary to ensure fair criminal process. If you were scanning a thesaurus for a single word to describe the decision, you would stop when you came to "watershed."

Yet the Court insists that *Ramos*'s holding does not count as a "watershed" procedural rule under Teague v. Lane, 489 U.S. 288, 311 (1989) (plurality opinion). The result of today's ruling is easily stated. *Ramos* will not apply retroactively, meaning that a prisoner whose appeals ran out before the decision can receive no aid from the change in law it made. So Thedrick Edwards, unlike Evangelisto Ramos, will serve the rest of his life in prison based on a 10-to-2 jury verdict. Only the reasoning of today's holding resists explanation. The majority cannot (and indeed does

---

[1]   I dissented in *Ramos* precisely because of its abandonment of stare decisis. [Citing the Alito dissent in *Ramos* that she joined and] Kimble v. Marvel Entertainment, LLC, 576 U.S. 446, 455 (2015) ("Respecting stare decisis means sticking to some wrong decisions"). Now that *Ramos* is the law, stare decisis is on its side. I take the decision on its own terms, and give it all the consequence it deserves.

not) deny, given all *Ramos* said, that the jury unanimity requirement fits
to a tee *Teague*'s description of a watershed procedural rule. . . .

                                   I

[E]verything rests on the majority's last move—the overturning of
Teague's watershed exception. If there can never be *any* watershed
rules—as the majority here asserts out of the blue—then, yes, jury unanimity cannot be one. The result follows trippingly from the premise. But
adopting the premise requires departing from judicial practice and principle. In overruling a critical aspect of *Teague*, the majority follows none
of the usual rules of stare decisis. It discards precedent without a party
requesting that action. And it does so with barely a reason given, much
less the "special justification" our law demands. The majority in that way
compounds its initial error: Not content to misapply *Teague*'s watershed
provision here, the majority forecloses any future application. It prevents
any procedural rule ever—no matter how integral to adjudicative fairness—from benefiting a defendant on habeas review. Thus does a settled
principle of retroactivity law die, in an effort to support an insupportable
ruling. . . .

The first clue that the unanimity rule falls within *Teague*'s small
core is that the Court thought its adoption justified overturning precedent. *Ramos* didn't just announce a new rule. It reversed a prior, well-
settled one. . . . Such a toppling of precedent needs a special justification—more than a run-of-the-mill claim of error. To meet that demand,
the *Ramos* majority described *Apodaca* as flouting the essential "meaning of the Sixth Amendment's jury trial right," as revealed in both historical practice and judicial decisions. Two concurring Justices added, to
support discarding this "egregiously wrong" precedent, that the unanimity rule prevents improper verdicts: *Apodaca* "sanctions the conviction"
of some defendants who would otherwise defeat the State's efforts "to
[meet] its burden" of proving guilt. [Citing opinions by Justices Kavanaugh and Sotomayor.] And the majority and concurrences alike invoked racial justice to support abandoning stare decisis, explaining how
a non-unanimity rule has posed a special danger of canceling Black jurors' votes. [Again citing opinions by Justices Kavanaugh and Sotomayor.] At bottom, then, the Court took the unusual step of overruling
precedent for the most fundamental of reasons: the need to ensure, in
keeping with the Nation's oldest traditions, fair and dependable adjudi-
cations of a defendant's guilt. In this much alone, *Ramos*'s reasoning
evokes this Court's descriptions of watershed rules.[3]

---

[3]   The majority misunderstands my point about the interaction between stare decisis and
Teague. I am not saying that if a "right is important enough to justify overruling" precedent,
then it is "important enough to apply retroactively." . . . Rather, the overruling of precedent—
and more, the justifications given to support that overruling—are elements to consider when
deciding on a rule's watershed status. . . . *Ramos* overturned precedent (rather than just announcing a new rule) on grounds strikingly reminiscent of *Teague*'s criteria for watershed status. . . .

And putting talk of stare decisis aside, there remains much more in *Ramos* to echo *Teague*. If, as today's majority says, *Teague* is full of "adjectives," so too is *Ramos*—and mostly the same ones. Jury unanimity, the Court pronounced, is an "essential element[ ]" of the jury trial right, and thus is "fundamental to the American scheme of justice." The Court discussed the rule's "ancient" history—"400 years of English and American cases requiring unanimity" leading up to the Sixth Amendment. As early as the 14th century, English common law recognized jury unanimity as a "vital right." Adopting that view, the early American States likewise treated unanimity as an "essential feature of the jury trial." So by the time the Framers drafted the Sixth Amendment, "the right to a jury trial *meant* a trial in which the jury renders a unanimous verdict." Because that was so, no jury verdict could stand (or in some metaphysical sense, even exist) absent full agreement: "A verdict, taken from eleven, was no verdict at all." Unanimity served as a critical safeguard, needed to protect against wrongful deprivations of citizens' "hard-won liberty." Or as Justice Story summarized the law a few decades after the Founding: To obtain a conviction, "unanimity in the verdict of the jury is indispensable."

If a rule so understood isn't a watershed one, then nothing is. (And that is, of course, what the majority eventually says.) Once more, from the quotations just above: "fundamental," "essential," "vital," "indispensable." No wonder today's majority declares a new-found aversion to "adjectives" . . . The unanimity rule, as *Ramos* described it, is as "bedrock" as bedrock comes. It is as grounded in the Nation's constitutional traditions—with centuries-old practice becoming part of the Sixth Amendment's original meaning. And it is as central to the Nation's idea of a fair and reliable guilty verdict. . . . For only then is the jury's finding of guilt certain enough—secure enough, mistake-proof enough—to take away the person's freedom. . . .

And something still more supports retroactivity here, for the opinions in *Ramos* . . . relied on a strong claim about racial injustice. The Court detailed the origins of Louisiana's and Oregon's non-unanimity rules, locating them (respectively) in a convention to "establish the supremacy of the white race" and "the rise of the Ku Klux Klan." Those rules, the Court explained, were meant "to dilute the influence [on juries] of racial, ethnic, and religious minorities"—and particularly, "to ensure that African-American juror service would be meaningless." Two concurring opinions linked that history to current practice. "In light of the[ir] racist origins," Justice Kavanaugh stated, "it is no surprise that non-unanimous juries can make a difference"—that "[t]hen and now" they can "negate the votes of black jurors, especially in cases with black defendants."[a] But that statement precludes today's result. If the old rule

---

[a] The jury in Edwards' case consisted of JonRe Taylor, a Black woman, and "six older white men and five older white women." Brief of Amicus Curiae JonRe Taylor in Support of Petitioner, *Edwards v. Vannoy*, p. 3. Taylor was the only one to vote not guilty on all charges. Her brief makes the case, inter alia, for her not guilty vote.—[Footnote by eds.]

functioned "as an engine of discrimination against black defendants," [quoting the Kavanaugh concurrence], its replacement must "implicat[e]" (as watershed rules do) "the fundamental fairness and accuracy of the criminal proceeding," Or as Justice Kavanaugh put the point more concretely, the unanimity rule then helps prevent "racial prejudice" from resulting in wrongful convictions. The rule should therefore apply not just forward but back, to all convictions rendered absent its protection.

II

The majority argues in reply that the jury unanimity rule is not so fundamental because . . . . Well, no, scratch that. Actually, the majority doesn't contest anything I've said about the foundations and functions of the unanimity requirement. Nor could the majority reasonably do so. For everything I've said about the unanimity rule comes straight out of *Ramos*'s majority and concurring opinions. Just check the citations: I've added barely a word to what those opinions (often with soaring rhetoric) proclaim. Start with history. The ancient foundations of the unanimous jury rule? Check. The inclusion of that rule in the Sixth Amendment's original meaning? Check. Now go to function. The fundamental (or bedrock or central) role of the unanimous jury in the American system of criminal justice? Check. The way unanimity figures in ensuring fairness in criminal trials and protecting against wrongful guilty verdicts? Check. The link between those purposes and safeguarding the jury system from (past and present) racial prejudice? Check. In sum: As to every feature of the unanimity rule conceivably relevant to watershed status, *Ramos* has already given the answer— check, check, check—and today's majority can say nothing to the contrary.[5]

Instead, the majority relies on decisions holding non-retroactive various other—even though dissimilar—procedural rules. In making that argument from past practice, the majority adopts two discrete tactics. Call the first "throw everything against the wall." Call the second "slice and dice." Neither can avail to render the jury unanimity rule anything less than what *Ramos* thought it—as the majority concedes, "momentous."

As its first move, the majority lists as many decisions holding rules non-retroactive as it can muster. The premise here is that sheer volume matters: The majority presents the catalog as if every rule is as important as every other and as if comparing any to the unanimity requirement is

---

[5] The majority does try to say that the plurality opinion in *Ramos* nonetheless "plainly foreshadowed today's decision" by noting that *Teague*'s watershed test was "demanding by design," in recognition of the States' reliance interests. But the *Ramos* plurality's description of the watershed test was nothing more than objective fact: Yes, the watershed test was purposefully demanding. As to whether the watershed test was *so* demanding as to exclude the jury unanimity rule, here is what the plurality had to say: "Whether the right to jury unanimity applies to cases on collateral review is a question for a future case where the parties will have a chance to brief the issue and we will benefit from their adversarial presentation." Not a lot of "plain[ ] foreshadow[ing]" there. Only a fair bit of wisdom about how to resolve legal issues— which, as I'll later discuss, the majority could usefully have considered before overruling the watershed exception.

beside the point. But that idea founders on this Court's constant refrain that watershed rules are only a small subset of procedural rules. For under that view (as under the very meaning of "watershed"), nothing could be less surprising than that non-watershed rules greatly outnumber watershed ones. That inexorable fact cannot refute the designation of any given rule—much less of jury unanimity—as watershed. And the majority's kitchen-sink list becomes yet less probative of the issue here because most of its bulk comes from decisions on sentencing. But *Teague* itself explains why sentencing procedures are not watershed: A watershed rule, the Court said there, must go to the jury's "determination of innocence or guilt." So the majority's indiscriminate inventory of non-retroactive rules cannot get it home.

Enter the majority's second stratagem, which tries to conquer by dividing. Here, the majority picks out "three aspects of *Ramos*" pointing toward watershed status, and names one prior decision to match each of the three. So in addressing the unanimity rule's "significance," the majority notes that the Court once held the jury-trial right non-retroactive. In tackling *Ramos*'s return to "original meaning," the majority points to our decision that an originalist rule about hearsay evidence should not apply backward. And in discussing *Ramos*'s role in "prevent[ing] racial discrimination," the majority invokes our denial of retroactivity to a rule making it easier to prove race-based peremptory strikes.

What the majority doesn't find—or even pretend to—is any decision corresponding to *Ramos* on all of those dimensions. Take just a pair of examples. The Court has never suggested that requiring a bench trial has race-based purposes or effects.[6] Similarly, the Court thought its new rule on hearsay evidence of less than towering import: Calling the rule "limited in scope," we doubted that it would have any effect on the "accuracy of factfinding." I'll resist making like points about other permutations because the main point here is a general one. The majority must slice and dice in this way—dividing *Ramos* into three for purposes of comparison—because it cannot find any rule analogous to jury unanimity on all relevant fronts. And that is for a simple reason: No procedure adopted since *Teague* so comprehensively fulfills that decision's criteria for retroactivity. If any rule is watershed, it is jury unanimity.

So the majority is left to overrule *Teague*'s holding on watershed rules.[7] On the last page or so of its merits discussion (before it turns to pre-butting this dissent), the majority eliminates the watershed

---

[6] Even on the metric of significance alone, the Court has not previously ranked the jury-unanimity and jury-trial rights as today's majority does. [Justice Kagan referred to a prior case where a plurality opinion suggested that "the accuracy and fairness concerns raised by divided juries—where, by definition, at least one person retains reasonable doubt—exceed those arising from judicial verdicts."] In insisting otherwise, the majority falls prey to a common greater-includes-the-lesser fallacy—akin to the view that if a State can eliminate a jury, it can impose jury rules of whatever kind it likes.

[7] In describing the majority as overruling *Teague*, I do not mean it overrules only *Teague*. That decision doesn't stand alone in stating the watershed exception as governing law. As I count, the Court has recited the exception 17 more times before today. [Citing cases.]

exception, declaring it "long past time" to do so. *Teague* had said there would not be "many" (retroactive) watershed rules. The majority now says there will be none at all. If that is so, of course, jury unanimity cannot be watershed. Finally, the majority offers an intelligible reason for declining to apply *Ramos* retroactively.

But in taking that road, the majority breaks a core judicial rule: respect for precedent. Stare decisis is a foundation stone of the rule of law, "promot[ing] the evenhanded, predictable, and consistent development of legal principles, foster[ing] reliance on judicial decisions, and contribut[ing] to the actual and perceived integrity of the judicial process." Payne v. Tennessee, 501 U.S. 808, 827 (1991). Adherence to precedent is, of course, "not an inexorable command." Id. at 828. *Ramos* itself teaches that much. But *Ramos* also shows how high stare decisis sets the bar for overruling a prior decision. To reverse course, we insist on compelling reasons, thorough explanation, and careful attention to competing interests. But not here. The majority crawls under, rather than leaps over, the stare decisis bar.

To begin with, no one here asked us to overrule *Teague*. This Court usually confines itself to the issues raised and briefed by the parties. There may be reasons to ignore that rule in one or another everyday case. But to do so in pursuit of overturning precedent is nothing short of extraordinary. Cf. *Ramos*, 590 U.S. at ___, n. 4 (Kavanaugh, J.) (An "important factor" protecting stare decisis "is that the Court typically does not overrule a precedent unless a party requests overruling"). We are supposed to (fairly) apply the prevailing law until a party asks us to change it. And when a party does make that request, we are supposed to attend to countervailing arguments—which no one here had a chance to make. That orderly process, skipped today, is what enables a court to arrive at a considered decision about whether to overthrow precedent.

Equally striking, the majority gives only the sketchiest of reasons for reversing *Teague*'s watershed exception. In deciding whether to depart from precedent, the Court usually considers—and usually at length—a familiar set of factors capable of providing the needed special justification. The majority can't be bothered with that customary, and disciplining, practice; it barely goes through the motions. Seldom has this Court so casually, so off-handedly, tossed aside precedent. In its page of analysis, the majority offers just one ground for its decision—that since *Teague*, the Court has not identified a new rule as watershed, and so "the purported exception has become an empty promise." But even viewed in the abstract, that argument does not fly. That the Court has not found a watershed rule since *Teague* does not mean it could or would not in the future. *Teague* itself understood that point: It saw value in the watershed exception even while recognizing that watershed rules would be few and far between. And viewed in the context of this case, the majority's argument positively craters. For the majority today comes face-to-face with a rule that perfectly fits each of *Teague*'s criteria: Jury unanimity, as described in *Ramos*, is watershed—even though no prior rule was. That airtight match between *Ramos* and *Teague* refutes the majority's one stated reason for overruling the latter decision. The majority could not rely on the absence of watershed rules to topple *Teague* if it had just faithfully applied that decision to this case.

In choosing otherwise, the majority imposes a steep price for over-ruling *Apodaca* in *Ramos*. Taking with one hand what it gave with the other, the Court curtails *Ramos*'s effects by expunging *Teague*'s provision for watershed rules. And so too the Court limits the consequences of any similarly fundamental change in criminal procedure that may emerge in the future. For the first time in many decades . . ., those convicted under rules found not to produce fair and reliable verdicts will be left without recourse in federal courts.[8]

I would not discard *Teague*'s watershed exception and so keep those unfairly convicted people from getting new trials. Instead, I would accept the consequences of last Term's holding in *Ramos*. A decision like that comes with a promise, or at any rate should. If the right to a unanimous jury is so fundamental—if a verdict rendered by a divided jury is "no ver-dict at all"—then Thedrick Edwards should not spend his life behind bars over two jurors' opposition. I respectfully dissent.

NOTES ON THE TEAGUE "WATERSHED" EXCEPTION

1. *TEAGUE V. LANE*

Teague v. Lane, 489 U.S. 288 (1989), established the proposition that the Court normally will not develop or apply new constitutional rules in fed-eral habeas review of state convictions. The Court had held in Taylor v Lou-isiana, 419 U.S. 522 (1975), that the Sixth Amendment required that the jury venire be drawn from a fair cross-section of the community. The question in *Teague* was whether this requirement should be extended to the petit jury. The case came to the Supreme Court after lower federal courts had denied habeas corpus relief following the affirmance of Taylor's state court convic-tions for six serious felonies.

Writing for four Justices,[a] Justice O'Connor began by noting that the Court had in the past adopted new constitutional rules of criminal procedure in habeas cases. Although the new rule was always applied in the case before

---

[8] The majority's final claim is that it is properly immune from this criticism—that I can-not "turn around and impugn" its ruling—because "criminal defendants as a group are better off under *Ramos* and today's decision, taken together, than they would have been if [my] dis-senting view had prevailed in *Ramos*." The suggestion is surprising. It treats judging as score-keeping—and more, as scorekeeping about how much our decisions, or the aggregate of them, benefit a particular kind of party. I see the matter differently. Judges should take cases one at a time, and do their best in each to apply the relevant legal rules. And when judges err, others should point out where they went astray. No one gets to bank capital for future cases; no one's past decisions insulate them from criticism. The focus always is, or should be, getting the case before us right.

[a] She was joined by Chief Justice Rehnquist and Justices Scalia and Kennedy. The O'Con-nor approach became the Court's view when Justice White added his support in Penry v. Lynaugh, 492 U.S. 302 (1989).

the Court, it was sometimes held non-retroactive and therefore unavailable to later habeas petitioners. These "non-retroactivity" pronouncements were usually left to later cases, but occasionally the Court addressed retroactivity when announcing the new rule. Hereafter, O'Connor said, the approach should be different:

> Retroactivity is properly treated as a threshold question, for, once a new rule is applied to the defendant in the case announcing the rule, evenhanded justice requires that it be applied retroactively to all who are similarly situated. Thus, before deciding whether the fair cross section requirement should be extended to the petit jury, we should ask whether such a rule would be applied retroactively to the case at issue.

O'Connor then applied the analysis outlined in *Edwards*, holding that the petitioner's claim sought a "new" rule that should not be applied retroactively. The lower court denial of relief, she concluded, was therefore correct regardless of the merits of the underlying Sixth Amendment question.

2.   THE GORSUCH CONCURRENCE IN *EDWARDS*

The Gorsuch concurrence in *Edwards* summarized the history of habeas at common law and in the federal courts:

> Leading up to the English Civil War, monarchs sometimes jailed their subjects summarily and indefinitely, with little explanation and even less process. In response, common law courts developed the [habeas corpus] ad subjiciendum writ to force the Crown to provide reasons for its actions and, if necessary, to ensure adequate process—like a criminal trial—to justify any further detention.

> Great though it was, the writ's power was never limitless. A prisoner confined under a final judgment of conviction by a court of competent jurisdiction stood on different footing than one confined by the King without trial. A court might issue the writ asking, "What is the reason for confinement?" But if the return came back: "Because he's serving a custodial sentence after being convicted of a crime," the inquiry was usually at an end. Custody pursuant to a final judgment was *proof* that a defendant had received the process due to him.

He added that "one important exception existed both here and in England. A habeas court could grant relief if the court of conviction lacked jurisdiction over the defendant or his offense."

He noted that the federal courts adhered to this structure when Congress authorized habeas for federal prisoners, and continued to do so after the Civil War when Congress granted federal courts the power to issue habeas writs to state authorities: "If a prisoner was in custody pursuant to a final state court judgment, a federal court was powerless to revisit those proceedings unless the state court had acted without jurisdiction."

When he reached *Brown v. Allen* in his historical progression, Gorsuch said that habeas corpus was transformed into "little more than an ordinary appeal with an extraordinary Latin name." And the "proliferation of new federal procedural rights, combined with a federal post-conviction mechanism that functioned like an ordinary appeal, soon yielded a giant haystack of habeas petitions." "It was only in this world," he said, "that *Teague*'s question about the retroactive application of new 'watershed' rules of criminal procedure could even begin to make sense." He continued:

> Exercising [its] remedial discretion, the Court began to develop doctrines aimed at returning the Great Writ closer to its historic office. It decided that some claims are not cognizable on federal habeas review if state courts provide a mechanism for review. Stone v. Powell, 428 U.S. 465 (1976). It established procedural default rules to prevent habeas petitioners from evading independent and adequate state law grounds for sustaining their convictions. Wainwright v. Sykes, 433 U.S. 72 (1977). It crafted a heightened harmless error standard, calibrated to reflect the finality interests at stake in the post-conviction context. Brecht v. Abrahamson, 507 U.S. 619 (1993). And it applied abuse-of-the-writ rules to prevent an endless cycle of petition and re-petition by prisoners with nothing but time on their hands. McCleskey v. Zant, 499 U.S. 467 (1991).
>
> Chief among these new-but-old developments was *Teague*. . . .

Gorsuch then described *Teague* and its "watershed" exception, and concluded:

> If so many other highly consequential rulings have failed to clear *Teague*'s bar, it's hard to see how *Ramos* might. One could even say that any other result would defy this Court's recent precedents.
>
> At the same time, though, one might *also* say these precedents illustrate how mystifying the whole *Teague* project has been from its inception. If *Teague* only prohibits the retroactive application of *new* rules of criminal procedure, after all, it's not exactly obvious why that prohibition applies to cases like *Crawford* or *Ramos*. Both decisions sought to realign this Court's decisions with the original meaning of the Sixth Amendment; in that sense, the rights they recognized were anything but new. And to the extent *Teague* asks whether a new rule is "fundamental" or "bedrock," it's hard to see how rights originally memorialized in the Constitution could fail to qualify. Certainly, this Court is in no position to second-guess the judgment of those who wrote and ratified the Constitution. Surely, too, many of the other rules of criminal procedure this Court has found less than "fundamental" since *Teague* seem anything but that to those whose lives they affect. Nor is it only *Teague*'s results that mystify. The test itself has been fraught with contradictions from the start. It asks litigants to be on the lookout for new procedural protections "implicit in the concept of ordered liberty." At the

same time, we have been told, the fact that "a new procedural rule is 'fundamental' in some abstract sense is not enough."

For me, it's here where the history canvassed above matters. This Court's (in)activity since *Teague* only begins to make sense when viewed against the backdrop of the traditional rule that old judgments are impervious to new challenges. Yes, this Court's decisions should apply to all cases pending in trial courts and on direct appeal. But they should not apply retroactively in habeas. The reason has nothing to do with whether Members of this Court happen to think the rules they announce are "new" in some sense or insufficiently "fundamental" in another. It's simpler than that: The writ of habeas corpus does not authorize federal courts to reopen a judgment issued by a court of competent of jurisdiction once it has become final.

Earlier, Gorsuch had added his sixth footnote:

Teague also discussed an exception to the finality rule for certain "substantive rules." Because the parties agree that *Ramos* involved only a new rule of criminal procedure, little need be said about *Teague*'s "substantive rule" exception. But it is worth noting that substantive rules, which place certain conduct " 'beyond the power of the criminal law-making authority to prescribe' " bear at least some resemblance to this Court's early cases finding a lack of jurisdiction over a defendant or an offense. Perhaps this aspect of *Teague* can be understood as accurately invoking the jurisdictional exception to the finality rule; perhaps not. But that question is for another day.

Note the potential significance of Justice Gorsuch's conclusion. Joined by Justice Thomas, he all but says that the regime of *Brown v. Allen* should no longer be followed—*all* merits review of a state criminal conviction that has become final should be foreclosed on federal habeas corpus. The *only* clear exception is a lack of jurisdiction in the convicting court, a situation that according to his footnote 6 might (but might not) exist if it failed properly to apply a new (or presumably old) "substantive" rule of federal constitutional law. Whether a lack of jurisdiction under state law would qualify would raise a tantalizing possibility, but presumably would be extremely rare in any event.

The Gorsuch position also suggests an intriguing irony. The Antiterrorism and Effective Death Penalty Act of 1996 (AEDPA), considered in Section 2 of this Chapter, is usually regarded as enacting significant limitations on the scope of merits review permitted by the *Brown v. Allen* regime. If Justice Gorsuch's view were to prevail, however, AEDPA would not have this effect. Rather, its effect would be to *enlarge* federal habeas by permitting review of state criminal cases on grounds other than a lack of jurisdiction. Since AEDPA authorized reviews of state convictions on the merits, albeit by a highly deferential standard, it might have ratified a modest version of *Brown v. Allen* and therefore undermined Justice Gorsuch's reliance on limitations inherent in the historical function of habeas corpus. Stay tuned.

3. QUESTIONS AND COMMENTS ON *EDWARDS*

The Gorsuch concurrence described *Teague* as saying that a "watershed" rule "would do two things: (1) 'significantly improve' existing procedures for determining factual guilt or innocence and (2) 'implicate the fundamental fairness of the trial.'" It is hard to say, as he added, that all, or perhaps even many, of the situations where the Court declined to hold new rights retroactive under this formula did not satisfy this inquiry.

Plainly something else is going on, most likely the traditional trade-off between the protections afforded by the newly announced rights and the state's interest in the finality of its criminal convictions. Justice Kavanaugh's opinion for the Court in *Edwards* all but makes plain that the state's finality interest is the Court's primary motivation. How should this balance be struck? Who has the better of the debate between the Court and Justice Kagan? From another perspective, given the fact that virtually no rulings have satisfied the *Teague* standard in the past or are likely to do so in the foreseeable future, was the Court right to put the issue to rest? Will the *Edwards* result tie the hands of a future Court with a different composition? Was that the point?

Consider another angle. The Court acknowledged with apparent approval that the *Gideon v. Wainwright* right-to-counsel requirement satisfied the "watershed" standard. Does this conclusion survive *Edwards*? If the Court at some point recognizes a new wrinkle to the *Gideon* requirement, should it be applied retroactively on habeas?

NOTES ON THE TEAGUE "SUBSTANTIVE" EXCEPTION

1. INTRODUCTION

The scope of *Teague*'s "substantive" exception has been actively disputed. In describing the new "substantive" rule exception to its limitation on retroactivity, the *Teague* plurality said that "a new rule should be applied retroactively if it places 'certain kinds of primary, private individual conduct beyond the power of the criminal law-making authority to proscribe.'" The Court added in Penry v. Lynaugh, 492 U.S. 302, 330 (1989):

> [T]he first exception set forth in *Teague* should be understood to cover not only rules forbidding criminal punishment of certain primary conduct but also rules prohibiting a certain category of punishment for a class of defendants because of their status or offense. Thus, if we held, as a substantive matter, that the Eighth Amendment prohibits the execution of mentally retarded persons . . . regardless of the procedures followed, such a rule . . . would be applicable to defendants on collateral review.

Application of the exception involves two steps. The first is whether the rule sought to be applied is "new." The second is whether it is "substantive" or "procedural."

2.   *CHAIDEZ V. UNITED STATES*

When, under *Teague*, is a rule "new"? Justice O'Connor said in *Teague* that "[i]n general . . . a case announces a new rule when it breaks new ground or imposes a new obligation on the States or the Federal Government. . . . To put it differently, a case announces a new rule if the result was not dictated by precedent existing at the time the defendant's conviction became final."

The Court elaborated in Lambrix v. Singletary, 520 U.S. 518 (1997). Justices Stevens, Ginsburg, and Breyer argued that the rule sought to be applied by the habeas applicant was "nothing more than an application of well-settled principles." Speaking for a majority of five (Justice O'Connor dissented on other grounds), Justice Scalia responded:

> Most of [the] dissent is devoted to making a forceful case that [the decision on which the habeas applicant relied] was a reasonable interpretation of prior law—perhaps even the most reasonable one. But the *Teague* inquiry—which is applied to Supreme Court decisions that are, one must hope, usually the most reasonable interpretation of prior law—requires more than that. It asks whether [the decision] was *dictated* by precedent—i.e., whether *no other* interpretation was reasonable.

The Court affirmed this approach in Chaidez v. United States, 568 U.S. 342 (2013). Padilla v. Kentucky, 559 U.S. 356 (2010), held that the Sixth Amendment right to effective assistance of counsel requires that a defendant's attorney provide advice about the risk of deportation arising from a guilty plea. The issue in *Chaidez* was whether *Padilla* applied retroactively to cases that had already become final.

In an opinion by Justice Kagan, the Court said that *Padilla* developed a "new" rule. The majority began by noting that the mere application of a settled principle to a new set of facts does not produce a new rule. That was not, however, the situation here. *Padilla* did not involve merely an application of the standard set forth in the Court's canonical ineffectiveness assistance of counsel decision, Strickland v. Washington, 466 U.S. 668 (1984). Before addressing whether an attorney's failure to provide advice about deportation "fell below an objective standard of reasonableness" under *Strickland*, the majority explained, *Padilla* decided a "threshold question" of whether advice about deportation even falls within the Sixth Amendment right to effective assistance of counsel. Prior to *Padilla*, courts had held that the right to effective assistance of counsel did not apply to advice about "collateral" consequences of a conviction, including deportation, and the Court itself had left that question open. "[W]hen we decided *Padilla*," the majority observed, "we answered a question about the Sixth Amendment's reach that we had left open, in a way that altered the law of most jurisdictions."[a]

---

[a]   In a footnote, the Court added that *Teague* stated two exceptions, but that "Chaidez does not argue that either of those exceptions is relevant here."

3. *BOUSLEY V. UNITED STATES*

When, under *Teague*, is a new rule "substantive"? Bousley v. United States, 523 U.S. 614 (1998), is often cited as an illustration of the substantive-new-rule exception to the *Teague* limitation on retroactivity. An enhanced penalty is provided in 18 U.S.C. § 924(c)(1)(A) for "any person who, during and in relation to any crime of violence or drug trafficking crime . . . for which the person may be prosecuted in a court of the Unites States, uses . . . a firearm. . . ." The Supreme Court held in Bailey v. United States, 516 U.S. 137 (1995), that the phrase "uses . . . a firearm" means "active employment of the firearm," not mere possession. One question in *Bousley* was whether *Bailey* should be applied retroactively to a conviction that occurred five years before *Bailey* was decided. The weapons involved were in close proximity to the site of the drug trafficking, but were not in active use.

The case came to the Supreme Court in review of Bousley's application for post-conviction relief under 28 U.S.C. § 2255.[b] The Court held that "petitioner's claim is not *Teague*-barred":

> [P]etitioner contends that the record reveals that neither he, nor his counsel, nor the court correctly understood the essential elements of the crime with which he was charged. Were this contention proved, petitioner's plea would be . . . constitutionally invalid. . . .
>
> Amicus urges us to apply the rule of *Teague v. Lane* to petitioner's claim that his plea was not knowing and intelligent. In *Teague*, we held that "new constitutional rules of criminal procedure will not be applicable to those cases which have become final before the new rules are announced," unless the new rule "places 'certain kinds of primary, private individual conduct beyond the power of the criminal law-making authority to proscribe,'" or could be considered a "watershed rul[e] of criminal procedure." But we do not believe that *Teague* governs this case. The only constitutional claim made here is that petitioner's guilty plea was not knowing and intelligent. There is surely nothing new about this principle . . . . And because *Teague* by its terms applies only to procedural rules, we think it is inapplicable to the situation in which this Court decides the meaning of a criminal statute enacted by Congress.
>
> This distinction between substance and procedure is an important one in the habeas context. The *Teague* doctrine is founded on the notion that one of the "principal functions of habeas corpus [is] 'to assure that no man has been incarcerated under a procedure which creates an impermissibly large risk that the innocent will be convicted.' Teague v. Lane, 489 U.S. 288, 312 (1989). Consequently, unless a new rule of criminal procedure is of such a nature that "without [it] the likelihood of an accurate conviction is seriously diminished," id. at 313, there is no reason to apply the rule

---

[b]   Although developed in the context of federal habeas for state prisoners, *Teague* has routinely been applied by the Court in the analogous context of § 2255 challenges to federal convictions.

retroactively on habeas review. By contrast, decisions of this Court holding that a substantive federal criminal statute does not reach certain conduct, like decisions placing conduct " 'beyond the power of the criminal law-making authority to proscribe,' " id. at 311, necessarily carry a significant risk that a defendant stands convicted of "an act that the law does not make criminal." Davis v. United States, 417 U.S. 333, 346 (1974). For under our federal system it is only Congress, and not the courts, which can make conduct criminal. Accordingly, it would be inconsistent with the doctrinal underpinnings of habeas review to preclude petitioner from relying on our decision in *Bailey* in support of his claim that his guilty plea was constitutionally invalid.

4.   *SCHRIRO V. SUMMERLIN*

At issue in Schriro v. Summerlin, 542 U.S. 348 (2004), was whether the rule of Ring v. Arizona, 536 U.S. 584 (2002), applied retroactively. *Ring* extended Apprendi v. New Jersey, 530 U.S. 466 (2000), to sentencing criteria applicable in capital cases. *Apprendi* had held that "[o]ther than the fact of a prior conviction, any fact that increases the penalty for a crime beyond the prescribed statutory maximum must be submitted to a jury, and proved beyond a reasonable doubt." Arizona law authorized the death penalty only where there was an aggravating factor. *Ring* held that the *Apprendi* jury-trial and beyond-a-reasonable-doubt requirements applied to such aggravating factors.

One question in *Schriro* was whether *Ring* should be retroactively applied as a new "watershed" rule of criminal procedure. As noted in *Edwards*, the Court said "no." *Schriro* also raised the issue whether the rule of *Ring* fell within the "substantive" rule exception to *Teague* non-retroactivity. In an opinion by Justice Scalia, the Court said:

> New *substantive* rules generally apply retroactively. This includes decisions that narrow the scope of a criminal statute by interpreting its terms, see Bousley v. United States, 523 U.S. 614, 620–621 (1998), as well as constitutional determinations that place particular conduct or persons covered by the statute beyond the State's power to punish. Such rules apply retroactively because they "necessarily carry a significant risk that a defendant stands convicted of 'an act that the law does not make criminal' " or faces a punishment that the law cannot impose upon him. . . . New rules of procedure, on the other hand, generally do not apply retroactively. They do not produce a class of persons convicted of conduct the law does not make criminal, but merely raise the possibility that someone convicted with use of the invalidated procedure might have been acquitted otherwise. Because of this more speculative connection to innocence, we give retroactive effect to only a small set of [new procedures].

The *Ring* rule might well have been considered "substantive." The effect of *Apprendi*, one could argue, was to transform the sentencing factors to which it applied into "elements" of the offense, thus changing the substantive definition of the crime for which the defendant was convicted. Indeed, the Court in *Ring* had said that "[b]ecause Arizona's enumerated aggravating factors operate as 'the functional equivalent of an element of a greater offense,' the Sixth Amendment requires that they be found by a jury."

The Court held otherwise:

> A rule is substantive rather than procedural if it alters the range of conduct or the class of persons that the law punishes. In contrast, rules that regulate only the *manner of determining* the defendant's culpability are procedural.

> Judged by this standard, Ring's holding is properly classified as procedural. *Ring* . . . did not alter the range of conduct Arizona law subjected to the death penalty. It could not have; it rested entirely on the Sixth Amendment's jury-trial guarantee, a provision that has nothing to do with the range of conduct a State may criminalize. Instead, *Ring* altered the range of permissible methods for determining whether a defendant's conduct is punishable by death, requiring that a jury rather than a judge find the essential facts bearing on punishment. Rules that allocate decisionmaking authority in this fashion are prototypical procedural rules . . . .

> A decision that modifies the elements of an offense is normally substantive rather than procedural. New elements alter the range of conduct the statute punishes, rendering some formerly unlawful conduct lawful or vice versa. But that is not what *Ring* did; the range of conduct punished by death in Arizona was the same before *Ring* as after. *Ring* held that, *because* Arizona's statutory aggravators restricted (as a matter of state law) the class of death-eligible defendants, those aggravators *effectively were* elements for federal constitutional purposes, and so were subject to the procedural requirements the Constitution attaches to trial of elements. This Court's holding that, *because Arizona* has made a certain fact essential to the death penalty, that fact must be found by a jury, is not the same as *this Court's* making a certain fact essential to the death penalty. The former was a procedural holding; the latter would be substantive.

5. *WELCH V. UNITED STATES*

Welch pleaded guilty in 2010 to a single count of being a felon in possession of a firearm and was sentenced to a mandatory minimum of 15 years. He argued on appeal that the provision of the Armed Career Criminal Act under which he was sentenced, known as the "residual clause," was not applicable to his situation, but he lost and his conviction and sentence ultimately became final. It was later held in Johnson v. United States, 576 U.S. 591 (2015), that the residual clause was void for vagueness. The question in Welch v. United States, 578 U.S. ___, 136 S.Ct. 1257 (2016), was whether Welch could take advantage of *Johnson* in a § 2255 challenge to his conviction. The ordinary maximum term for his sentence if the Career Criminal Act provision was not applicable was 10 years.

Justice Thomas argued that *Johnson* should not be applied retroactively to Welch's sentence:

> Time and again, the Court has articulated the test for defining a substantive constitutional rule as follows: The rule must "place particular conduct or persons covered by the statute beyond the State's power to punish." Schriro v. Summerlin, 542 U.S. 348, 352 (2004). . . . *Johnson* announced a new constitutional rule, but it is not substantive. . . . It does not preclude the Government from prohibiting particular conduct or deem any conduct constitutionally protected. The Government remains as free to enhance sentences for federal crimes based on the commission of previous violent felonies after *Johnson* as it was before. Nor does *Johnson*'s vagueness rule place any class of persons or punishment off limits. There is no category of offender that Congress cannot subject to an enhanced sentence after *Johnson*. The only constraint *Johnson* imposes is on the *manner* in which the Government can punish offenders. To avoid "fail[ing] to give ordinary people fair notice" or "invit[ing] arbitrary enforcement" [quoting *Johnson*], Congress must be clearer in describing what conduct [will warrant an enhanced sentence].

Thomas recognized a second category of cases that should be applied retroactively:

> *Johnson* also does not fit within the second type of substantive rule this Court has recognized, which consists of "decisions that narrow the scope of a criminal statute by interpreting its terms." *Schriro*, 542 U.S. at 351.
>
> The Court has invoked this subset of new rules just once, in Bousley v. United States, 523 U.S. 614 (1998). *Bousley* held that Bailey v. United States, 516 U.S. 137 (1995), which interpreted a federal firearms sentencing enhancement to require proof of "active employment of the firearm" as an element, applied retroactively. The Court . . . reasoned, "decisions of this Court holding that a substantive federal criminal statute does not reach certain conduct" share a key commonality with "decisions placing conduct beyond the power of the criminal law-making authority to proscribe": both "necessarily carry a significant risk that a defendant stands convicted of an act that the law does not make criminal." The Court thus classified decisions "holding that a substantive federal criminal statute does not reach certain conduct" as substantive.
>
> I would not so readily assume that *Bousley* applies here. Until today, *Bousley* applied only to new rules reinterpreting the text of federal criminal statutes in a way that narrows their reach. *Johnson* announced no such rule.

Justice Thomas was, however, speaking only for himself in dissent. The Court, in an opinion by Justice Kennedy, disagreed:

> By striking down the residual clause as void for vagueness, *Johnson* changed the substantive reach of the Armed Career Criminal Act, altering "the range of conduct or the class of persons that

the [Act] punishes." Schriro v. Summerlin, 542 U.S. 348, 353 (2004). Before *Johnson*, [a person in Welch's situation] faced 15 years to life in prison. After *Johnson*, the same person engaging in the same conduct . . . faces at most 10 years in prison. The [provision under which Welch was sentenced] is invalid under *Johnson*, so it can no longer mandate or authorize any sentence. *Johnson* establishes, in other words, that "even the use of impeccable factfinding procedures could not legitimate" a sentence based on that clause. United States v. United States Coin & Currency, 401 U.S. 715, 724 (1971). It follows that *Johnson* is a substantive decision.

By the same logic, *Johnson* is not a procedural decision. *Johnson* had nothing to do with the range of permissible methods a court might use to determine whether a defendant should be sentenced under the Armed Career Criminal Act. It did not, for example, "allocate decision-making authority" between judge and jury, *Schriro*, 542 U.S. at 353, or regulate the evidence that the court could consider in making its decision, see Whorton v. Bockting, 549 U.S. 406, 413–14, 417 (2007). Unlike those cases, *Johnson* affected the reach of the underlying statute rather than the judicial procedures by which the statute is applied. *Johnson* is thus a substantive decision and so has retroactive effect under *Teague* in cases on collateral review.

As to the meaning of *Bousley*, the Court added:

Although this Court has put great emphasis on substantive decisions that place certain conduct, classes of persons, or punishments beyond the legislative power of Congress, the Court has also recognized that some substantive decisions do not impose such restrictions. The clearest example comes from *Bousley* . . . . The Court in *Bousley* had no difficulty concluding that *Bailey* was substantive, as it was a decision "holding that a substantive federal criminal statute does not reach certain conduct." *Bousley*, 523 U.S. at 620; see *Schriro*, supra, at 354 ("A decision that modifies the elements of an offense is normally substantive rather than procedural"). The Court reached that conclusion even though Congress could (and later did) reverse *Bailey* by amending the statute to cover possession as well as use. See United States v. O'Brien, 560 U.S. 218, 232–33 (2010) (discussing statutory amendment known as the "*Bailey* fix"). *Bousley* thus contradicts the contention that the *Teague* inquiry turns only on whether the decision at issue holds that Congress lacks some substantive power.

6. QUESTIONS AND COMMENTS ON *TEAGUE*'S "SUBSTANTIVE" EXCEPTION

Given the history of *Teague*'s "watershed" exception prior to *Edwards*, might one expect that there would be pressure to force holdings into the "substantive" category in order to provide relief in sympathetic cases? And after *Edwards* might that pressure be increased?

It is hard, for example, to fit *Johnson*'s holding that the residual clause of the Armed Career Criminal Act was unconstitutionally vague into the *Teague* "substantive" exception. The statement in Schriro v. Summerlin, 542 U.S. 348 (2004), that the substantive exception applies to "constitutional determinations that place particular conduct or persons covered by the statute beyond the State's power to punish" does not appear to embrace the *Johnson* holding. The majority in *Welch*, however, concluded that *Johnson* fell within the first *Teague* exception because *Johnson* "affected the reach of the underlying statute rather than the judicial procedures by which the statute is applied." Accordingly, it was "a substantive decision and so has retroactive effect under *Teague* in cases on collateral review." Does this conclusion fit the *Teague* inquiry as it evolved? Or is the Thomas opinion more faithful to its spirit? Should *Johnson* have been given retroactive effect? Is it relevant—perhaps controlling—that the state's finality interest differs because a retroactivity holding would involve resentencing (and to a potentially significant sentence at that) rather than retrial?

Also consider *Bousley* and *Schriro*. Is it clear that the new rule in the one case is substantive and the other procedural? Are these two cases consistent? Do they match up with *Welch*?

In the end, has the Court taken the right approach to the availability in federal collateral attack of new constitutional decisions that go beyond previously established law? A related question is the appropriate impact of the Court's approach to retroactivity in *state* post-conviction proceedings. That topic is postponed for now but addressed in Subsection A of Section 5 of this Chapter.

ADDITIONAL NOTES ON THE TEAGUE "SUBSTANTIVE" EXCEPTION

1.   MONTGOMERY V. LOUISIANA

Henry Montgomery was convicted in 1963 of a murder committed when he was 17. He was sentenced to a mandatory term of life without parole. Many years later, the Court held in Miller v. Alabama, 567 U.S. 460 (2012), that life without parole could not be imposed on a juvenile for a homicide offense without consideration of his or her particular circumstances. One question in Montgomery v. Louisiana, 577 U.S. 190 (2016), was whether *Miller* fit *Teague*'s substantive-new-rule exception to non-retroactivity. In an opinion by Justice Kennedy, the Court held that it did:

> *Miller* requires that before sentencing a juvenile to life without parole, the sentencing judge take into account "how children are different, and how those differences counsel against irrevocably sentencing them to a lifetime in prison." The Court recognized that a sentencer might encounter the rare juvenile offender who exhibits such irretrievable depravity that rehabilitation is impossible and life without parole is justified. But in light of "children's diminished culpability and heightened capacity for change," *Miller* made clear that "appropriate occasions for sentencing juveniles to this harshest possible penalty will be uncommon."

Miller, then, did more than require a sentencer to consider a juvenile offender's youth before imposing life without parole . . . . Because *Miller* determined that sentencing a child to life without parole is excessive for all but " 'the rare juvenile offender whose crime reflects irreparable corruption,' " it rendered life without parole an unconstitutional penalty for "a class of defendants because of their status"—that is, juvenile offenders whose crimes reflect the transient immaturity of youth. As a result, *Miller* announced a substantive rule of constitutional law. Like other substantive rules, *Miller* is retroactive because it " 'necessarily carr[ies] a significant risk that a defendant' "—here, the vast majority of juvenile offenders—" 'faces a punishment that the law cannot impose upon him.' " Schriro v. Summerlin, 542 U.S. 348, 352 (2004) (quoting Bousley v. United States, 523 U.S. 614, 620 (1998)).

Louisiana nonetheless argues that *Miller* is procedural because it did not place any punishment beyond the State's power to impose; it instead required sentencing courts to take children's age into account before condemning them to die in prison. In support of this argument, Louisiana points to *Miller*'s statement that the decision "does not categorically bar a penalty for a class of offenders or type of crime . . . . Instead, it mandates only that a sentencer follow a certain process considering an offender's youth and attendant characteristics—before imposing a particular penalty." . . .

To be sure, *Miller*'s holding has a procedural component. *Miller* requires a sentencer to consider a juvenile offender's youth and attendant characteristics before determining that life without parole is a proportionate sentence. . . . A hearing where "youth and its attendant characteristics" are considered as sentencing factors is necessary to separate those juveniles who may be sentenced to life without parole from those who may not. The hearing does not replace but rather gives effect to *Miller*'s substantive holding that life without parole is an excessive sentence for children whose crimes reflect transient immaturity.

Louisiana suggests that *Miller* cannot have made a constitutional distinction between children whose crimes reflect transient immaturity and those whose crimes reflect irreparable corruption because *Miller* did not require trial courts to make a finding of fact regarding a child's incorrigibility. That this finding is not required, however, speaks only to the degree of procedure *Miller* mandated in order to implement its substantive guarantee. When a new substantive rule of constitutional law is established, this Court is careful to limit the scope of any attendant procedural requirement to avoid intruding more than necessary upon the States' sovereign administration of their criminal justice systems. Fidelity to this important principle of federalism, however, should not be construed to demean the substantive character of the federal right at issue. That *Miller* did not impose a formal factfinding requirement does not leave States free to sentence a child whose crime reflects transient immaturity to life without parole. To the contrary, *Miller* established that this punishment is disproportionate under the Eighth Amendment.[a]

2.   *JONES V. MISSISSIPPI*

Jones, a 15-year-old who was convicted of murdering his grandfather, was sentenced to a mandatory term of life without parole. *Miller v. Alabama* was decided while his case was pending before the Mississippi Supreme Court on state collateral review. That court decided that *Miller* was retroactive, and ordered a new sentencing hearing. After the hearing, the sentencing judge acknowledged that he had discretion to impose a sentence of less than life without parole, but "after considering the factors 'relevant to the child's culpability,'" decided that life without parole was the appropriate sentence.

Jones argued on appeal that *Miller* required the sentencing judge to do more—to "either (i) make a separate factual finding of permanent incorrigibility, or (ii) at least provide an on-the-record sentencing explanation with an 'implicit finding' of permanent incorrigibility." The Mississippi Supreme Court held that the sentencing judge had done enough. The Supreme Court granted certiorari, it said, because lower courts had disagreed about how *Miller* should be interpreted.

In an opinion by Justice Kavanaugh in Jones v. Mississippi, 593 U.S. ___, 141 S.Ct. 1307 (2021), the Supreme Court agreed that the sentencing judge had done enough. It said that the "problem for Jones is that *Miller* and *Montgomery* squarely rejected such a requirement," quoting in a footnote the last paragraph from *Montgomery* reproduced in Note 1 above. It added that "because a discretionary sentencing procedure suffices to ensure individualized consideration of a defendant's youth, we should not now add still more procedural requirements."

In the course of its opinion, the Court spoke of the relationship between *Miller* and *Montgomery*: "Despite the procedural function of *Miller*'s rule, *Montgomery* held that the *Miller* rule was substantive for retroactivity purposes and therefore applied retroactively on collateral review." It added in a footnote:

> As the Court has stated in cases both before and after *Montgomery*, the Court determines whether a rule is substantive or procedural for retroactivity purposes "by considering the function of the rule" itself—not "by asking whether the constitutional right underlying the new rule is substantive or procedural." Welch v. United States, 578 U.S. 120, 130–31 (2016). For purposes of

---

[a]   The Court also spoke to the appropriate remedy:

A State may remedy a *Miller* violation by permitting juvenile homicide offenders to be considered for parole, rather than by resentencing them. Allowing those offenders to be considered for parole ensures that juveniles whose crimes reflected only transient immaturity—and who have since matured—will not be forced to serve a disproportionate sentence in violation of the Eighth Amendment.

Joined by Justices Thomas and Alito, Justice Scalia dissented. Justice Thomas also wrote a separate dissent on another issue.

Teague, a rule is procedural if it regulates " 'only the manner of determining the defendant's culpability.' " *Welch*, 578 U. S. at 129 (quoting Schriro v. Summerlin, 542 U.S. 348, 353 (2004). A rule is substantive and applies retroactively on collateral review, by contrast, if it " 'alters the range of conduct or the class of persons that the law punishes.' " *Welch*, 578 U.S. at 129 (quoting *Summerlin*, 542 U.S. at 353). As the Court's post-*Montgomery* decision in *Welch* already indicates, to the extent that *Montgomery's* application of the *Teague* standard is in tension with the Court's retroactivity precedents that both pre-date and post-date *Montgomery*, those retroactivity precedents—and not *Montgomery*—must guide the determination of whether rules other than *Miller* are substantive. To be clear, however, our decision today does not disturb *Montgomery's* holding that *Miller* applies retroactively on collateral review. By now, most offenders who could seek collateral review as a result of *Montgomery* have done so and, if eligible, have received new discretionary sentences under *Miller*.

The effect of this footnote and its accompanying text, said Justice Thomas in a concurring opinion in *Jones*, is that "*Montgomery* gave a good-for-one-ride ticket to a class of juvenile offenders, and its errors will never be repeated." The Court "candidly admits," he added, "both that *Miller's* rule was 'procedural' and that *Montgomery* 'ma[de] the rule retroactive.' " It "closes the door to courts following *Montgomery* in the future," he said, and "in doing so . . . tacitly admits that the horses have already left the barn [because] 'most offenders who could seek collateral review as a result of *Montgomery* have done so.' "

Joined by Justices Breyer and Kagan, Justice Sotomayor dissented, arguing for a more formal finding at the sentencing hearing. She added: "How low this Court's respect for stare decisis has sunk":

> [T]he Court . . . rewrites *Miller* and *Montgomery* to say what the Court now wishes they had said, and then denies that it has done any such thing. . . . Rather than try to harmonize its decision today with *Montgomery's* retroactivity holding, it confesses in a footnote that its rewriting of precedent is inconsistent with *Montgomery* and basic retroactivity principles. The Court's solution? It urges lower courts to simply ignore *Montgomery* going forward . . . . Instead of "disturb[ing]" *Montgomery's* retroactivity holding the Court attempts to bury it.

She described the effect of the Court's holding in these terms:

> [T]he Court transforms *Miller* into a decision requiring only a "discretionary sentencing procedure." At the same time, the Court insists that it "does not disturb" *Montgomery's* holding "that *Miller* applies retroactively on collateral review." In other words, the Court rewrites *Miller* into a procedural rule and, paradoxically, maintains that *Miller* was nevertheless "substantive for retroactivity purposes."

3.   QUESTIONS AND COMMENTS ON *MONTGOMERY* AND *JONES*

It is argued in Dov Fox and Alex Stein, Constitutional Retroactivity in Criminal Procedure, 91 Wash. L. Rev. 463, 468 (2016), that:

> The *Montgomery* majority reached a just result for the wrong reason. Justice required that the constitutional rule announced in *Miller* apply retroactively to prisoners who did not get the benefit of that rule by the time that their sentences were finalized. But the reason underlying this intuition is not that a right to individualized sentencing places particular conduct or persons beyond the power to punish. Rather, it is that *Miller* afforded juvenile defendants a fundamentally important due process protection. . . . The Court's "rewriting" of the *Miller* rule from procedural to substantive made that constitutional holding retroactive through the back door that its *Teague* jurisprudence left open.

Is their point well taken? On its own terms, on what rationale is *Montgomery* based? Is there an element of doubletalk in the Court's reasoning? Should it be important that there are easy fixes to the retroactive application of *Miller* short of a complete retrial on the question of guilt, i.e., a "just result" can be reached (especially after *Jones*) at a relatively low cost to state interests?

From another perspective, is *Montgomery* consistent with *Schriro*? Citing *Apprendi* and *Ring*, the Court in *Jones* added in a footnote that "[i]f permanent incorrigibility were a factual prerequisite to a life-without-parole sentence, this Court's Sixth Amendment precedents might require that a jury, not a judge, make such a finding." Since *Ring* was not retroactive, does it follow that the lesser "procedural" requirement of consideration rather than a formal finding should also not be retroactive?

What is going on in *Montgomery* and *Jones*? One explanation might be changes in the composition of the Court. In *Montgomery*, the Court's opinion was written by Justice Kennedy, who was joined by Chief Justice Roberts and by Justices Ginsburg, Breyer, Sotomayor, and Kagan. In dissent were Justices Scalia, Thomas, and Alito.[b] In *Jones*, the Court's opinion was written by Justice Kavanaugh, who was joined by Chief Justice Roberts and Justices Alito, Gorsuch, and Barrett. Justice Thomas concurred in the judgment. In dissent were Justices Sotomayor, Breyer, and Kagan. Is that all there is to it?

Jones was decided roughly three weeks before *Edwards* and Justice Kavanaugh wrote both opinions, so it was undoubtedly known when *Jones* was released to the public that part of *Teague* was going to be completely abandoned. Why not completely abandon *Montgomery* too? Because the horses were out of the barn, *Montgomery* could be neutralized, the impact of *Miller* could be limited, and a retroactive *Miller* was unlikely to have any more effect?

---

[b]   The Court's opinion in *Miller* was written by Justice Kagan, who was joined by Justices Kennedy, Ginsburg, Breyer, and Sotomayor. In dissent were Chief Justice Roberts and Justices Scalia, Thomas, and Alito. In *Welch*, Justice Thomas was the sole dissenter. The Kennedy opinion for the majority was joined by Chief Justice Roberts and by Justices Ginsburg, Breyer, Alito, Sotomayor, and Kagan.

4. BIBLIOGRAPHY

Edwards will surely provoke a lively literature. For an early entry, see Richard M. Re, Reason and Rhetoric in *Edwards v. Vannoy* (June 11, 2021). Available at SSRN: https://ssrn.com/abstract=3865178.

[The Bibliography in the Casebook, pages 961–62, can be referred to here for articles on *Teague*.]

SECTION 2. REVIEW OF STATE COURT DECISIONS ON THE MERITS: AEDPA

Page 964, add a footnote at the end of the first sentence after the quotation at the top of the page:

ᵃ Eve Brensike Primus, Equitable Gateways: Toward Expanded Federal Habeas Corpus Review of State Court Criminal Convictions, 61 Ariz. L. Rev. 591 (2019), begins with the recitation of statistics from an empirical study showing that "fewer than 0.3% of noncapital state petitioners get any form of federal habeas relief, and more than half of the prisoners who file habeas petitions have their petitions dismissed on procedural grounds without a federal court ever considering the merits of the underlying constitutional claims." Her thesis is that all is not lost, and that one who focuses on "equitable gateways" and "litigates toward them has a better chance of getting through." She identifies two basic categories of such gateways: petitioners who show innocence and petitioners who show that they "did not have a full and fair opportunity to have their federal claims adjudicated in the convicting state's system." The substance of her article offers guidelines for how this second gateway can be exploited.

Page 966, delete Note 3 and substitute the following:

3. DOES *TEAGUE* SURVIVE AEDPA?

The possibility that AEDPA might foreclose review in a case where *Teague* might permit it was suggested in a concurring opinion in *Edwards v. Vannoy.* The Court's opinion is excerpted earlier in this Supplement. The Court discarded the "watershed" exception to *Teague v. Lane,* holding that new procedural rules could no longer be applied retroactively on federal collateral attack, period. The result was that Ramos v. Louisiana, 590 U.S. ___, 140 S.Ct. 1390 (2020), which held that a state jury must be unanimous to convict a criminal defendant of a serious offense, would not be applied retroactively to Louisiana and Oregon rules that had previously allowed non-unanimous jury verdicts.

Joined by Justice Gorsuch, Justice Thomas took the position in his concurring opinion that the same result was required by AEDPA:

> I write separately to highlight that we could also have resolved this case by applying the statutory text of the Antiterrorism and Effective Death Penalty Act of 1996 (AEDPA). AEDPA directs federal courts to deny "any claim that was adjudicated on the merits in State court" unless the state court's decision "was contrary to, or involved an unreasonable application of, clearly established Federal law, as determined by the Supreme Court." 28 U.S.C. § 2254(d)(1). In 2011, petitioner urged a Louisiana court to hold that the Federal Constitution requires jury unanimity, and the court rejected that claim on the merits. That conclusion was consistent with Apodaca v. Oregon, 406 U.S. 404 (1972), in which this

Court determined that the Constitution does not require unanimous jury verdicts for state criminal convictions. AEDPA thus leaves no room for this Court—or any federal court—to grant relief. . . . It is not enough for a federal court to disagree with the state court—much less disagree on a point of law that this Court had not yet settled when the state court issued its judgment. Rather, the state court's decision must conflict with clearly established law and be obviously wrong "beyond any possibility for fairminded disagreement." Harrington v. Richter, 562 U.S. 86, 103 (2011). . . . Our analysis could have begun and ended there—with § 2254(d)(1)'s plain text. Congress, through AEDPA, has made clear that federal courts cannot provide relief in this case. [I]t does not contemplate retroactive rules upsetting a state court's adjudication of an issue that reasonably applied the law at the time. Section 2254(d)—the absolute bar on claims that state courts reasonably denied—has no exception for retroactive rights.

It would seem to follow that, even if the Court were to hold a new rule to be "substantive" and therefore retroactive under *Teague*, Justices Thomas and Gorsuch would deny relief based on AEDPA.

Recall that Justice Gorsuch, joined by Justice Thomas, also wrote a separate concurring opinion in *Edwards*. That opinion is summarized in the Notes following the *Edwards* excerpts in this Supplement. Are the two concurrences consistent with each other? Can they both be right?

The Court has applied the *Teague* "substantive" exception to non-retroactivity in numerous cases since AEDPA without addressing the possibility that AEDPA might foreclose relief. Examples are *Schriro v. Summerlin*, *Welch v. United States*, and *Montgomery v. Louisiana*, all of which are summarized in the Notes following the excerpts from *Edwards v. Vannoy* included in this Supplement. The Court has, however, addressed the relationship between *Teague* and AEDPA in another context.

In Horn v. Banks, 536 U.S. 266 (2002), and the successor decision in the same case, Beard v. Banks, 542 U.S. 406 (2004), it held that federal habeas courts are required to apply *Teague* even though a state post-conviction court addressed the criminal defendant's claims on the merits and even though the state court decision may have made an "unreasonable" mistake in its application of federal law that would allow review under AEDPA. In *Horn*, the Court said in a unanimous per curiam opinion:

> While it is of course a necessary prerequisite to federal habeas relief that a prisoner satisfy the AEDPA standard of review set forth in 28 U.S.C. § 2254(d) . . ., none of our post-AEDPA cases have suggested that a writ of habeas corpus should automatically issue if a prisoner satisfies the AEDPA standard, or that AEDPA relieves courts from the responsibility of addressing properly raised *Teague* arguments. To the contrary, if our post-AEDPA cases suggest anything about AEDPA's relationship to *Teague*, it is that the AEDPA and *Teague* inquiries are distinct. . . . Thus, in addition to performing any analysis required by AEDPA, a federal court considering a

habeas petition must conduct a threshold *Teague* analysis when the issue is properly raised by the state.

On remand, the Circuit Court held that the habeas petitioner's claim did not rely on a "new" rule and that the state Supreme Court had unreasonably applied the state of the law existing at the time of conviction. The Supreme Court reversed again. In a five-to-four decision, the majority concluded that the petitioner's claim was indeed based on a "new" rule and that neither *Teague* exception applied. Habeas was therefore foreclosed under *Teague* without regard to whether AEDPA would have allowed review.

Page 980, add to the list of other literature on AEDPA in Note 4:

LeRoy Pernell, Racial Justice and Federal Habeas Corpus as Postconviction Relief from State Convictions, 69 Mercer L. Rev. 453 (2018);

Page 986, add at the end of footnote b:

Daniel Epps, Harmless Errors and Substantial Rights, 131 Harv. L. Rev. 2117 (2018), points out that "all prior attempts to understand harmless error have proceeded from the premise that it involves a remedies question: what should a court do about a violation of the defendant's constitutional rights?" Epps argues instead that

harmless error is inexorably tied up in the process of defining and enforcing constitutional *rights*. When asking whether an error is harmless, an appellate court should not think of itself as asking whether a particular violation of the defendant's rights is serious enough to demand the remedy of reversal. Instead, it is really asking whether a defendant's constitutional rights have been violated at all.

He concludes that this "rights-based approach" has at least one important practical payoff:

[I]t would require courts to be clearer about the values at stake when adjudicating claims of harmless error. No longer could a court declare a broad scope of a constitutional right while in the same breath undercutting that right's effective value through the use of harmless error analysis. That would be a step forward, even if only a small one.

Page 989, add a new Note:

3A. DECISIONS ON THE MERITS WITHOUT OPINION

Both state and federal appellate courts frequently make decisions on the merits without elaborating the reasons for their decision. Usually they are summary affirmances of a lower court decision, and usually the lower court will have given reasons for its decision. Is it fair to assume that the appellate court adopted the lower court's reasoning when it affirmed the decision?

The answer to this question when a federal court makes a summary affirmance is "no," as reflected in the following passage from Justice Gorsuch's dissent in Wilson v. Sellers, 584 U.S. ___, 138 S.Ct. 1188 (2018):

Appellate courts usually have an independent duty to review the facts and law in the cases that come to them. Often they see errors in lower court opinions. But often, too, they may affirm on alternative bases either argued by the parties or (sometimes) apparent to them on the face of the record. See, e.g., SEC v. Chenery Corp., 318 U.S. 80, 88 (1943) (noting "the settled rule that, in reviewing the decision of a lower court, it must be affirmed if the result is correct 'although the lower court relied upon a wrong ground or gave a wrong reason' "). And a busy appellate court sometimes may not see the profit in devoting its limited resources to explaining the error and the alternative basis for affirming when the outcome is sure to remain the same, so it issues a summary affirmance instead. To reflect these realities, this Court has traditionally warned readers *against* presuming our summary affirmance orders rest on reasons articulated in lower court opinions. Comptroller of Treasury of Md. v. Wynne, 575 U.S. 542, ___, 135 S.Ct. 1787, 1801 (2015) (" '[A] summary affirmance is an affirmance of the judgment only,' and 'the rationale of the affirmance may not be gleaned solely from the opinion below' "). The courts of appeals have issued similar warnings for similar reasons about their own summary orders.

Typically, the reason for seeking to determine the rationale for a summary affirmance by the Supreme Court or a federal Circuit Court will be to learn whether it should have precedential effect. Is the situation different when federal courts are confronted in habeas cases with state court summary affirmances? The answer is "yes," it is different. A federal habeas court will be interested in the rationale of a state court summary disposition for an entirely different reason.

AEDPA permits federal courts to grant habeas only where a relevant state court decision "was contrary to, or involved an unreasonable application of, clearly established Federal law." In order to determine whether a state supreme court summary affirmance was "unreasonable" in its application of federal law, a federal habeas court would be obligated, one would assume, to discover how the state courts applied the applicable federal law. How should it do so when the state's highest court has said nothing?

(i) Federal Claim Rejected Because of Procedural Foreclosure: Ylst v. Nunnemaker

One possible rationale for the state court disposition in such a situation is an adequate and independent state ground resulting in a procedural foreclosure. Such a decision by a state court then would not involve a controlling determination of federal law in the first place.

In Ylst v. Nunnemaker, 501 U.S. 797 (1991), a federal habeas petitioner's constitutional claim had been rejected on direct appeal from his conviction because he had not raised it at trial. "[A]n objection based upon a *Miranda* violation cannot be raised for the first time on appeal," the court said. He later sought collateral review in several state courts, all of which summarily denied relief without opinion. The question before the Supreme Court was how lower federal habeas courts should understand the reasoning of the state habeas courts in such circumstances. Justice Scalia's opinion for the Court said:

> The problem we face arises, of course, because many formulary orders are not meant to convey *anything* as to the reason for the decision. Attributing a reason is therefore both difficult and artificial. We think that the attribution necessary for federal habeas purposes can be facilitated, and sound results more often assured, by applying the following presumption: Where there has been one reasoned state judgment rejecting a federal claim, later unexplained

orders upholding that judgment or rejecting the same claim rest upon the same ground. If an earlier opinion "fairly appear[s] to rest primarily upon federal law," we will presume that no procedural default has been invoked by a subsequent unexplained order that leaves the judgment or its consequences in place. Similarly where, as here, the last reasoned opinion on the claim explicitly imposes a procedural default, we will presume that a later decision rejecting the claim did not silently disregard that bar and consider the merits.

(ii) Federal Claim Rejected on the Merits: Wilson v. Sellers

In Wilson v. Sellers, 584 U.S. ___, 138 S.Ct. 1188 (2018), the last reasoned state court opinion rejected a federal claim on the merits. The ultimate question before federal habeas courts was whether a summary affirmance of that decision by a state appellate court "unreasonably" applied federal law. A preliminary question was whether the state appellate court should be taken to have relied on the same reasoning that was reflected in the lower state court disposition. The Supreme Court addressed only this preliminary question, leaving the ultimate issue for Circuit Court determination on remand.

Wilson was sentenced to death following a conviction for murder. He claimed in a state habeas proceeding that his counsel was ineffective. This claim was rejected on the ground that his counsel was not deficient and that, in any event, the alleged error (failure to offer mitigating evidence at sentencing) was not prejudicial because the evidence was "inadmissible on evidentiary grounds." The state Supreme Court summarily affirmed without explanation. In an opinion by Justice Breyer, the Court said:

> What then is the federal habeas court to do? We hold that the federal court should "look through" the unexplained decision to the last related state-court decision that does provide a relevant rationale. It should then presume that the unexplained decision adopted the same reasoning. But the State may rebut the presumption by showing that the unexplained affirmance relied or most likely did rely on different grounds than the lower state court's decision, such as alternative grounds for affirmance that were briefed or argued to the state supreme court or obvious in the record it reviewed.

The Court elaborated:

> The State points out that there could be many cases in which a "look through" presumption does not accurately identify the grounds for the higher court's decision. And we agree. We also agree that it is more likely that a state supreme court's single word "affirm" rests upon alternative grounds where the lower state court decision is unreasonable than, e.g., where the lower court rested on a state-law procedural ground, as in Ylst. But that is why we have set forth a presumption and not an absolute rule. And the unreasonableness of the lower court's decision itself provides some

evidence that makes it less likely the state supreme court adopted the same reasoning. Thus, additional evidence that might not be sufficient to rebut the presumption in a case like *Ylst* would allow a federal court to conclude that counsel has rebutted the presumption in a case like this one. For instance, a federal habeas court may conclude that counsel has rebutted the presumption on the basis of convincing alternative arguments for affirmance made to the State's highest court or equivalent evidence presented in its briefing to the federal court similarly establishing that the State's highest court relied on a different ground than the lower state court, such as the existence of a valid ground for affirmance that is obvious from the state-court record. . . . A presumption that can be rebutted by evidence of, for instance, an alternative ground that was argued or that is clear in the record was the likely basis for the decision is in accord with full and proper respect for state courts. . . .

The Court then remanded the case to the Circuit Court to follow this approach in determining whether the state appellate court was "unreasonable" in its application of federal law.

Joined by Justices Thomas and Alito, Justice Gorsuch dissented. He began:

> After a state supreme court issues a summary order sustaining a criminal conviction, should a federal habeas court reviewing that decision presume it rests only on the reasons found in a lower state court opinion? The answer is no. The statute governing federal habeas review permits no such "look through" presumption. Nor do traditional principles of appellate review. In fact, we demand the *opposite* presumption for our work—telling readers that we independently review each case and that our summary affirmances may be read only as signaling agreement with a lower court's judgment and not necessarily its reasons. Because I can discern no good reason to treat the work of our state court colleagues with less respect than we demand for our own, I would reject [the Court's] presumption and must respectfully dissent.

Gorsuch reasoned:

> As the text [of AEDPA] and our precedent make clear, a federal habeas court must focus its review on the final state court decision on the merits, not any preceding decision by an inferior state court. Nor does it matter whether the final state court decision comes with a full opinion or in a summary order: the same deference is due all final state court decisions. Harrington v. Richter, 562 U.S. 86, 98 (2011).
>
> The upshot of these directions is clear. Even when the final state court decision "is unaccompanied by an explanation, the habeas petitioner's burden still must be met by showing *there was no reasonable basis* for the state court to deny relief." *Richter,* 562 U.S. at 98 (emphasis added). And before a federal court can disregard a

final summary state court decision, it "must determine what arguments or theories . . . *could have supporte[d]* the state court's decision; and then it must ask whether it is possible fair-minded jurists could disagree that those arguments or theories are inconsistent with the holding in a prior decision of this Court." Id. at 102 (emphasis added). Far from suggesting federal courts should presume a state supreme court summary order rests on views expressed in a lower court's opinion, then, AEDPA and our precedents require more nearly the *opposite* presumption: federal courts must presume the order rests on any reasonable basis the law and facts allow.

If this standard seems hard for a habeas petitioner to overcome, "that is because it was meant to be." Ibid. In AEDPA, Congress rejected the notion that federal habeas review should be "a substitute for ordinary error correction." Id. at 102–03.

There is, Gorsuch added, "some good news" in the Court's approach. The Court's elaboration of the force of its presumption "reveals just how futile this whole business really is":

> [I]f, as the Court . . . tells us, a federal habeas court can always deny relief on a basis that is apparent from the record or on the basis of alternative arguments presented by the parties in state or federal proceedings, then the "look through" presumption truly means nothing and we are back where we started. . . . [A]federal habeas court is neither obliged to *look through* exclusively to the reasons given by a lower state court, nor required to *presume* that a summary order adopts those reasons.

> All this is welcome news of a sort. The Court may promise us a future of foraging through presumptions and rebuttals. But at least at the end of it we rest knowing that what was true before remains true today: a federal habeas court should look at all the arguments presented in state and federal court and examine the state court record. And a federal habeas court should sustain a state court summary decision denying relief if those materials reveal a basis to do so reasonably consistent with this Court's holdings. Exactly what a federal court applying the statute and *Richter* has had to do all along. . . .

(iii) Questions and Comments

What is the debate in *Wilson* all about? At the end of the day, is there any operational difference between the majority and the dissent? Both opinions permit the denial of habeas relief if the state can show a plausible basis in federal law to justify the state court disposition, whatever the state court's reasoning may have been in fact. And both illustrate how hard it will be for a federal habeas petitioner to overcome a state court summary denial of relief. Might the message be, indeed, that appellate state courts will be better off if they say nothing?

SECTION 3. PROCEDURAL LIMITATIONS

SUBSECTION A. PROCEDURAL FORECLOSURE

Page 1008, add to the end of the third full paragraph:

As explained in Eve Brensike Primus, Federal Review of State Criminal Convictions: A Structural Approach to Adequacy Doctrine, 116 Mich. L. Rev. 75, 83 (2017), "[c]ause and prejudice asks whether an individual defendant had a legitimate excuse for failing to comply with state procedures." The adequacy prong of the adequate and independent state ground doctrine "asks not whether the defendant should be forgiven for failing to comply with legitimate rules but whether the state's rules are legitimate in the first place—whether they warrant the respect and deference that justify procedural default."

Primus argues for a broader adequacy inquiry in addition to the one the Court is accustomed to making: "what is needed is a structural approach to adequacy, one that would consider how the interaction of multiple procedural rules unfairly burdens federal rights." She concludes:

> Rather than looking in each case only at the particular procedural rule that the petitioner is said to have violated, the federal courts should consider how that one rule is situated in the overall state procedural system and ask a larger question: Is the state system structured in such a way that this litigant will not have, in practice, a real opportunity to raise a federal constitutional claim? Unless the federal court is willing to look at the labyrinth, there is little chance that petitioners will ever find their way through it.

SUBSECTION B. EXHAUSTION OF STATE REMEDIES AND TIMELINESS OF PETITIONS

Page 1020, add a footnote at the end of Note 4:

ᵉ Once a judgment has been entered by a district court, the petitioner's rights of appeal are also controlled by AEDPA, as described in the final note in Section 2 of this Chapter. Prior to an appeal, Federal Rule of Civil Procedure 59(e) allows the petitioner to make a motion in the district court "to alter or amend" the judgment. This motion must be made within 28 days, and has the effect of suspending the finality of the judgment until the disposition of the motion. It is at that point that the time to take an appeal begins to run.

The grounds open for contention under such a motion are extremely limited, basically allowing the district court only to correct a mistake rather than address new evidence or arguments. The Court held in Banister v. Davis, 590 U.S. ___, 140 S.Ct. 1698 (2020), that a Rule 59(e) motion did *not* constitute a successive petition under AEDPA, but instead should be treated as a continuing part of the underlying habeas petition. It doing so, it distinguished Gonzalez v. Crosby, 545 U.S. 524 (2005), which held that a motion for "relief from a final judgment" under Rule 60(b) *did* constitute a successive petition and was thus subject to the AEDPA limitations. Functionally, as the Court in *Banister* described *Gonzalez*, a Rule 60(b) motion serves as a "collateral attack [on an] already completed judgment."

SECTION 4. CLAIMS OF INNOCENCE

Page 1049, add to the list of articles in the first paragraph of Note 4:

Diane P. Wood, The Enduring Challenges for Habeas Corpus, 95 Notre Dame L. Rev. 1805 (2020) (revisiting Friendly's *Is Innocence Irrelevant* article and suggesting that relief should be available for freestanding claims of innocence); William H. Pryor, Jr., The Great Writ and Federal Courts: Judge Wood's Solution in Search of a Problem, 95 Notre Dame L. Rev. 1847 (2020) (disagreeing with Judge Wood's proposal).

Page 1050, add at the end of Note 4:

Finally, for discussion of the treatment of claims of *legal* innocence, i.e., convictions or sentences under an unconstitutional or inapplicable statute, in which the author notes that the Supreme Court's reception in recent years to such claims "is noteworthy because it runs against the general trend of judges narrowing the scope of federal habeas review," see Leah M. Litman, Legal Innocence and Federal Habeas, 104 Va. L. Rev. 417, 420 (2018).

SECTION 5. INTERSECTING ISSUES

SUBSECTION A. APPLICABILITY OF *TEAGUE* IN STATE COURTS

Page 1051, omit Note 1 and substitute the following:

1. INTRODUCTION

Recall, as developed previously in this Supplement, that Teague v. Lane, 489 U.S. 288 (1989), held that "new" rules of constitutional law adopted (discovered?) by the Supreme Court should not be applied retroactively in federal post-conviction proceedings if the conviction had become final before the decision announcing the new rule. The default is non-retroactivity. There were two exceptions: for new "substantive" rules; and for new "watershed" rules of criminal procedure that affected the fundamental fairness and accuracy of the underlying conviction. Litigation over application of the first exception is active and controversial, and new "substantive" rules continue to be announced. Litigation over application of the second exception was settled in *Edwards v. Vannoy*, which is excerpted earlier in this Supplement.

Teague was developed in the context of federal habeas corpus for state prisoners. It also applies in § 2255 proceedings for federal prisoners. The first two cases discussed below involve the relevance of *Teague* to *state* post-conviction proceedings.[a] Must the state courts follow *Teague*? Or are the states free to chart their own course? Subsection A concludes by considering application of the independence prong of the adequate-and-independent-state-ground doctrine in both state and federal post-conviction proceedings.

[a] Lee Kovarsky, Structural Change in State Post-Conviction Review, 98 Notre Dame L. Rev. 443 (2017), considers the increased importance of state post-conviction review caused by the juxtaposition of expanding constitutional rights that, for one reason or another, cannot be resolved at trial and the declining availability of federal habeas relief: "In economic phrasing,

demand for collateral process is rising at the same time that federal supply is falling." See also Z. Payvand Ahdout, Direct Collateral Review, 121 Colum. L. Rev. 159 (2021) (defining "direct collateral review" as Supreme Court review of state collateral proceedings, and noting the increase in recent years of Supreme Court decisions in such cases in spite of an earlier presumption against taking them; "Direct collateral review is a way for the Court to keep law current, correct course, and do justice.").

Page 1054, add at the end of footnote e:

See also Ruthanne M. Deutsch, Federalizing Retroactivity Rules: The Unrealized Promise of *Danforth v. Minnesota* and the Unmet Obligation of State Courts to Vindicate Federal Constitutional Rights, 44 Fla. St. U. L. Rev. 53 (2016).

Page 1054, insert after the first paragraph in Note 2(iii):

Note that while *Teague* has been substantially modified by subsequent decisions, it appears that *Danforth*, however it is to be read, remains good law. *Edwards v. Vannoy*, which is excerpted earlier in this Supplement, discarded the *Teague* "watershed" exception and held flatly that "[n]ew procedural rules do not apply retroactively on federal collateral review." But in footnote 6 of its opinion, the Court said:

> The *Ramos* rule does not apply retroactively on *federal* collateral review. States remain free, if they choose, to retroactively apply the jury-unanimity rule as a matter of state law in state postconviction proceedings. See Danforth v. Minnesota, 552 U.S. 264, 282 (2008).

Page 1054, delete the second paragraph of Note 3 and substitute the following:

Miller barred a sentence of mandatory life without parole for juvenile offenders who had been convicted of a homicide offense. As a matter of federal law, deciding whether *Miller* applied retroactively required consideration of whether it was a "new" rule that fell within an exception to the *Teague* default of non-retroactivity. That is one of the issues debated and decided in the opinion below. That aspect of the decision is discussed above in the Notes following *Edwards v. Vannoy*, which is excerpted earlier in this Supplement. The Court held that *Miller* fit the "substantive" *Teague* exception and therefore was applicable retroactively.

Page 1060, omit the sentence in brackets in the first paragraph of Part III and substitute the following:

[This aspect of the Court's holding in *Montgomery* is considered in the Notes following *Edwards v. Vannoy* in the new Subsection B of Section 1 of this Chapter included in this Supplement. The Court concluded:]

CHAPTER VIII

STATE SOVEREIGN IMMUNITY AND THE ELEVENTH AMENDMENT

SECTION 1. NATURE OF THE LIMITATION

Page 1100, add a new Note after Note 5:

5A. PROPER TERMINOLOGY

The sovereign immunity of the states in federal courts has often been referred to as "Eleventh Amendment immunity." This term has frequently been used by the Supreme Court,[h] and it is sometimes used in the Notes in this Chapter. It reflects the fact that the Eleventh Amendment is the only part of the Constitution that directly limits suits against states in a federal court. But ever since *Hans*, it has been clear that the Supreme Court's conception of state sovereign immunity is broader than the terms of the Eleventh Amendment.

The Court now conceives of the Eleventh Amendment as merely clarifying that, contrary to *Chisholm v. Georgia*, the Constitution's grant of Article III power to hear disputes between out-of-state citizens and states did not displace state sovereign immunity. The source of immunity, under this view, is not the Eleventh Amendment, but rather the constitutional structure as informed by the sovereign rights that the states would have had at the time the Constitution was adopted.

The Court explained this point in Alden v. Maine, 527 U.S. 706, 713 (1999):

> We have . . . sometimes referred to the States' immunity from suit as "Eleventh Amendment immunity." The phrase is convenient shorthand but something of a misnomer, for the sovereign immunity of the States neither derives from, nor is limited by, the terms of the Eleventh Amendment. Rather, as the Constitution's structure, its history, and the authoritative interpretations by this Court make clear, the States' immunity from suit is a fundamental aspect of the sovereignty which the States enjoyed before the ratification of the Constitution, and which they retain today (either literally or by virtue of their admission into the Union upon an equal footing with the other States) except as altered by the plan of the Convention or certain constitutional Amendments.

As a result, the term that probably best accords with the Court's current approach to this topic is simply "state sovereign immunity." This is the language that the Court used, for example, in its most recent decision in this area, *Franchise Tax Board v. Hyatt*, which is excerpted as a main case below.

ʰ   See, for example, Seminole Tribe of Florida v. Florida, 517 U.S. 44, 58, 59 (1996). *Seminole Tribe* is a main case in Section 2 of this Chapter.

Page 1105, add after the final citation in the first footnote a:

See also James E. Pfander and Jacob Wentzel, The Common Law Origins of *Ex parte Young*, 72 Stan. L. Rev. 1269 (2020).

Page 1125, add a new Note after Note 3:

3A. FEDERAL INJUNCTIONS TO ENFORCE STATE LAW: *PENNHURST STATE SCHOOL AND HOSPITAL V. HALDERMAN*

The Pennhurst State School and Hospital was a Pennsylvania institution for the care of the mentally retarded. A class action was brought in federal court on behalf of residents of Pennhurst against the Hospital, some of its officials, the state Department of Public Welfare, and a number of other defendants to enforce rights alleged to arise from the federal Constitution, from federal legislation, and from state legislation. After long and complex litigation, the Circuit Court approved an injunction requiring comprehensive changes in living conditions at the Hospital on the basis of rights found to have been created by the *state* legislation.

In Pennhurst State School and Hospital v. Halderman, 465 U.S. 89 (1984), the Supreme Court held the injunction forbidden by the Eleventh Amendment:

> We first address the contention that respondents' state law claim is not barred by the Eleventh Amendment because it seeks only prospective relief as defined in *Edelman v. Jordan*. The Court of Appeals held that if the judgment below rested on federal law, it could be entered against petitioner state officials under the doctrine established in *Edelman* and *Ex parte Young* even though the prospective financial burden was substantial and on-going. The court assumed, and respondents assert, that this reasoning applies as well when the official acts in violation of state law. This argument misconstrues the basis of the doctrine established in *Young* and *Edelman*.

> [T]he injunction in *Ex parte Young* was justified, notwithstanding the obvious impact on the state itself, on the view that sovereign immunity does not apply because an official who acts unconstitutionally is "stripped of his official or representative character." . . . Our decisions repeatedly have emphasized that the *Young* doctrine rests on the need to promote the vindication of federal rights.

> The Court also has recognized, however, that the need to promote the supremacy of federal law must be accommodated to the constitutional immunity of the states. This is the significance of *Edelman v. Jordan*. We recognized that the prospective relief authorized by *Young* "has permitted the Civil War amendments to the Constitution to serve as a sword, rather than merely a shield, for those whom they were designed to protect." But we declined to extend the fiction of *Young* to encompass retroactive relief, for to do

so would effectively eliminate the constitutional immunity of the states. . . . In sum *Edelman*'s distinction between prospective and retroactive relief fulfills the underlying purpose of *Ex parte Young* while at the same time preserving to an important degree the constitutional immunity of the states.

The need to reconcile competing interests is wholly absent, however, when a plaintiff alleges that a state official has violated *state* law. In such a case the entire basis for the doctrine of *Young* and *Edelman* disappears. A federal court's grant of relief against state officials on the basis of state law, whether prospective or retroactive, does not vindicate the supreme authority of federal law. On the contrary, it is difficult to think of a greater intrusion on state sovereignty than when a federal court instructs state officials on how to conform their conduct to state law. Such a result conflicts directly with the principles of federalism that underlie the Eleventh Amendment. We conclude that *Young* and *Edelman* are inapplicable in a suit against state officials on the basis of state law.

Justice Stevens, joined by Justices Brennan, Marshall, and Blackmun, dissented.

A footnote in Justice Powell's *Pennhurst* opinion states that "[a]t the time the suit was filed, suits against Pennsylvania were permitted only where expressly authorized by the legislature," and further that Pennsylvania later enacted a statute on sovereign immunity, "including an express preservation of its immunity from suit in federal court." The dissent made no mention of this point, but as David Shapiro points out in Comment, Wrong Turns: The Eleventh Amendment and the *Pennhurst* Case, 98 Harv. L. Rev. 61, 76–78 (1984), the story is more complicated than at first appears.

The *Pennhurst* litigation began in 1974. At that time, Pennsylvania's sovereign immunity was apparently intact. In 1978, however, the state Supreme Court abrogated the doctrine retroactively. The legislature overturned that decision, but the Pennsylvania Supreme Court held that the statute could not bar litigation of a cause of action that had already accrued at the time of its passage. Thus, it is at least arguable that, under the decisions of the Pennsylvania Supreme Court (and contrary to the wishes of the legislature), there was no state doctrine of sovereign immunity applicable to the *Pennhurst* litigation.

Should state law have mattered? *Erie* would seem to require that federal courts use state law to decide questions of state sovereign immunity from state law claims. Martha Field takes exactly that position. See Martha Field, The Eleventh Amendment and Other Sovereign Immunity Doctrines: Congressional Imposition of Suit upon the States, 126 U. Pa. L. Rev. 1203, 1254 n.240 (1978). Does it follow that if state law permits an action against the state, the federal courts should be free to entertain it? In Atascadero State Hospital v. Scanlon, 473 U.S. 234, 241 (1985), the Court said:

The test for determining whether a state has waived its immunity from federal-court jurisdiction is a stringent one. Although a state's general waiver of sovereign immunity may subject it to

suit in state court, it is not enough to waive the immunity guaran-
teed by the Eleventh Amendment. As we explained just last term,
"a state's constitutional interest in immunity encompasses not
merely *whether* it may be sued, but *where* it may be sued."
Pennhurst State School and Hospital v. Halderman, 465 U.S. 89,
99 (1984). Thus, in order for a state statute or constitutional provision to constitute a waiver of Eleventh Amendment immunity, it
must specify the state's intention to subject itself to suit in *federal
court*.

Does it follow from *Atascadero* that *Pennhurst* was right?

**Pages 1129–33, delete the Notes on the Intersection of the Eleventh
Amendment and State Law, and add the following:**

Franchise Tax Board v. Hyatt

Supreme Court of the United States, 2019.
587 U.S. ___, 139 S.Ct. 1485.

■ JUSTICE THOMAS delivered the opinion of the Court.

This case, now before us for the third time, requires us to decide
whether the Constitution permits a State to be sued by a private party
without its consent in the courts of a different State. We hold that it does
not and overrule our decision to the contrary in Nevada v. Hall, 440 U.S.
410 (1979).

I

In the early 1990s, respondent Gilbert Hyatt earned substantial income from a technology patent for a computer formed on a single inte-
grated circuit chip. Although Hyatt's claim was later canceled, his royal-
ties in the interim totaled millions of dollars. Prior to receiving the patent, Hyatt had been a long-time resident of California. But in 1991, Hyatt sold his house in California and rented an apartment, registered to
vote, obtained insurance, opened a bank account, and acquired a driver's
license in Nevada. When he filed his 1991 and 1992 tax returns, he
claimed Nevada—which collects no personal income tax, as his primary
place of residence.

Petitioner Franchise Tax Board of California (Board), the state
agency responsible for assessing personal income tax, suspected that Hyatt's move was a sham. Thus, in 1993, the Board launched an audit to
determine whether Hyatt underpaid his 1991 and 1992 state income
taxes by misrepresenting his residency. In the course of the audit, employees of the Board traveled to Nevada to conduct interviews with Hyatt's estranged family members and shared his personal information
with business contacts. In total, the Board sent more than 100 letters and
demands for information to third parties. The Board ultimately concluded that Hyatt had not moved to Nevada until April 1992 and owed
California more than $10 million in back taxes, interest, and penalties.
Hyatt protested the audit before the Board, which upheld the audit after

an 11-year administrative proceeding. The appeal of that decision remains pending before the California Office of Tax Appeals.

In 1998, Hyatt sued the Board in Nevada state court for torts he alleged the agency committed during the audit. After the trial court denied in part the Board's motion for summary judgment, the Board petitioned the Nevada Supreme Court for a writ of mandamus ordering dismissal on the ground that the State of California was immune from suit. The Board argued that, under the Full Faith and Credit Clause, Nevada courts must apply California's statute immunizing the Board from liability for all injuries caused by its tax collection. The Nevada Supreme Court rejected that argument and held that, under general principles of comity, the Board was entitled to the same immunity that Nevada law afforded Nevada agencies—that is, immunity for negligent but not intentional torts. We granted certiorari and unanimously affirmed, holding that the Full Faith and Credit Clause did not prohibit Nevada from applying its own immunity law to the case. Franchise Tax Bd. of Cal. v. Hyatt, 538 U.S. 488, 498–99 (2003) (*Hyatt I*). Because the Board did not ask us to overrule *Nevada v. Hall*, we did not revisit that decision.

On remand, the trial court conducted a 4-month jury trial that culminated in a verdict for Hyatt that, with prejudgment interest and costs, exceeded $490 million. On appeal, the Nevada Supreme Court rejected most of the damages awarded by the lower court, upholding only a $1 million judgment on one of Hyatt's claims and remanding for a new damages trial on another. Although the court recognized that tort liability for Nevada state agencies was capped at $50,000 under state law, it nonetheless held that Nevada public policy precluded it from applying that limitation to the California agency in this case. We again granted certiorari and this time reversed, holding that the Full Faith and Credit Clause required Nevada courts to grant the Board the same immunity that Nevada agencies enjoy. Franchise Tax Bd. of Cal. v. Hyatt, 578 U.S. ___, ___–___, 136 S.Ct. 1277, 1281–83 (2016) (*Hyatt II*). Although the question was briefed and argued, the Court was equally divided on whether to overrule *Hall* and thus affirmed the jurisdiction of the Nevada Supreme Court. On remand, the Nevada Supreme Court instructed the trial court to enter damages in accordance with the statutory cap for Nevada agencies.

We granted, for a third time, the Board's petition for certiorari. The sole question presented is whether *Nevada v. Hall* should be overruled.[1]

II

Nevada v. *Hall* is contrary to our constitutional design and the understanding of sovereign immunity shared by the States that ratified the Constitution. Stare decisis does not compel continued adherence to this

---

[1]   Hyatt argues that the law-of-the-case doctrine precludes our review of this question, but he failed to raise that nonjurisdictional issue in his brief in opposition. We therefore deem this argument waived. . . .

erroneous precedent. We therefore overrule *Hall* and hold that States retain their sovereign immunity from private suits brought in the courts of other States.

A

Hall held that the Constitution does not bar private suits against a State in the courts of another State. The opinion conceded that States were immune from such actions at the time of the founding, but it nonetheless concluded that nothing "implicit in the Constitution" requires States "to adhere to the sovereign-immunity doctrine as it prevailed when the Constitution was adopted." 440 U.S. at 417–18, 424–27. Instead, the Court concluded that the Founders assumed that "prevailing notions of comity would provide adequate protection against the unlikely prospect of an attempt by the courts of one State to assert jurisdiction over another." Id. at 419. The Court's view rested primarily on the idea that the States maintained sovereign immunity vis-à-vis each other in the same way that foreign nations do, meaning that immunity is available only if the forum State "voluntar[ily]" decides "to respect the dignity of the [defendant State] as a matter of comity." Id. at 416.

The *Hall* majority was unpersuaded that the Constitution implicitly altered the relationship between the States. In the Court's view, the ratification debates, the Eleventh Amendment, and our sovereign-immunity precedents did not bear on the question because they "concerned questions of federal-court jurisdiction." Id. at 420. The Court also found unpersuasive the fact that the Constitution delineates several limitations on States' authority, such as Article I powers granted exclusively to Congress and Article IV requirements imposed on States. Despite acknowledging "that ours is not a union of 50 wholly independent sovereigns," *Hall* inferred from the lack of an express sovereign immunity granted to the States and from the Tenth Amendment that the States retained the power in their own courts to deny immunity to other States.

Chief Justice Burger, Justice Blackmun, and Justice Rehnquist dissented.

B

Hall's determination that the Constitution does not contemplate sovereign immunity for each State in a sister State's courts misreads the historical record and misapprehends the "implicit ordering of relationships within the federal system necessary to make the Constitution a workable governing charter and to give each provision within that document the full effect intended by the Framers." Id. at 433 (Rehnquist, J., dissenting). As Chief Justice Marshall explained, the Founders did not state every postulate on which they formed our Republic—"we must never forget, that it is *a constitution* we are expounding." McCulloch v. Maryland, 17 U.S. (4 Wheat.) 316, 407 (1819). And although the Constitution assumes that the States retain their sovereign immunity except as otherwise provided, it also fundamentally adjusts the States' relationship with each other and curtails their ability, as sovereigns, to decline to recognize each other's immunity.

1

After independence, the States considered themselves fully sovereign nations. As the Colonies proclaimed in 1776, they were "Free and Independent States" with "full Power to levy War, conclude Peace, contract Alliances, establish Commerce, and to do all other Acts and Things which Independent States may of right do." Declaration of Independence ¶ 4. Under international law, then, independence "entitled" the Colonies "to all the rights and powers of sovereign states." McIlvaine v. Coxe's Lessee, 8 U.S. (4 Cranch) 209, 212 (1808).

"An integral component" of the States' sovereignty was "their immunity from private suits." Federal Maritime Comm'n v. South Carolina Ports Authority, 535 U.S. 743, 751–52 (2002); see Alden v. Maine, 527 U.S. 706, 713 (1999) ("[A]s the Constitution's structure, its history, and the authoritative interpretations by this Court make clear, the States' immunity from suit is a fundamental aspect of the sovereignty which the States enjoyed before the ratification of the Constitution, and which they retain today . . ."). This fundamental aspect of the States' "inviolable sovereignty" was well established and widely accepted at the founding. . . .

The Founders believed that both "common law sovereign immunity" and "law-of-nations sovereign immunity" prevented States from being amenable to process in any court without their consent. See James E. Pfander, Rethinking the Supreme Court's Original Jurisdiction in State-Party Cases, 82 Cal. L. Rev. 555, 581–88 (1994); see also Caleb Nelson, Sovereign Immunity as a Doctrine of Personal Jurisdiction, 115 Harv. L. Rev. 1559, 1574–79 (2002). The common-law rule was that "no suit or action can be brought against the king, even in civil matters, because no court can have jurisdiction over him." 1 W. Blackstone, Commentaries on the Laws of England 235 (1765) (Blackstone). The law-of-nations rule followed from the "perfect equality and absolute independence of sovereigns" under that body of international law. Schooner Exchange v. McFaddon, 11 U.S. (7 Cranch) 116, 137 (1812). . . .

The founding generation thus took as given that States could not be haled involuntarily before each other's courts. See Ann Woolhandler, Interstate Sovereign Immunity, 2006 S.Ct. Rev. 249, 254–59. . . .

In short, at the time of the founding, it was well settled that States were immune under both the common law and the law of nations. The Constitution's use of the term "States" reflects both of these kinds of traditional immunity. And the States retained these aspects of sovereignty, "except as altered by the plan of the Convention or certain constitutional Amendments." *Alden*, 527 U.S. at 713.

2

One constitutional provision that abrogated certain aspects of this traditional immunity was Article III, which provided a neutral federal forum in which the States agreed to be amenable to suits brought by other States. Art. III, § 2; see *Alden*, 527 U.S. at 755. . . .

The States, in ratifying the Constitution, similarly surrendered a portion of their immunity by consenting to suits brought against them by the United States in federal courts. See Principality of Monaco v. Mississippi, 292 U.S. 313, 328 (1934). "While that jurisdiction is not conferred by the Constitution in express words, it is inherent in the constitutional plan." *Monaco*, 292 U.S. at 329. . . .

The Antifederalists worried that Article III went even further by extending the federal judicial power over controversies "between a State and Citizens of another State." They suggested that this provision implicitly waived the States' sovereign immunity against *private* suits in federal courts. But "[t]he leading advocates of the Constitution assured the people in no uncertain terms" that this reading was incorrect. *Alden*, 527 U.S. at 716. According to Madison:

> "[A federal court's] jurisdiction in controversies between a state and citizens of another state is much objected to, and perhaps without reason. It is not in the power of individuals to call any state into court. The only operation it can have, is that, if a state should wish to bring a suit against a citizen, it must be brought before the federal court. This will give satisfaction to individuals, as it will prevent citizens, on whom a state may have a claim, being dissatisfied with the state courts." Elliot's Debates 533. . . .

Not long after the founding, however, the Antifederalists' fears were realized. In Chisholm v. Georgia, 2 U.S. (2 Dall.) 419 (1793), the Court held that Article III allowed the very suits that the "Madison-Marshall-Hamilton triumvirate" insisted it did not. *Hall*, 440 U.S. at 437 (Rehnquist, J., dissenting). That decision precipitated an immediate "furor" and "uproar" across the country. Congress and the States accordingly acted swiftly to remedy the Court's blunder by drafting and ratifying the Eleventh Amendment.

The Eleventh Amendment confirmed that the Constitution was not meant to "rais[e] up" any suits against the States that were "anomalous and unheard of when the Constitution was adopted." Hans v. Louisiana, 134 U.S. 1, 18 (1890). Although the terms of that Amendment address only "the specific provisions of the Constitution that had raised concerns during the ratification debates and formed the basis of the *Chisholm* decision," the "natural inference" from its speedy adoption is that "the Constitution was understood, in light of its history and structure, to preserve the States' traditional immunity from private suits." *Alden*, at 723–24. . . .

Consistent with this understanding of state sovereign immunity, this Court has held that the Constitution bars suits against nonconsenting States in a wide range of cases. See, e.g., *Federal Maritime Comm'n*, supra (actions by private parties before federal administrative agencies); *Alden*, supra (suits by private parties against a State in its own courts); Blatchford v. Native Village of Noatak, 501 U.S. 775 (1991) (suits by Indian tribes in federal court); *Monaco*, supra (suits by foreign states in federal court); Ex parte New York, 256 U.S. 490 (1921) (admiralty suits by private parties in federal court); Smith v. Reeves, 178 U.S. 436 (1900) (suits by federal corporations in federal court).

3

Despite this historical evidence that interstate sovereign immunity is preserved in the constitutional design, Hyatt insists that such immunity exists only as a "matter of comity" and can be disregarded by the forum State. He reasons that, before the Constitution was ratified, the States had the power of fully independent nations to deny immunity to fellow sovereigns; thus, the States must retain that power today with respect to each other because "nothing in the Constitution or formation of the Union altered that balance among the still-sovereign states." Brief for Respondent 14. . . .

The problem with Hyatt's argument is that the Constitution affirmatively altered the relationships between the States, so that they no longer relate to each other solely as foreign sovereigns. Each State's equal dignity and sovereignty under the Constitution implies certain constitutional "limitation[s] on the sovereignty of all of its sister States." World-Wide Volkswagen Corp. v. Woodson, 444 U.S. 286, 293 (1980). One such limitation is the inability of one State to hail another into its courts without the latter's consent. The Constitution does not merely allow States to afford each other immunity as a matter of comity; it embeds interstate sovereign immunity within the constitutional design. Numerous provisions reflect this reality.

To begin, Article I divests the States of the traditional diplomatic and military tools that foreign sovereigns possess. Specifically, the States can no longer prevent or remedy departures from customary international law because the Constitution deprives them of the independent power to lay imposts or duties on imports and exports, to enter into treaties or compacts, and to wage war. Compare Art. I, § 10, with Declaration of Independence ¶ 4 (asserting the power to "levy War, conclude Peace, contract Alliances, [and] establish Commerce").

Article IV also imposes duties on the States not required by international law. The Court's Full Faith and Credit Clause precedents, for example, demand that state-court judgments be accorded full effect in other States and preclude States from "adopt[ing] any policy of hostility to the public Acts" of other States. *Hyatt II*, 578 U.S. at ___ 136 S.Ct. at 1281; see Art. IV, § 1. States must also afford citizens of each State "all Privileges and Immunities of Citizens in the several States" and honor extradition requests upon "Demand of the executive Authority of the State" from which the fugitive fled. Art. IV, § 2. Foreign sovereigns cannot demand these kinds of reciprocal responsibilities absent consent or compact. . . .

The Constitution also reflects implicit alterations to the States' relationships with each other, confirming that they are no longer fully independent nations. For example, States may not supply rules of decision governing "disputes implicating the[ir] conflicting rights." Texas Industries, Inc. v. Radcliff Materials, Inc., 451 U.S. 630, 641 (1981). Thus, no State can apply its own law to interstate disputes over borders, Cissna v. Tennessee, 246 U.S. 289, 295 (1918), water rights, Hinderlider v. La Plata River & Cherry Creek Ditch Co., 304 U.S. 92, 110 (1938), or the interpretation of interstate compacts, Petty v. Tennessee-Missouri Bridge Comm'n, 359 U.S. 275, 278–79 (1959). The States would have had the raw power to apply their own law to such matters before they entered the Union, but the Constitution implicitly forbids that exercise of power because the "interstate . . . nature of the controversy makes it inappropriate for state law to control." *Texas Industries*, supra, at 641. Some subjects that were decided by pure "political power" before ratification now turn on federal "rules of law." Rhode Island v. Massachusetts, 37 U.S. (12 Pet.) 657, 737 (1838). See Bradford R. Clark, Federal Common Law: A Structural Reinterpretation, 144 U. Pa. L. Rev. 1245, 1322–31 (1996).

Interstate sovereign immunity is similarly integral to the structure of the Constitution. Like a dispute over borders or water rights, a State's assertion of compulsory judicial process over another State involves a direct conflict between sovereigns. The Constitution implicitly strips States of any power they once had to refuse each other sovereign immunity, just as it denies them the power to resolve border disputes by political means. Interstate immunity, in other words, is "implied as an essential component of federalism." *Hall*, 440 U.S. at 430–31 (Blackmun, J., dissenting).

Hyatt argues that we should find no right to sovereign immunity in another State's courts because no constitutional provision explicitly grants that immunity. But this is precisely the type of "ahistorical literalism" that we have rejected when "interpreting the scope of the States' sovereign immunity since the discredited decision in *Chisholm*." *Alden*, 527 U.S. at 730; see id. at 736 ("[T]he bare text of the Amendment is not an exhaustive description of the States' constitutional immunity from suit"). In light of our constitutional structure, the historical understanding of state immunity, and the swift enactment of the Eleventh Amendment after the Court departed from this understanding in *Chisholm*, "[i]t is not rational to suppose that the sovereign power should be dragged before a court." Elliot's Debates 555 (Marshall). Indeed, the spirited historical debate over Article III courts and the immediate reaction to *Chisholm* make little sense if the Eleventh Amendment were the only source of sovereign immunity and private suits against the States could already be brought in "partial, local tribunals." Elliot's Debates 532 (Madison). Nor would the Founders have objected so strenuously to a neutral federal forum for private suits against States if they were open to a State being sued in a different State's courts. Hyatt's view thus inverts the Founders' concerns about state-court parochialism. *Hall*, supra, at 439 (Rehnquist, J., dissenting).

Moreover, Hyatt's ahistorical literalism proves too much. There are many other constitutional doctrines that are not spelled out in the Constitution but are nevertheless implicit in its structure and supported by historical practice—including, for example, judicial review, Marbury v. Madison, 5 U.S. (1 Cranch) 137, 176–80 (1803); intergovernmental tax immunity, *McCulloch*, 17 U.S. (4 Wheat.) at 435–36; executive privilege, United States v. Nixon, 418 U.S. 683, 705–06 (1974); executive immunity, Nixon v. Fitzgerald, 457 U.S. 731, 755–58 (1982); and the President's removal power, Myers v. United States, 272 U.S. 52, 163–64 (1926). Like these doctrines, the States' sovereign immunity is a historically rooted principle embedded in the text and structure of the Constitution.

C

With the historical record and precedent against him, Hyatt defends *Hall* on the basis of stare decisis. But stare decisis is " 'not an inexorable command,' " Pearson v. Callahan, 555 U.S. 223, 233 (2009), and we have held that it is "at its weakest when we interpret the Constitution because our interpretation can be altered only by constitutional amendment," Agostini v. Felton, 521 U.S. 203, 235 (1997). The Court's precedents identify a number of factors to consider, four of which warrant mention here: the quality of the decision's reasoning; its consistency with related decisions; legal developments since the decision; and reliance on the decision.

The first three factors support our decision to overrule *Hall*. We have already explained that *Hall* failed to account for the historical understanding of state sovereign immunity and that it failed to consider how the deprivation of traditional diplomatic tools reordered the States' relationships with one another. We have also demonstrated that *Hall* stands as an outlier in our sovereign-immunity jurisprudence, particularly when compared to more recent decisions.

As to the fourth factor, we acknowledge that some plaintiffs, such as Hyatt, have relied on *Hall* by suing sovereign States. Because of our decision to overrule *Hall*, Hyatt unfortunately will suffer the loss of two decades of litigation expenses and a final judgment against the Board for its egregious conduct. But in virtually every case that overrules a controlling precedent, the party relying on that precedent will incur the loss of litigation expenses and a favorable decision below. Those case-specific costs are not among the reliance interests that would persuade us to adhere to an incorrect resolution of an important constitutional question.

* * *

Nevada v. *Hall* is irreconcilable with our constitutional structure and with the historical evidence showing a widespread preratification understanding that States retained immunity from private suits, both in their own courts and in other courts. We therefore overrule that decision.

Because the Board is thus immune from Hyatt's suit in Nevada's courts, the judgment of the Nevada Supreme Court is reversed, and the case is remanded for proceedings not inconsistent with this opinion.

It is so ordered.

■ JUSTICE BREYER, with whom JUSTICE GINSBURG, JUSTICE SOTOMAYOR, and JUSTICE KAGAN join, dissenting.

Can a private citizen sue one State in the courts of another? Normally the answer to this question is no, because the State where the suit is brought will choose to grant its sister States immunity. But the question here is whether the Federal Constitution *requires* each State to grant its sister States immunity, or whether the Constitution instead *permits* a State to grant or deny its sister States immunity as it chooses.

We answered that question 40 years ago in Nevada v. Hall, 440 U.S. 410 (1979). The Court in *Hall* held that the Constitution took the permissive approach, leaving it up to each State to decide whether to grant or deny its sister States sovereign immunity. Today, the majority takes the contrary approach—the absolute approach—and overrules *Hall*. I can find no good reason to overrule *Hall*, however, and I consequently dissent.

I

Hall involved a suit brought by a California resident against the State of Nevada in the California courts. We rejected the claim that the Constitution entitled Nevada to absolute immunity. We first considered the immunity that States possessed as independent sovereigns before the Constitution was ratified. And we then asked whether ratification of the Constitution altered the principles of state sovereign immunity in any relevant respect. At both steps, we concluded, the relevant history and precedent refuted the claim that States are entitled to absolute immunity in each other's courts.

A

Hall first considered the immunity that States possessed before ratification. "States considered themselves fully sovereign nations" during this period, and the Court in *Hall* therefore asked whether sovereign nations would have enjoyed absolute immunity in each other's courts at the time of our founding.

The answer was no. At the time of the founding, nations granted other nations sovereign immunity in their courts not as a matter of legal obligation but as a matter of choice, i.e., of comity or grace or consent. Foreign sovereign immunity was a doctrine "of implied consent by the territorial sovereign . . . deriving from standards of public morality, fair dealing, reciprocal self-interest, and respect." National City Bank of N.Y. v. Republic of China, 348 U.S. 356, 362 (1955). Since customary international law made the matter one of choice, a nation could withdraw that sovereign immunity if it so chose. . . .

. . . Drawing on the comparison to foreign nations, the Court in *Hall* emphasized that California had made a sovereign decision not to "exten[d] immunity to Nevada as a matter of comity." 440 U.S. at 418. Unless some constitutional rule required California to grant immunity that it had chosen to withhold, the Court "ha[d] no power to disturb the judgment of the California courts." Id.

B

The Court in *Hall* next held that ratification of the Constitution did not alter principles of state sovereign immunity in any relevant respect. The Court concluded that express provisions of the Constitution—such as the Eleventh Amendment and the Full Faith and Credit Clause of Article IV—did not require States to accord each other sovereign immunity. And the Court held that nothing "implicit in the Constitution" treats States differently in respect to immunity than international law treats sovereign nations. Id. at 418.

To the contrary, the Court in *Hall* observed that an express provision of the Constitution undermined the assertion that States were absolutely immune in each other's courts. Unlike suits brought against a State in the State's own courts, *Hall* noted, a suit against a State in the courts of a different State "necessarily implicates the power and authority of" both States. Id. at 416. The defendant State has a sovereign interest in immunity from suit, while the forum State has a sovereign interest in defining the jurisdiction of its own courts. The Court in *Hall* therefore justified its decision in part by reference to "the Tenth Amendment's reminder that powers not delegated to the Federal Government nor prohibited to the States are reserved to the States or to the people." Id. at 425. Compelling States to grant immunity to their sister States would risk interfering with sovereign rights that the Tenth Amendment leaves to the States. . . .

II

The majority disputes both *Hall*'s historical conclusion regarding state immunity before ratification and its conclusion that the Constitution did not alter that immunity. But I do not find the majority's arguments convincing.

A

The majority asserts that before ratification "it was well settled that States were immune under both the common law and the law of nations." The majority thus maintains that States were exempt from suit in each other's courts.

But the question in *Hall* concerned the *basis* for that exemption. Did one sovereign have an absolute right to an exemption from the jurisdiction of the courts of another, or was that exemption a customary matter, a matter of consent that a sovereign might withdraw? As to that question, nothing in the majority's opinion casts doubt on *Hall*'s conclusion that

States—like foreign nations—were accorded immunity as a matter of consent rather than absolute right. . . .

B

The majority next argues that "the Constitution affirmatively altered the relationships between the States" by giving them immunity that they did not possess when they were fully independent. The majority thus maintains that, whatever the nature of state immunity before ratification, the Constitution accorded States an absolute immunity that they did not previously possess.

The most obvious problem with this argument is that no provision of the Constitution gives States absolute immunity in each other's courts. The majority does not attempt to situate its newfound constitutional immunity in any provision of the Constitution itself. Instead, the majority maintains that a State's immunity in other States' courts is "implicit" in the Constitution, "embed[ded] . . . within the constitutional design," and reflected in " 'the plan of the Convention.' " . . .

. . . I can find nothing in the "plan of the Convention" or elsewhere to suggest that the Constitution converted what had been the customary practice of extending immunity by consent into an absolute federal requirement that no State could withdraw. None of the majority's arguments indicates that the Constitution accomplished any such transformation.

The majority argues that the Constitution sought to preserve States' "equal dignity and sovereignty." That is true, but tells us nothing useful here. When a citizen brings suit against one State in the courts of another, both States have strong sovereignty-based interests. In contrast to a State's power to assert sovereign immunity in its own courts, sovereignty interests here lie on both sides of the constitutional equation. . . .

[W]here the Constitution alters the authority of States vis-à-vis other States, it tends to do so explicitly. The Import-Export Clause cited by the majority, for example, creates "harmony among the States" by preventing them from "burden[ing] commerce . . . among themselves." Michelin Tire Corp. v. Wages, 423 U.S. 276, 283, 285 (1976). The Full Faith and Credit Clause, also invoked by the majority, prohibits States from adopting a "policy of hostility to the public Acts" of another State. Franchise Tax Bd. of Cal. v. Hyatt, 578 U.S. ___, ___, 136 S.Ct. 1277, 1281 (2016). By contrast, the Constitution says nothing explicit about interstate sovereign immunity. . . .

III

In any event, stare decisis requires us to follow *Hall*, not overrule it. See Planned Parenthood of Southeastern Pa. v. Casey, 505 U.S. 833, 854–55 (1992); see also Kimble v. Marvel Entertainment, LLC, 576 U.S. 446, 455–56, 135 S.Ct. 2401, 2409 (2015). Overruling a case always requires " 'special justification.' " *Kimble*, 576 U.S. at 456, 135 S.Ct. at 2409. What could that justification be in this case? The majority does not find one.

The majority believes that *Hall* was wrongly decided. But "an argument that we got something wrong—even a good argument to that effect—cannot by itself justify scrapping settled precedent." *Kimble,* 576 U.S. at 455, 135 S.Ct. at 2409. Three dissenters in *Hall* also believed that *Hall* was wrong, but they recognized that the Court's opinion was "plausible." 440 U.S. at 427 (opinion of Blackmun, J.). While reasonable jurists might disagree about whether *Hall* was correct, that very fact—that *Hall* is not obviously wrong—shows that today's majority is obviously wrong to overrule it. . . .

The dissenters in *Hall* feared its "practical implications." 440 U.S. at 443 (opinion of Rehnquist, J.). But I can find nothing in the intervening 40 years to suggest that this fear was well founded. The Board and its amici have, by my count, identified only 14 cases in 40 years in which one State has entertained a private citizen's suit against another State in its courts. See Brief for Petitioner 46–47; Brief for State of Indiana et al. as Amici Curiae 13–14. In at least one of those 14 cases, moreover, the state court eventually agreed to dismiss the suit against its sister State as a matter of comity. How can it be that these cases, decided over a period of four decades, show *Hall* to be unworkable?

The *Hall* issue so rarely arises because most States, like most sovereign nations, are reluctant to deny a sister State the immunity that they would prefer to enjoy reciprocally. Thus, even in the absence of constitutionally mandated immunity, States normally grant sovereign immunity voluntarily. States that fear that this practice will be insufficiently protective are free to enter into an interstate compact to guarantee that the normal practice of granting immunity will continue. . . .

Perhaps the majority believes that there has been insufficient reliance on *Hall* to justify preserving it. But any such belief would ignore an important feature of reliance. The people of this Nation rely upon stability in the law. Legal stability allows lawyers to give clients sound advice and allows ordinary citizens to plan their lives. Each time the Court overrules a case, the Court produces increased uncertainty. To overrule a sound decision like *Hall* is to encourage litigants to seek to overrule other cases; it is to make it more difficult for lawyers to refrain from challenging settled law; and it is to cause the public to become increasingly uncertain about which cases the Court will overrule and which cases are here to stay. . . .

* * *

It is one thing to overrule a case when it "def[ies] practical workability," when "related principles of law have so far developed as to have left the old rule no more than a remnant of abandoned doctrine," or when "facts have so changed, or come to be seen so differently, as to have robbed the old rule of significant application or justification." *Casey,* 505 U.S. at 854–55. It is far more dangerous to overrule a decision only because five Members of a later Court come to agree with earlier dissenters on a difficult legal question. The majority has surrendered to the temptation to overrule *Hall* even though it is a well-reasoned decision that has caused no serious practical problems in the four decades since we decided it. Today's decision can only cause one to wonder which cases the Court will overrule next. I respectfully dissent.

NOTES ON FRANCHISE TAX BOARD V. HYATT

1. *NEVADA V. HALL*

California residents were injured when their car was struck by a vehicle being driven on official business by an employee of the state of Nevada. The accident occurred in California. The plaintiffs sued in a California state court, naming as defendants the Nevada employee's estate (he was killed in the accident) and the state. Personal jurisdiction was acquired over the state under a California statute authorizing service of process on nonresident motorists. The California courts upheld a jury verdict against Nevada for more than $1 million, notwithstanding a Nevada statute limiting recoveries against the state to $25,000. In Nevada v. Hall, 440 U.S. 410 (1979), the Supreme Court affirmed.

In an opinion by Justice Stevens, the Court denied that California was bound by federal law to respect Nevada's sovereign immunity. The Court observed that there was nothing in either the Eleventh Amendment or in Article III that "provide[s] any basis, explicit or implicit, for this Court to impose limits on the powers of California exercised in this case." The Court also reasoned that the constitutional Founders appeared to have assumed that "prevailing notions of comity would provide adequate protection against the unlikely prospect of an attempt by the courts of one State to assert jurisdiction over another." As for broader principles of state sovereignty, the Court reasoned:

> It may be wise policy, as a matter of harmonious interstate relations, for States to accord each other immunity or to respect any established limits on liability. They are free to do so. But if a federal court were to hold, by inference from the structure of our Constitution and nothing else, that California is not free in this case to enforce its policy of full compensation, that holding would constitute the real intrusion on the sovereignty of the States—and the power of the people—in our Union.

Justice Blackmun, joined by Chief Justice Burger and by Justice Rehnquist, dissented, saying that, although the majority's decision was "plausible," he would find "a constitutional doctrine of interstate sovereign immunity" implied as an essential component of the federal system. Justice Rehnquist, joined by the Chief Justice, wrote separately, adding that the result reached by the majority "destroys the framers' careful allocation of responsibility among the state and federal judiciaries, and makes nonsense of the effort embodied in the Eleventh Amendment to preserve the doctrine of sovereign immunity."

For criticism of *Nevada v. Hall*, see Ann Woolhandler, Interstate Sovereign Immunity, 2006 Sup. Ct. Rev. 249. For a defense of *Hall*, see William Baude, Sovereign Immunity and the Constitutional Text, 103 Va. L. Rev. 1 (2017). For discussion of the case in the broader context of choice of law generally, see Patrick J. Borchers, Is the Supreme Court Really Going to Regulate Choice of Law Involving States?, 50 Creighton L. Rev. 7 (2016).

2. *ALDEN V. MAINE*

The Supreme Court's conception of state sovereign immunity has evolved significantly since *Nevada v. Hall*. This is especially evident in decisions addressing Congress's authority to abrogate immunity, which are addressed in Section 2 of this chapter. A noteworthy example is Alden v. Maine, 527 U.S. 706 (1999), a 5–4 decision in which the Court held that Congress lacked authority under Article I of the Constitution to abrogate a state's immunity in the state's own courts. This was true, reasoned the Court, even though the Eleventh Amendment does not apply to state courts. The Court explained:

> [The Court's] holdings reflect a settled doctrinal understanding, consistent with the views of the leading advocates of the Constitution's ratification, that sovereign immunity derives not from the Eleventh Amendment but from the structure of the original Constitution itself. . . . The Eleventh Amendment confirmed rather than established sovereign immunity as a constitutional principle; it follows that the scope of the States' immunity from suit is demarcated not by the text of the Amendment alone but by fundamental postulates implicit in the constitutional design.

The Court proceeded to conclude, based on "history, practice, precedent, and the structure of the Constitution," that "the States retain immunity from private suit in their own courts, an immunity beyond the congressional power to abrogate by Article I legislation." The Court distinguished *Nevada v. Hall* as follows:

> Our opinion in *Hall* did distinguish a State's immunity from suit in federal court from its immunity in the courts of other States; it did not, however, address or consider any differences between a State's sovereign immunity in federal court and in its own courts. Our reluctance to find an implied constitutional limit on the power of the States cannot be construed, furthermore, to support an analogous reluctance to find implied constitutional limits on the power of the Federal Government. The Constitution, after all, treats the powers of the States differently from the powers of the Federal Government. . . .
>
> Our decision in *Hall* thus does not support the argument urged by petitioners here. The decision addressed neither Congress' power to subject States to private suits nor the States' immunity from suit in their own courts. In fact, the distinction drawn between a sovereign's immunity in its own courts and its immunity in the courts of another sovereign, as well as the reasoning on which this

distinction was based, are consistent with, and even support, the proposition urged by the respondent here—that the Constitution reserves to the States a constitutional immunity from private suits in their own courts which cannot be abrogated by Congress.

3.   QUESTIONS AND COMMENTS ON *FRANCHISE TAX BOARD V. HYATT*

According to the Court in *Franchise Tax*, what is the source of the states' sovereign immunity? To what extent, if at all, is the text of the Eleventh Amendment relevant to this immunity? The Court contends that the Constitution treated the relationship between U.S. states differently than the way that international law at that time treated the relationship between sovereign nations. How, according to the Court, is this historical point relevant to the immunity issue in this case? What is the dissent's response? Both the majority and dissent invoke considerations relating to state sovereignty: the majority invokes a sovereign right of a state not to be hailed into a sister state court without its consent, and the dissent invokes a sovereign right of a state to open its courts up to suits against other states. What is the majority's rationale for favoring the first sovereignty interest over the second?

In overturning *Nevada v. Hall*, what justifications does the Court give for departing from stare decisis? Is it simply that a new Court majority has concluded that *Hall* was wrongly decided, as the dissent contends? The Court notes, among other things, that "*Hall* stands as an outlier in our sovereign-immunity jurisprudence, particularly when compared to more recent decisions." If the reasoning of a decision is inconsistent with the reasoning of subsequent decisions, should stare decisis still apply? Does overturning a decision in order to make the case law more coherent undermine legal stability, as suggested by the dissent?[a]

  [a]   For an extremely critical discussion of the result and reasoning in *Franchise Tax Board v. Hyatt*, see Louise Weinberg, Sovereign Immunity and Interstate Government Tort, 54 U. Mich. J.L. Reform 17 (2020).

SECTION 2. CONSENT AND CONGRESSIONAL ABROGATION

Page 1177, add to footnote b:

Graham K. Bryant, The Historical Argument for State Sovereign Immunity in Bankruptcy Proceedings, 87 Miss. L.J. 49 (2018).

Page 1214, add a new Note after Note 4:

4A. *ALLEN V. COOPER*

In 1996, a private marine salvage company, Intersal, discovered the remains of Blackbeard's pirate ship, which had sunk off the North Carolina coast in the early 1700s. Under federal and state law, the shipwreck belonged to North Carolina. But the state contracted with Intersal to have it take charge of the recovery operations, and Intersal in turn contracted with Frederick Allen, a local videographer, to document the operations through photos and videos. Allen registered copyrights in the works. In 2013, Allen protested that the state was uploading the works to its website without permission, and he and the state agreed to a settlement that set forth the parties' respective rights in the materials. After the settlement, Allen complained that the state was again using his videos and photos without permission, and he filed suit against the state (and a variety of other defendants) in a federal district court, seeking damages for alleged copyright infringement. In his suit, he invoked the Copyright Remedy Clarification Act of 1990 (CRCA), which provides that a state "shall not be immune, under the Eleventh Amendment [or] any other doctrine of sovereign immunity, from suit in Federal court" for copyright infringement and that in such a suit a state is liable "in the same manner and to the same extent as" a private party.

In Allen v. Cooper, 589 U.S. ___, 140 S.Ct. 994 (2020), the Supreme Court unanimously agreed that the state was entitled to sovereign immunity. Justice Kagan wrote the lead opinion. The Court first rejected Allen's argument that Congress's Article I authority to regulate copyrights gives it the authority to abrogate state sovereign immunity. This argument, the Court reasoned, was foreclosed by the Court's 1999 decision in *Florida Prepaid Postsecondary Ed. Expense Bd.* v. *College Savings Bank* (discussed at pages 1192–93 of the casebook). In that case, the Court held that Congress's effort to abrogate state sovereign immunity in the Patent Remedy Act, which was modeled on the CRCA and had similar language, was unconstitutional. Congress's authority over copyrights stems from the same clause in Article I as its authority to regulate patents, i.e., the clause that gives Congress the power "[t]o promote the Progress of Science and useful Arts, by securing for limited Times to Authors and Inventors the exclusive Right to their respective Writings and Discoveries." "[T]o extend the point to this case," said the Court, if Congress lacks the power to abrogate sovereign immunity in the Patent Remedy Act, it would lack the same power with respect to copyrights "and for the same reason. Here too, the power to 'secur[e]' an intellectual property owner's 'exclusive Right' under Article I stops when it runs into sovereign immunity."

Nothing in the Court's 2006 decision in *Central Va. Community College* v. *Katz*, concerning the Article I Bankruptcy Clause, changes this conclusion. (*Katz* is discussed at pages 1174–77 of the casebook.) The Court explained: "[E]verything in *Katz* is about and limited to the Bankruptcy Clause; the opinion reflects what might be called bankruptcy exceptionalism. . . . [The decision] points to a good-for-one-clause-only holding." The Court also emphasized the importance of stare decisis:

> [W]e would have to overrule *Florida Prepaid* if we were to decide this case Allen's way. But stare decisis, this Court has understood, is a "foundation stone of the rule of law." Michigan v. Bay Mills Indian Community, 572 U.S. 782, 798 (2014). To reverse a decision, we demand a "special justification," over and above the belief "that the precedent was wrongly decided." Halliburton Co. v. Erica P. John Fund, Inc., 573 U.S. 258, 266 (2014). Allen offers us nothing special at all; he contends only that if the Court were to use a clause-by-clause approach, it would discover that *Florida Prepaid* was wrong (because, he says again, the decision misjudged Congress's authority under the Intellectual Property Clause). And with that charge of error alone, Allen cannot overcome stare decisis.

Next, the Court rejected Allen's argument that Congress had authority to enact the CRCA under Section 5 of the Fourteenth Amendment. Although the Court accepted that copyrights are a form of property entitled to protection under the Fourteenth Amendment's Due Process Clause, it reasoned that, in order to be unconstitutional, a state's copyright violation would have to be intentional or at least reckless, and there would also have to be a lack of an adequate state remedy for the violation. The CRCA is not limited to those situations, however, and thus is valid, reasoned the Court, only if it meets the "congruence and proportionality" test from *Boerne*.

Again, the Court looked to its decision in *Florida Prepaid*. In that case, the Court had concluded that there was an insufficient record before Congress of state patent violations to justify the abrogation of immunity. In this case, said the Court, "the concrete evidence of States infringing copyrights (even ignoring whether those acts violate due process) is scarcely more impressive than what the *Florida Prepaid* Court saw." Moreover, as in *Florida Prepaid*, the Court noted that the legislative record here did not reflect any focus on whether the relatively few state infringements that were identified violated the Due Process Clause. As a result:

> [T]he evidence of Fourteenth Amendment injury supporting the CRCA and the Patent Remedy Act is equivalent—for both, that is, exceedingly slight. And the scope of the two statutes is identical—extending to every infringement case against a State. It follows that the balance the laws strike between constitutional wrong and statutory remedy is correspondingly askew.

The Court concluded its opinion by observing that nothing in its analysis prevented Congress from passing a valid copyright abrogation statute in the future: "if it detects violations of due process, then it may enact a proportionate response. That kind of tailored statute can effectively stop States from behaving as copyright pirates."

Justice Thomas concurred in part and concurred in the judgment. Although agreeing that the CRCA was not a valid abrogation of immunity, he took issue with three aspects of the majority opinion. First, he rejected the idea that a "special justification" is needed for overturning precedent. In his view, the Court has a duty under Article III to overturn precedents that it concludes are demonstrably erroneous, and he observed in a footnote that he continues to believe that *Katz* was wrongly decided. Second, he did not think it appropriate for the Court to suggest potential legislation to Congress. Finally, he did not think that it was clear that copyrights should be considered property for purposes of the Due Process Clause of the Fourteenth Amendment, although he was willing to accept that proposition for the sake of argument in this case.

Justice Breyer concurred in the judgment, and was joined by Justice Ginsburg. Breyer noted that he continues to believe that the Court took a wrong turn in the *Seminole Tribe* line of cases, but "recognizing that my longstanding view has not carried the day, and that the Court's decision in *Florida Prepaid* controls this case, I concur in the judgment."

Page 1216, add at the end of Note 5:

For an argument that the Eleventh Amendment "means what it says," see William Baude and Stephen E. Sachs, The Misunderstood Eleventh Amendment, 169 U. Pa. L. Rev. 609 (2021). According to Baude and Sachs, the Eleventh Amendment "eliminates federal judicial power over one set of cases: suits pled against states, in law or equity, by diverse plaintiffs"; "[i]t strips subject-matter jurisdiction in all such cases, regardless of why or how the plaintiffs are in federal court, and in only such cases"; "[i]t can't be waived"; "[i]t can't be abrogated"; and "[i]t applies in the Supreme Court." They also contend that, in addition to the Eleventh Amendment, there is "a common-law immunity from compulsory process, one that prevents states from being forced into court without their consent" and that this immunity "largely can't be abrogated by Congress under Article I." Although they note that the Supreme Court's reasoning in its state sovereign immunity decisions has not reflected their proposed literal reading of the Eleventh Amendment, they find that the Court nevertheless "has arrived at mostly right answers in its sovereign immunity cases, most of the time."

SECTION 3. CONSTITUTIONALLY REQUIRED REMEDIES IN STATE COURT

Page 1231, add at the end of footnote b:

For discussion of the questions raised in Note 4, see Ann Woolhandler and Michael G. Collins, State Jurisdictional Independence and Federal Supremacy, 72 Fla. L. Rev. 73 (2020). The authors conclude that the *Crain* line of cases "is concerned with constitutionally adequate remedies" and that "the requirements tend to surface when lower federal court jurisdiction is disfavored or unavailable." They see the decisions in *Haywood v. Drown* (a main case in Chapter I, Section 2) and *Montgomery v. Louisiana* (discussed in the Notes following *Haywood*), however, as having the "potential to make the *Crain* line largely superfluous" by "possibly requiring greater state conformity with federal-court versions of causes of action raising constitutional claims."

CHAPTER IX

42 U.S.C. § 1983

SECTION 2. OFFICIAL IMMUNITIES

Page 1272, add a footnote at the end of Note 8:

[d] For an argument against *Mitchell v. Forsyth*, see Michael E. Solimine, Are Interlocutory Qualified Immunity Appeals Lawful?, 94 Notre Dame Online Rev. 169 (2019).

Page 1274, add a footnote at the end of Note 10:

[f] For a rare analysis of qualified immunity that differentiates between *Bivens* and § 1983, see Katherine Mims Crocker, Qualified Immunity and Constitutional Structure, 117 Mich. L. Rev. 1405 (2019). Crocker argues that the extension of qualified immunity in *Harlow* might be viewed as a "compensating adjustment" for the "judicial overreach" of creating *Bivens* in the first place. Qualified immunity in actions authorized by § 1983 would necessarily stand on different ground, perhaps influenced by considerations of federalism.

Page 1274, add a new Note:

11. BIBLIOGRAPHY

In addition to the many articles on specific aspects of qualified immunity (see, for example, the articles on the "order-of-battle" issue in the next section), there is continuing, indeed accelerating, debate about qualified immunity in general. Prominent critics of qualified immunity include William Baude, Is Qualified Immunity Unlawful?, 106 Cal. L. Rev. 45 (2018); Alan K. Chen, The Intractability of Qualified Immunity, 93 Notre Dame L. Rev. 1937 (2018); Joanna C. Schwartz, The Case Against Qualified Immunity, 93 Notre Dame L. Rev. 1797 (2018); and Fred O. Smith, Jr., Formalism, Ferguson, and the Future of Qualified Immunity, 93 Notre Dame L. Rev. 2093 (2018).

Scott Michelman, The Branch Best Qualified to Abolish Immunity, 93 Notre Dame L. Rev. 1999 (2018), assumes that qualified immunity should be eliminated and argues that the judiciary should do so. Karen M. Blum, Qualified Immunity: Time to Change the Message, 93 Notre Dame L. Rev. 1887 (2018), argues that the Court should embrace respondeat superior for government employers and thus "fix" qualified immunity by making it irrelevant. John F. Preis, Qualified Immunity and Fault, 93 Notre Dame L. Rev. 1969 (2018), argues that qualified immunity as currently applied does not accurately assess fault and perhaps cannot do so.

A partial defense of qualified immunity appears in Aaron L. Nielson and Christopher J. Walker, A Qualified Defense of Qualified Immunity, 93 Notre Dame L. Rev. 1853 (2018). And an empirical assessment of how it works at trial appears in Alexander A. Reinert, Qualified Immunity at Trial, 93 Notre Dame L. Rev. 2065 (2018) (partly joining issue with Joanna Schwartz, supra). The application of qualified immunity in a particular context is explored in David M. Shapiro and Charles Hogle, The Horror Chamber: Unqualified Immunity in Prison, 93 Notre Dame L. Rev. 2021 (2018).

Finally, Michael L. Wells, Qualified Immunity After *Ziglar v. Abbasi*: The Case for a Categorical Approach, 68 Am. U. L. Rev. 379 (2018), proposes that qualified immunity should be scrapped as a comprehensive doctrine but retained for some specific constitutional violations based on analysis of the costs and benefits in particular contexts.

Page 1281, add a footnote at the end of Note 1:

[aa] For a recent decision that follows *Hope v. Pelzer*, see Taylor v. Riojas, 592 U.S. ___, 141 S.Ct. 52 (2020). Inmate Trent Taylor alleged that he had been held in a shockingly unsanitary cell, covered in feces, for several days. When moved to a second cell, he had to relieve himself in a clogged floor drain, causing "raw sewage to spill across the floor." Left without clothes or a bunk, he was forced to sleep naked in the sewage.

Despite these allegations, a federal district court granted summary judgment to the defendant officers based on qualified immunity, saying the law was not clearly established. The Fifth Circuit affirmed, but the Supreme Court reversed, saying, à la *Hope v. Pelzer*, that "no reasonable corrections officer could have concluded that, under the extreme conditions of this case, it was constitutionally permissible to house Taylor in such deplorably unsanitary conditions for such an expended period of time." The per curiam opinion was unanimous, save for Justice Barrett, who did not participate, and Justice Thomas, who dissented without opinion.

Page 1282, add at the end of Note 2:

In the aftermath of the murder of George Floyd by a Minneapolis police officer in May 2020, the role of qualified immunity in limiting liability for excessive force became a cause célèbre. Suddenly, a strong political constituency emerged to demand curtailment of qualified immunity, at least for law enforcement. Several bills to that effect were introduced in Congress. The one that gained the most traction was H.R. 1280, called the George Floyd Justice in Policing Act of 2021. This bill, running to 136 pages in the large-type format of proposed legislation, has a wide variety of provisions, ranging from data reporting and compilation; to limitations of specific police practices (no-knock warrants in drug cases and chokeholds); to requiring police use of body cameras; to authorizing Department of Justice investigations; to policies to eliminate racial profiling.

Title I of the statute, on Police Accountability, has two provisions of direct relevance here. Section 101 would lower the mens rea required for prosecution under 18 U.S.C. § 242, which is the criminal counterpart of § 1983. Section 242 punishes anyone who, under color of law, "subjects any person . . . to the deprivation of any rights, privileges, or immunities secured or protected by the Constitution or laws of the United States . . . ." The statute requires that such acts be done "willfully," which has been construed to require a "purpose to deprive a person of a specific constitutional right . . . made definite by decision or other rule of law . . . ." Screws v. United States, 325 U.S. 91, 101 (1945). (The narrowing construction in *Screws* was adopted to address vagueness concerns that would arise if the statute were applied to unclear or recently announced federal rights.) Section 101 of the proposed George Floyd Act would strike "willfully" and insert "knowingly or recklessly." The practical effect of this change might not be great, but it plainly would make criminal prosecution of police officers for civil-rights violations somewhat easier.

Section 102 of the proposed statute addresses qualified immunity. It would amend § 1983 by adding:

> It shall not be a defense or immunity in any action brought under this section against a local [or state] law enforcement officer

[or in a *Bivens* action against a federal investigative or law enforcement officer] that—

    (1)   the defendant was acting in good faith, or that the defendant believed, reasonably or otherwise, that his or her conduct was lawful at the time when the conduct was committed; or

    (2)   the rights, privileges, or immunities secured by the Constitution and laws were not clearly established at the time of their deprivation by the defendant, or that at such time, the state of the law was otherwise such that the defendant could not reasonably have been expected to know whether his or her conduct was lawful.

Note that this provision would go far beyond curtailing the excesses of qualified immunity applied to highly unreasonable acts not precisely covered by specific prior precedent. It would make even a completely reasonable belief in the lawfulness of one's actions irrelevant to liability under § 1983. This change would apply not only to excessive force, where it is often hard to imagine a completely reasonable belief in lawfulness, but also to other contexts, such as violations of the Fourth Amendment, where reasonable mistakes are more likely.

H.R. 1280 passed the House by a vote of 220–212 very shortly after being introduced. It was then sent to the Senate, where, so far, no action has been taken. The issue seems certain to arise again.

Page 1296, add at the end of Note 3:

For an important exploration of the petition and private bill system, see Maggie Blackhawk, Equity Outside the Courts, 120 Colum. L. Rev. 203 (2020).